The Entrepreneur's Guide to Starting a Successful Business

Other Books by James W. Halloran

*Why Entrepreneurs Fail: Avoid the 20 Fatal Pitfalls
of Running Your Business*

The Right Fit: The Entrepreneur's Guide to Finding the Perfect Business

The Entrepreneur's Guide to Starting a Successful Business

James W. Halloran

Second Edition

McGraw-Hill, Inc.

New York St. Louis San Francisco Auckland Bogotá
Caracas Lisbon London Madrid Mexico Milan
Montreal New Delhi Paris San Juan Singapore
Sydney Tokyo Toronto

There is one group that all entrepreneurs need to give special recognition—their families. Without the complete support and understanding of their families, entrepreneurs cannot reach their goals. My deepest gratitude goes out to Diane, Tim, and Andy.

 This book is printed on recycled, acid-free paper containing a minimum of 50% recycled de-inked fiber.

Library of Congress Cataloging-in-Publication Data

Halloran, James W.
    The entrepreneur's guide to starting a successful business / James
W. Halloran.—2nd ed.
        p.   cm.
    Includes index.
    ISBN 0-07-025799-X   —ISBN 0-07-025798-1 (pbk.)
    1. New business enterprises. 2. Entrepreneurship. I. Title.
HD62.5.H35 1992   91-33435
658.1′141—dc20   CIP

    2 3 4 5 6 7 8 9 0 DOH/DOH 9 8 7 6 5 4 3 2

ISBN 0-07-025798-1 {PBK}
ISBN 0-07-025799-X {HC}

The sponsoring editor for this book was David Conti, the editing supervisor was Jane Palmieri, and the production supervisor was Donald Schmidt. It was set in Helvetica by McGraw-Hill's Professional Book Group composition unit.

Printed and bound by R. R. Donnelley & Sons Company.

This publication is designed to provide accurate and authoritative information in regard to the subject matter covered. It is sold with the understanding that the publisher is not engaged in rendering legal, accounting, or other professional service. If legal advice or other expert assistance is required, the services of a competent professional person shoud be sought.

—from a declaration of principles jointly adopted by a committee of the American Bar Association and a committee of publishers

Contents

Preface

The entrepreneurial environment is one of constant change and opportunities. In the past five years, since the first edition of this book, changes have occurred that made a new edition mandatory. This new edition has been expanded by five chapters, in addition to numerous updates of previous material, to accommodate our changing marketplace. Subjects such as the environmental industry opportunities and the increased interest in international trade for small businesses are receiving greater attention. More entrepreneurs are finding profitable part-time businesses than ever before. You will find that this new edition of *The Entrepreneur's Guide to Starting a Successful Business* has addressed these and other developments to offer the reader a complete guide in ways to reach the entrepreneurial dream.

You can, if the desire is strong enough, break away from your routine and live the life of an entrepreneur. It takes desire and perseverance to be your own boss, not money. As an entrepreneur, teacher, and small business consultant, I have put my experiences and education in writing with the hope of inspiring and helping, in a realistic manner, those readers who have had the ambition, but not the confidence, to move ahead in pursuing their dreams.

The Entrepreneur's Guide to Starting a Successful Business is written from the experience of teaching and practicing small business management for almost twenty years. What has proven to be successful in the classroom and the small business world has been incorporated in this book. The reader will find it different in its approach and methods than previously written books in its field. Just as in a successful classroom, it demands participation by the reader. It is written with the intent of allowing the reader to discover if he or she possesses the "entrepreneur spirit."

Built into the book is a hypothetical project of creating a business. A course on entrepreneurship cannot be complete without requiring the reader to invest time into researching a business idea. Therefore, the book is written in the same chronological order as taken in opening a business.

The writing style is intended to make the reading enjoyable. Case studies, stories, and examples are written into the body of the reading in order to empha-size key points. They relate directly to what the reader is currently reading and should serve as a retention stimulus.

The book gives a fresh emphasis to some areas which have not been cov-ered sufficiently in current entrepreneurship books. To start with, the theme for this book is "the entrepreneur spirit." This terminology appears in each chapter as it conveys the objective of the book.

There is particular concentration on the marketing aspects of small business. The marketing strategies employed in designing a business layout, promotion and advertising, salesmanship, and when to expand a business are treated in sepa-rate chapters. These areas address the most current happenings in the market-place.

One feature that stands out in this book is the problem-solving techniques. There is a continuous flow of problems and situations presented with explanations on how they are solved. Real problems that the entrepreneurs are confronted with are discussed and analyzed. This is not a book of theories and principles; it is a very real explanation of the small business world.

The course from which this book has been derived has been consistently de-scribed as "exciting, challenging, a lot of work, and very worthwhile." It is intended for anyone who has experienced the thought, "I bet I could do it on my own." It is hoped that as the reader turns the pages he or she begins to feel the "entrepre-neur spirit."

James W. Halloran

PART ONE

Preliminary Planning: Exploring Opportunities

1

The Entrepreneur Spirit

The American dream—owning your own business, large profits, no boss, your own timetable—it is all out there, but how does one achieve it? It is a way of life—filled with risks and excitement—but worth trying to achieve, no matter how difficult the journey. It is not impossible, it takes the entrepreneur's spirit, a spirit of perseverance and adventure, a special drive that not everyone has. It is reserved for those who care more about controlling their own destiny than how much money they will make. The entrepreneur, more than anyone else in the business world, understands the meaning behind ABC's *Wide World of Sports* theme "the thrill of victory and the agony of defeat." Integrated within the book is a study of creating a hypothetical business. By following the step-by-step format, you will enjoy the adventure of opening an enterprise such as the projects listed in Appendixes A and B.

Characteristics of the entrepreneur

Individuals who are willing to take the risks of making their own profits and assuming their own losses are entrepreneurs. However, it takes certain personality traits or a large amount of money to be successful. You should not presume that because you passed an entrepreneur personality quiz in the Sunday morning newspaper that you will be successful in starting a business. There are many successful entrepreneurs who have failed such tests as the one shown here, while those who have passed have flunked the real test. See the following pages for the quiz and scoring.

Take this quiz and see how your score stacks up against 1500 entrepreneurs surveyed by the Center for Entrepreneurial Management. All are now running businesses that they started.

Circle the appropriate answer.

1. How were your parents employed?

   a. Both were self-employed most of their working lives.
   b. Both were self-employed for some part of their working lives.
   c. One parent was self-employed for most of his or her working life.
   d. One parent was self-employed at some point in his or her working life.
   e. Neither parent was ever self-employed.

2. Have you ever been fired from a job?

   a. Yes, more than once.
   b. Yes, once.
   c. No.

3. What is your family background?

   a. You were born outside the U.S.
   b. One or both parents were born outside the U.S.
   c. At least one grandparent was born outside the U.S.
   d. Your grandparents, parents, and you were born inside the U.S.

4. Describe your work career.

   a. Primarily in small business (under 100 employees).
   b. Primarily in medium-sized business (100 to 500 employees).
   c. Primarily in big business (over 500 employees).

5. Did you operate any businesses before you were 20?

   a. Many.
   b. A few.
   c. None.

6. What is your age?

   a. 21 to 30.
   b. 31 to 40.
   c. 41 to 50.
   d. 51 or over.

7. Where do you stand in your family?

   a. First child.
   b. Middle.
   c. Youngest.
   d. Other (foster, adopted).

8. What is your marital status?

   a. Married.
   b. Divorced.
   c. Single.

9. What level of formal education have you reached?

   a. Some high school.
   b. High school diploma.
   c. Bachelor's degree.
   d. Master's degree.
   e. Doctorate.

10. What is your primary motivation in starting a business?

    a. To make money.
    b. You don't like working for someone else.
    c. To be famous.
    d. As an outlet for excess energy.

11. Describe your relationship to the parent who provided most of the family's income.

    a. Strained.
    b. Comfortable.
    c. Competitive.
    d. Nonexistent.

12. How would you choose between working hard and working smart?

    a. Work hard.
    b. Work smart.
    c. Both.

13. On whom do you rely for crucial management advice?

    a. Internal management teams.
    b. External management professionals.
    c. External financial professionals.
    d. No one except yourself.

(Continued)

14. If you were at the racetrack, which would you bet on?

   a. The daily double—a chance to make a killing.
   b. A 10-to-1 shot.
   c. A 3-to-1 shot.
   d. The 2-to-1 favorite.

15. Name the one ingredient that you consider both **necessary** and **sufficient** for starting a business.

   a. Money.
   b. Customers.
   c. An idea or product.
   d. Motivation and hard work.

16. If you were an advanced tennis player and had a chance to play a top pro like Jimmy Connors, what would you do?

   a. Turn it down because he could easily beat you.
   b. Accept the challenge but not bet any money on it.
   c. Bet a week's pay that you would win.
   d. Get odds, bet a fortune and try for an upset.

17. With which do you tend to "fall in love" too quickly?

   a. New product ideas.
   b. New employees.
   c. New manufacturing ideas.
   d. New financial plans.
   e. All of the above.

18. Which of the following personality types is best suited to be your right-hand person?

   a. Bright and energetic.
   b. Bright and lazy.
   c. Dumb and energetic.

19. Why do you accomplish tasks better?

   a. You are always on time.
   b. You are super organized.
   c. You keep good records.

20. Which do you hate to discuss?

   a. Problems involving employees.
   b. Signing expense accounts.
   c. New management practices.
   d. The future of business.

21. Which would you prefer?

   a. Rolling dice with a 1-in-3 chance of winning.
   b. Working on a problem with a 1-in-3 chance of solving it in a set time.

22. If you could choose, which of the following competitive professions would you follow:

   a. Professional golf.
   b. Sales.
   c. Personnel counseling.
   d. Teaching.

23. Would you rather work with a partner who is a close friend or work with a stranger who is an expert in your field?

   a. The close friend.
   b. The expert.

24. When do you enjoy being with people?

   a. When you have something meaningful to do.
   b. When you can do something new and different.
   c. Even when you have nothing planned.

25. Do you agree with the following statement? In business situations that demand action, clarifying who is in charge will help produce results.

   a. Agree.
   b. Agree with reservations.
   c. Disagree.

26. In playing competitive games, what most concerns you?

   a. How well you play.
   b. Winning or losing.
   c. Both.
   d. Neither.

Scoring:

To determine your entrepreneurial profile, find the score for each of your answers on the following chart. Add them up for your total score.

   1. a = 10 b = 5 c = 5 d = 2 e = 0   5
   2. a = 10 b = 7 c = 0   0
   3. a = 5 b = 4 c = 3 d = 0   0
   4. a = 10 b = 5 c = 0   5
   5. a = 10 b = 7 c = 0   0
   6. a = 8 b = 10 c = 5 d = 2   8

(Continued)

7. a = 15 b = 2 c = 0 d = 0
8. a = 10 b = 2 c = 2
9. a = 2 b = 3 c = 10 d = 8 e = 4
10. a = 0 b = 15 c = 0 d = 0
11. a = 10 b = 5 c = 10 d = 5
12. a = 0 b = 5 c = 10
13. a = 0 b = 10 c = 0 d = 5
14. a = 0 b = 2 c = 10 d = 3
15. a = 0 b = 10 c = 0 d = 0
16. a = 0 b = 10 c = 3 d = 0
17. a = 5 b = 5 c = 5 d = 5 e = 15
18. a = 2 b = 10 c = 0
19. a = 5 b = 15 c = 5
20. a = 8 b = 10 c = 0 d = 0
21. a = 0 b = 15
22. a = 3 b = 10 c = 0 d = 0
23. a = 0 b = 10
24. a = 3 b = 3 c = 10
25. a = 10 b = 2 c = 0
26. a = 8 b = 10 c = 15 d = 0

Scoring

235–285—Successful entrepreneur. Someone who starts multiple businesses successfully.

200–234—Entrepreneur. Starts one business successfully.

185–199—Latent entrepreneur. Always wanted to start a business.

170–184—Potential entrepreneur. Has the ability but has not started thinking about starting a business yet.

155–169—Borderline entrepreneur. No qualifications but still in the running. Would need a lot of training to succeed.

Below 155—Hired hand.

The average score for the entrepreneurs in the survey was 239. The Center of Entrepreneur Management found that entrepreneurs often come from homes where one parent was self-employed for most of his or her working life. Many had been enterprising as youngsters. Nearly 60 percent are the oldest child in the family and more than 75 percent were married. Fifty-six percent said they wanted to start a business primarily because they disliked working for others.

Decision making is a must. In a small business the individual makes the decision. There are no neatly typed research reports, no large support staff to call in for consultations, no passing the buck—the entrepreneur is it. Too many aspiring entrepreneurs, just out of the corporate world, find themselves unable to make a decision to take advantage of an opportunity because they have become too dependent on others in evaluating possible expansion offerings or acquisitions. What the entrepreneur says goes, all responsibility rests on the shoulders of the owner.

It takes the confidence of a person who can bounce back. The decisions made *must* be made with confidence. When they are wrong and the world comes tumbling down, you must be able to look ahead to the next decision as being the right one.

Entrepreneurs need to be determined. It is a must or else during the hard times the individual will fold up his or her tent and say "Well, I gave it a try." A try is not enough. It takes constant trying and the willingness to hang in there until the final result is declared. Keep in mind that no one ever said it was going to be easy, particularly in the beginning stages.

Creativity is of the essence. A small business is no different from a large business. Those who market their goods or services differently, better, and with a flair will come out ahead. You will need all the creativity you can muster to get out of some of the jams you are liable to get yourself into. Quick thinking and the ability to move fast and act fast is a prerequisite.

Successful entrepreneurs are goal-oriented individuals. The desire to achieve a goal and then seek a higher one is how businesses are built. The constant challenge of reaching for new heights is an ever-present motivation. The truly successful entrepreneurs of today do not stop after they have achieved wealth. They continue pursuing challenging goals.

The small businessperson does everything from unloading trucks to putting together complex financial packages. When an employee is sick, guess who fills in? There is no leaving the problems at the office for entrepreneurs, they go with them. Some days are long and tedious, and vacations are short because it is difficult to leave a young business, so dependent on one source of leadership, for a long period of time.

Why

Most individuals are looking for three things when they venture out on their own: profits, independence, and the desire to control their own destiny. All three can be reached, but they should be ranked in terms of achievement and importance.

Controlling your own destiny

This is the foremost reason you should be interested in owning your own business. There can be no value assigned to the value of controlling when a task needs to be accomplished. The entrepreneur is not told he must attend the weekly sales meeting which forces him to miss his son's little league game or his daughter's dance recital. Entrepreneurs set the priorities in their lives, and above all this is the number one benefit of entrepreneurship. This benefit is the motivation that keeps the business idea alive.

Independence

This means freedom from direct supervision. It does not mean the entrepreneur is free to do whatever she wishes. There are still people to answer to, whether it be bankers, franchisors, landlords, or suppliers. There will be financial statements that the bank will demand, periodic reports to the parent company if you are a franchise, tax reports to the government, and numerous other obligations that will demand attention and action at certain set times. There is no direct boss however, and that is quite a benefit.

Profits

This is listed third because it is the hardest to achieve and usually the last objective you will accomplish. Profits take time to develop and are a test of patience and perseverance. Charles O'Meara, the owner of Absolute Sound, a highly specialized stereophonic retail store in Winter Park, Florida, achieved his success by never wavering in his confidence.

Charles gained his experience in the stereo industry by working for different stereo stores while attending college. After receiving his degree, he was disappointed with the career opportunities he was offered, so he continued on in college in pursuit of an MBA degree. During this time he continued to work and increase his expertise in the stereo business.

While taking courses in small business management and retailing, Charles became convinced the entrepreneurial life was for him. Equipped with the knowledge gained from completing a small business management project and with his professor's assistance, he found a location for a highly specialized stereo retail store. The site was on the main street of an exclusive shopping district in Winter Park, Florida. The financing became available through the help of a well-to-do friend who believed in Charles's ability. The friend helped secure a $55,000 bank loan and Absolute Sound became a reality.

First-year sales were $343,000, which was above initial expectations; however, due to bank debt and opening expenses, there were no profits. The second year's sales soared to $535,000, due in large part to the advent of a custom design installation service. Always customer-oriented, Charles followed this philosophy by designing and installing stereo systems in clients' homes. The store's customer relations programs offering personalized assistance, mailing newsletters, and having a stringent customer follow-up plan began to produce. After five years of operation, the business was generating sales in excess of $1,000,000, over $1000 per square foot of retail space.

With growth, more space and parking were needed. Absolute Sound moved to a new 4000-square-foot store, a short walk from the original store. Two years later Charles is closing in on a $2,000,000 sales volume, achieving substantial profits, and driving a new Mercedes Benz. He has built a strong customer base, a good relationship with his bank, recently opened a second store, and is ambitiously looking at the future.

Charles attributes his success to hard work and following the "customer is king" philosophy. "It is tougher than I thought. There have been some very difficult times. However, I never stopped believing I would succeed. No matter how rotten the day before, I have always considered tomorrow as a new opportunity. You never know what might happen. I still make mistakes, such as my inventory getting out of line or my ego getting ahead of good business sense, but when I do, I go back to the basics of running a customer-oriented business. The business has become part of me—an appendage I could not live without." He consistently builds on his established customers through newsletters, an established-customer charge-card system, and a strong follow-up-on-the-sale program. He budgets 5 percent of sales to advertising consistently, which allows exposure to potential new customers. His program of making the product easy to buy, as opposed to easy to sell, is designed to meet the customer's needs. A dramatic use of in-store colors has been designed to appeal to his male target market. He has done an outstanding job of thinking through his operation in terms of the basic details learned through his experience and education. Absolute Sound has been consistently recognized within its industry as one of the top-performing and innovative stores of its kind.

Usually the small business is out there competing with the giants. It is hard and entrepreneurs have to be good or they will not survive. Unless you are equipped with an abundance of money or a dynamite invention, you must be realistic in your profit expectations. Most new entrepreneurs sacrifice current income levels in order to achieve the two benefits mentioned above with the hope, but not the promise, of achieving large profits down the road. Caution is the key word in projecting a profit picture for a new venture. You must be honest in your approach to the importance you assign to each benefit.

When

There is rarely an ideal time for a prospective entrepreneur to throw up her hands and shout "I have had enough of everyone else's problems, just let me have my own!" There are some warnings and cautions to point out. The often-used phrase, "There is no time like the present," is not always appropriate in making this decision. The best time might be when you are not so tied into the company profit-sharing and pension plans that it costs a small fortune to leave that job. This might also be the time when you are not looking directly at such expenses as college education for the children. For most, this period of time falls between the ages of 25 to 35, after five to ten years of being on the job. During this working period, hopefully enough earnings have been put away to serve as seed money for a new venture. Many entrepreneurs are created through the loss of a job. Opening a business, however, is not recommended if the reason for doing so is out of desperation. Too many businesses are opened by inexperienced people trying to work in an area in which they are unfamiliar, simply because they became frustrated with the job-hunting process. It is a mistake to open any business that is not properly prepared for and researched. If you open a business in an area of work that you have no experience in, you run the risk that you will not like what you are doing. One thing worse than working for someone in a position or field that you do not like is working for yourself, using your personal monies, in a position that is not enjoyable.

Starting a business takes planning; many great businesses have been created in peoples' homes and garages during their spare time. Allowing a business investment or idea to grow into a full-time job is the ideal method of starting. It turns a hobby that you enjoy into a full-time occupation that you will love. Many successful mail-order businesses have begun this way.

Do not rush a business opening; if it is a good idea it will be around for many years. There is no reason that a few months, or even years, of waiting will cause it to fail. There are times when opportunities become available which must be acted upon immediately or lost forever. These types of opportunities are few and far between, and always deserve a very cautious investigation. The best course of action to follow is to let an idea grow and then bloom into the ideal occupation.

Look at the story of the birth of an idea and its possibilities. When Jeff Hancock arrived home from work he heard a familiar complaint from his wife Eleanor. "The next time I find the boys' baseball cards on their bedroom floor I am going to throw them away." He remembered his mother telling him the same thing thirty years earlier. He recently read where some of those old cards were now worth thousands of dollars in the collectors' market. He could easily envision the same thing happening to his sons' cards. "Boys come here," he exclaimed as he looked at their bedroom floor littered with cards. "Let's take these cards and mount them on the wall, on a plaque that shows a baseball diamond. We can put them in individual plastic sleeves to protect them, and stick them on the plaque to show the position they play." Everyone agreed Dad had a great idea, and within a few days a rough plaque was created. Looking with pride at his idea, Jeff wondered if he had just invented a salable product and decided it was worth investigating. He met with his old college friend, Bob Nance (who owned a small manufacturing plant), to see what was involved with producing the plaque. Bob was enthusiastic, and a partnership, H & N Products, was formed, with each partner committing $1000 to try and develop a market. The plaque design and first production run of 1000 units was made at a cost of $1500, the self-adhesive sleeves were purchased, and now they were ready to try the mail-order market.

Before placing the first ad, Jeff met with a patent attorney to inquire about the possibilities of obtaining a patent. The attorney questioned whether it was possible using a baseball diamond as artwork, because it was considered a public domain design. It would not hurt, however, to make a patent search for $250. The search found no patents on anything similar to Jeff's idea. The attorney still felt uncertain as to the feasibility of obtaining a utility or design patent. Confronted with the cost range from $800 to $2500 and a two- to three-year waiting period, Jeff decided against the patent application and registered a copyright for $90 instead. The first media advertisement H & N Products tried was a small, 1- by 3-inch column, mail-order ad in a national weekly sports publication, the *Sporting News*. The cost was $480 to reach a circulation of 650,000. Already over the original budgeted monies, the ad solicited 42 responses, at $4.95 plus postage and handling each. Disappointed and running low on funds, Jeff turned to another medium, the market of the *Sports Collectors Digest.* A full-page ad (see Fig. 1-1), at a cost of $160 for a circulation of 10,000, was run. The result was 64 responses at $4.95. The ad ran twice more, but each ad received less response. The next course of action was a direct mailer to over 400 baseball collector stores through the country. Nine dealers responded by ordering a dozen each at $42 wholesale. Reorders were never received from any of the dealers.

The partners traveled to visit an ex-major league pitcher who owned a company which made personalized baseball cards for businesses and organizations, whose clients used them as business cards, or to show off their company softball teams, etc. Jeff and Bob tried unsuccessfully to sell him on the idea of mounting the organization's cards on the plaque.

Out of money and out of the desire to invest more, Jeff made one more attempt. He visited the merchandising director of a major league team. A decision was made to purchase 1000 at $1.50 each if the plaques could be made in poster form, ready to mail. The cost of this potential order would be $1.30 per unit. The partners were confused whether to accept the order at a gross profit of 20 cents per unit or was it time to put the idea away?

They hadn't made an attempt at exploring the market of children who collect baseball cards. There was a long list of ideas to explore if they were willing to invest the money. It might not work, but imagine the profit potential of selling posters for a dollar or two net profit per unit to a market of millions of people who collect baseball cards. This is the spirit, the determination to explore all the alleys in an effort to launch a product or service in which a person believes. The risks are great and probabilities are long, but if they succeed they can end up with large profits, independence, and the right to control their own destiny.

A note of caution concerning when and if you are able to move into the world of entrepreneurship: Once a person leaves the job market for *any* extended period of time, he or she loses contacts and personal marketability within the industry. This makes it very difficult to get back into the job market without starting over. If a person operates a business for ten years and then throws in the towel, it is extremely difficult to go back to a former career.

Types of entrepreneurs

There are two broad classifications of entrepreneurs: the independent and the franchisee.

The independent relies totally on herself and the people she employs to build a profitable business. This individual is often the one who started in her garage at night with some preposterous idea at which her friends laughed. With a little encouragement and a small taste of success, the idea grew into a marketable product, service, or retail store. The independent entrepreneur relies on her own initiative in regard to financing, organizing, and operating her business. With the exception of banks, landlords, and other necessary associations, she is alone to develop the best method possible to operate her business.

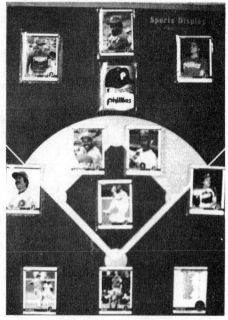
Figure 1-1. Advertisement—H & N Products.

The franchisee is the relatively new entrepreneur on the block. The individual works under a two-party legal agreement whereby one party is granted the privilege to conduct business as an individual owner, but must operate according to certain agreements and terms specified by the other party. This is franchising and the legal agreement is the franchise contract. The party who is the sponsor of the privileges is the franchisor, and the party who receives the privileges is the franchisee. Although the concept of franchising has been around since the nineteenth century, it has really boomed since the early 1950s. Everyone is familiar with the growth of McDonald's, 7-Eleven, and Fotomat, but there are thousands of smaller, less-known franchises in operation all across the United States and other parts of the world.

The advantage of the franchise is that you do not have to be an expert in the field to get started; you just need to be able to obtain the necessary capital. The franchise usually offers managerial training, financing assistance or guidance, and marketing experience and benefits.

The training program can be as elaborate as McDonald's Hamburger University, where the franchisee actually participates in a fully developed residential training program or as skimpy as an instruction manual. The financial assistance might come in the form of direct loans from the parent company or assistance in preparing your loan request for the bank. The marketing benefits might be a well-recognized name or trademark, including a total and tested marketing program. The franchisee might only receive some point-of-purchase materials and some suggested ad slicks to run in the local newspaper. Franchises come in all forms, shapes, and sizes and with different types of investment plans. The individual should keep the expression "you get what you pay for" in mind when evaluating franchise opportunities. It should also be pointed out that those who were among the first to take advantage of the franchise offerings of McDonald's, Burger King, and Pizza Hut now own very profitable businesses purchased with modest investments. The resale value of a prosperous franchise can be very substantial. The franchisee is a genuine entrepreneur because he is willing to take the risks of assuming profits and losses. However, franchisees are more securely blanketed and actually act as an arm of the parent company. These individuals will at times become exasperated at the feeling that they are still working for someone else due to following procedures, completing reports, and sharing profits.

Small businesses range from the mom and pop candy store to companies with the capacity to generate millions of dollars of sales. There is no single standard definition to classify a business as small. However, for the purpose of this book, certain criteria will be assumed:

- The number of employees is usually fewer than 100.
- The financing for the business originates from one individual or a small group which would usually number less than ten.
- The firm operates under a profit goal and, excluding marketing activities, is geographically centralized.
- The firm is considered small in relationship to the large firms in its industry.

Entrepreneurs are to be found in all segments of the business community, such as retail, wholesale, manufacturing, agriculture, finance, computer technology, construction, and transportation, as can be seen in Fig. 1-2.

Retailers are classified as any business engaged in selling products or services to the intended ultimate user. They can be merchandise marketers such as jewelry stores, shoe stores, and floral shops, or they can be consumer or business services, such as beauty salons, dry cleaners, accounting services, motels, restaurants, or automobile repair. Vending machine companies and mail-order houses are included in this category. They operate as independent units, franchises, or small chains. Small businesses dominate this category.

Wholesalers are classified as any businesses which act as a middleman between manufacturer and retailers, or who assemble, store, and distribute products to industrial users. Small businesses also dominate this category, selling everything from imported gift lines, produce, and hardware to heavy-duty industrial machinery. Full-function wholesalers take title to the products they sell, and limited-function wholesalers market the product before taking possession. Full-function wholesalers operate from their own warehouse facilities.

Manufacturing is dominated by the large businesses, although there are thousands of small businesses engaged in the manufacturing industry. Small machine shops, toy factories, packaging firms, cabinet shops, and clothing manufacturers are all examples of an important part of the industry. These are often family-owned operations trying to operate in an environment of big business and labor unions.

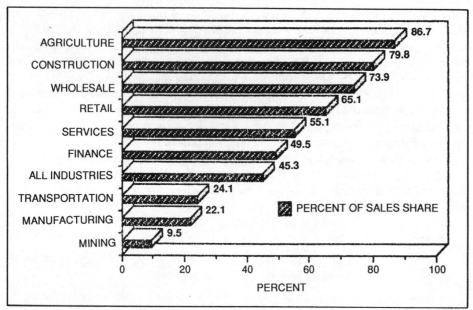

Figure 1-2. Sales share of firms with fewer than 100 employees by major industry. (Office of the President, State of Small Business, 1989)

Whitemarsh Paper and Specialties Company of Philadelphia is a small business principally involved in the sale and distribution of packaging materials. They design, cut, and assemble packaging for small and large consumer goods companies. The president of the 37-year-old family-owned company, George Neslie, Jr., has these comments concerning labor unions and competing with the large companies in the industry; "Since we became unionized twelve years ago it has made my job much more difficult and has driven up costs to the point of severely cutting into our profit margins. Union contracts have forced us into being less competitive and less flexible. For example, it was not unusual in the past for a salesman to make a delivery while making a sales call. This is no longer possible as it is stated in our union contract that only our truck drivers are permitted to make deliveries.

"As far as competing with the large businesses in our industry, the only way is through price. Even with the unions our overhead is still lower than the big company and on the specialized items, which we are equipped to produce, we are able to manufacture faster and cheaper than they. Our limitation is that it must be a product we are able to produce with our present equipment as we are not able to make the large capital expenditures of the conglomerates."

The insurance agency, the local realtor, small finance companies, small banks, and pawnbrokers are all examples of the presence of entrepreneurship in financial services. Many of these businesses are being taken over by large holding companies. There are many more who through creative and entrepreneurial risk taking compete quite well in their respective communities.

The growth of computer technology companies has created a new industry for the entrepreneur. Hundreds of computer software companies are springing up and adding to a new avenue for the would be entrepreneur. The future of this industry is filled with exciting opportunities for those individuals with the abilities to enter this fast-growing market. This industry is just in its infancy.

The construction industry includes thousands of small businesses, including painters, plumbers, general contractors, electricians, and home builders who are independent of the large developers. Small businesses are an important ingredient of this business sector. Architecture firms and land surveyors belong in this category.

Although the large businesses have a strong grip on the transportation and communication industry, there are many private charter airlines, local radio and TV stations, and taxicab companies which prosper in this group.

All the small businesses from all these categories constitute a formidable part of our industrial society. As shown in Fig. 1-2, roughly 45 percent of all business conducted in the United States is derived from the small business sector. Its contribution is immense in terms of the number of jobs that are created, the number of new products introduced, and competition stimulus it generates. Many times the small firm is able to act quicker and more efficiently than the large corporation. The lack of red tape and standard operating procedures allows the small business to react faster to the needs of the market. In the retailing segment they are able to offer personalization that the large merchandisers cannot compete with. The added value of personalized service is often worth the additional price the customer pays to deal with the small business. The entrepreneur is a very vital ingredient to our way of life, and opportunities are available to those who are willing to take the risks.

The entrepreneur spirit project

This project is a business plan for the prospective entrepreneur. A business plan is a written description of the steps needed to reach a business goal. Through this plan you will be able to discover your aptitude for pursuing your interest. As you proceed step by step through the project, you will have completed the planning stages of forming a business enterprise. You will

- Investigate the market for the opportunity you wish to pursue and that you are qualified to enter. The objective is to discover if conditions and opportunities are present for market entry.
- Analyze your objectives. Are your profit and career goals attainable?
- Search for a location for your business. It is necessary to be in the right place at the right time. Customer accessibility is a vital ingredient, particularly for certain retail establishments.
- Line up all necessary capital requirements. The financial plan that you will work under must be well planned. Financial restrictions serve as a great inhibitor. The type of organizational structure you choose will help you in your planning.
- Draw up an assistance reference guide. You will need the help of established businesspeople in your industry, suppliers and other professionals, in designing your business, marketing, and inventory control systems. Those suppliers who will benefit from your entry into a market will be willing to direct you in becoming established. Making contact with reputable organizations will be invaluable.
- Survey the market. Whether it is customer surveys or traffic counts, this will tell you a lot about your market.
- Educate yourself to the best techniques to use in selling your product. Consider taking a sales course if applicable. Also, learn the most effective merchandising techniques and promotional aids.
- Establish relationships with banks, lawyers, and accountants. Bring them into the planning stages; you will need them now and later. They will be necessary in financing plans, contract agreements, and designing bookkeeping systems.
- Plan your personnel needs. Personnel can be your greatest asset, or if you are not careful, your greatest headache.
- Study insurance needs. Acquire protection on only what you need and what you can afford.
- List necessary equipment and estimate cost. Decide on used or new. Too much unnecessary and sophisticated equipment is often purchased for new ventures.
- Draw a conclusion as to your aptitude and desire of someday becoming an entrepreneur.

The entrepreneur spirit project—step 1

Choose the avenue of entrepreneurship that holds the most interest for you. Remember these requirements:

- The enterprise should be one that is of personal interest and not totally foreign to you.
- Write out your goals in terms of what objectives you wish to achieve.
- Determine if there is a need or a market for your product or service.
- List all competitive factors in your market. Later on you will learn how to investigate and analyze your competition.
- Make a realistic statement of all assets available for your venture.

Best wishes for your new venture!

2

On Your Mark, Get Set, Go!

"Owning your own business has been compared to holding a tiger by its tail. It keeps throwing you back and forth, but you are afraid of what might happen if you let go." (Source unknown)

The decision to venture out comes in different ways, for different reasons, and at different times for the aspiring entrepreneur.

- The job has turned stale with no opportunities for advancement or challenge. This is the most common reason and indicates the ambition to be successful.

- An inheritance has been passed on allowing enough capital to pursue a long-held idea.

- A pink slip has arrived on your desk. Remember, however, not to act out of desperation.

- The idea you have been nurturing and developing is starting to catch on and demands more time and attention if it is to prove profitable.

- A change of circumstances has occurred in your personal life. For example, a pregnant woman takes a leave of absence from her job to start a family. During this time she spends more time on her hobby of making fashion jewelry for her friends. A salesperson friend talks her into allowing him to take samples of her jewelry to an upcoming gift and accessories show at the regional merchandise mart. He returns with 200 orders totaling $25,000 and she never returns to her previous job.

- An opportunity becomes available for you to buy an existing business. The price and terms are favorable and the opportunity seems excellent.

Finding the opportunity

Where are the opportunities? Are they in the classified section of the newspaper? Are they listed with real estate and business brokers? Do you ask friends and relatives? How do you search them out? If you are intent upon owning your own business and have no direct experience, you might be better off looking for an existing business for sale, or a franchise opportunity. The reasons are simple—it gives you more time to gain the necessary experience and knowledge, and it gives you a picture of your new career.

Franchising

The advantage of franchising is buying into a program that has been tried, supposedly with success. The entrepreneur enters into a financial arrangement with the franchisor, learns the business, and hopefully earns the profits. A word of caution: Many franchises are not the profit-making machines that they are advertised to be. As in all areas of the business world, there are many "fly-by-night" ventures lurking in the woods. Investigate franchise opportunities and agreements carefully. The franchise document should include the following:

1. The legal name of the franchisor and a concise history of the business for the preceding 15 years.

2. The names, titles, and occupations of all key people involved in the business of the franchisor for the past five years.

3. An account of all administrative, criminal, or material civil legal action currently pending or completed against the franchisor involving any alleged violation of franchise law, misrepresentation, or fraud.

4. A disclosure as to any bankruptcy filings made by any officers, general partners, or previous officers of the franchisor.

5. Disclosure of the full initial franchise fee and other initial payments. The entire initial investment should be clearly illustrated.

6. Disclosure of all additional fees. These might include service fees (advertising and royalty), training fees, lease payments, assistance fees, and insurance.

7. In the event the franchisor is the designated supplier of goods or services to the franchisee, there must be a list as to what is to be purchased and its cost.

8. If the franchisor is directly or indirectly providing financing, the franchisor must disclose what payments or items will be financed and the terms and conditions.

9. Explanation of assistance to be performed by the franchisor before the opening of the business and during its operation. Description of all training programs and the experience of the trainers. Also the process of selecting and approving the location of the business.

10. Description of the territory served and the rights to the territory. Is it protected? Can the territory rights be forfeited or lost?

11. Explanation of the rights to use a commercial symbol such as a trademark, service mark, or logo.

12. Explanation of the obligation to manage the operation. Does it allow absentee management?

13. Statement as to the term of the agreement. Are there renewal or extension provisions?

14. Explanation of any earnings clause. To make an earnings claim the franchisor must adhere to very stringent requirements. If these requirements are not met, any representations to sales, profits, or earnings are illegal.

15. Disclosure of all franchises currently and formerly operating. This must include addresses and telephone numbers. Contacting existing and former franchisees is an excellent evaluation tool.

16. Audited financial statements of the franchisor must be presented for review.

17. A statement of the acknowledgment of receipt of information. This statement must be signed by the prospective franchisee upon receipt of all disclosure documents. A sale cannot legally be final until ten days from the signing of this receipt.

It is not difficult to find franchise opportunities. You can attend regional franchise shows where you have the opportunity to visit with the sales representatives of many different franchisors or you can write for information. The local library will have plenty of publications such as *The Entrepreneur* and *Venture* magazines, and reference books, which will give the interested party the addresses and basic capital requirements for most national franchise offerings. A letter expressing interest will surely bring a response and possibly a salesperson to your doorstep. If the prospective franchisee possesses the necessary qualifications, the franchisor might even send an invitation and an airline ticket to visit them for a day of wining, dining, and education. Be wary of high-pressure sales tactics.

As shown in Fig. 2-1, franchising continued its impressive growth rate through the 1980s and is expected to continue to grow. Figure 2-2 shows that over one-third of all retail sales are through franchised operations.

Buying an existing business

If you seek more independence than owning a franchise allows, or if you object to sharing the profits, then a search for an existing business is in order. It is like finding a good job, the really great opportunities have a line of interested parties. However, it is possible and it cannot be overlooked. Let's look at some examples of classified opportunities.

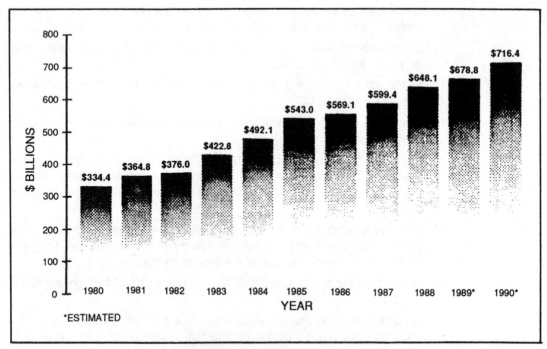

Figure 2-1. Growth of franchised sales of goods and services. (Franchising in the Economy: 1988–1990, published by the International Franchise Association Educational Foundation)

Seafood Market. A steal at $9800, $6000 down, low overhead, excellent profits, call _____.

A phone call to the seller revealed that he claimed profits of over $20,000 per year and was selling the business for just the cost price of his equipment. Common sense in this example would have you wonder why anyone who makes $20,000 per year would be willing to sell out for less than half of one year's profits. There might be all kinds of stories about retiring, illness, or other personal reasons, but the interested buyer should be interested only in sound financial reasoning.

Another classified opportunity might contain a more complex offering such as:

Private School. Florida location, excellent potential. Write PO Box XXX, WSJ.

A letter of inquiry to this ad resulted in an interesting situation. First, a letter of confidentiality had to be signed to assure that this offering would not become public knowledge. The school was owned and operated by an accountant and his wife. He served as the headmaster for this small, grade 6 through 12 private coed school. The school was located in a major Florida city on 6 acres of lakefront property. There were six buildings: two dormitories, two classroom buildings, an administrative house, and a small gymna-

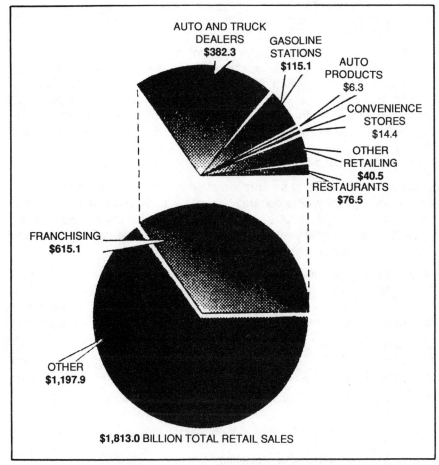

Figure 2-2. Percentage of retail sales sold through franchises. (Franchising in the Economy: 1988–1990, published by the International Franchise Association Educational Foundation)

sium. The real estate is considered to be quite valuable. The asking price is $750,000, which could be purchased with $150,000 cash and assumed first and second mortgages of $600,000. The problem with the school was declining enrollment. Present enrollment was 90 students, down from a previous high of 125. The present owners had been forced to raise tuition fees to compensate for the loss of students, therefore it is considered to be an expensive school. There were no profits on the current income statement.

It appears the owners are asking $150,000 to have a problem taken away from them. Presuming the property is mortgaged to the limit, it is not a fair price. However, although this might appear outrageous, it is not out of the question that someone might pay close to the asking price for this business. The reason—it is in Florida and represents a convenient lifestyle. Businesses are often bought on the desire to own something desirable and not because it is a good investment. Given two identical businesses, one in

Florida and the other in Oklahoma, the Florida business can sell much more quickly, at a much higher price, due to its location in the Sun Belt.

At the same time the prospective buyer is looking through the classifieds, she should consult with a business broker who will have a list of available business opportunities, including the basic financial information. A good broker will give helpful suggestions and possibly lead the prospective buyer in the right direction, bringing the two parties together. The broker should also have existing and new franchise offerings available for sale. It is well to remember the broker is employed by the seller.

So what does constitute a good opportunity and what is important to know?

Any opportunity must be in an area in which you feel comfortable.
Former guidance counselors generally have little background to be considering a computer-oriented business. However, an engineer who has tinkered with computers as a hobby might be a candidate. Let your education and experience be your guide.

How much capital is required and how much do you have?
The book will address financial planning in a later chapter, but for now keep in mind that one of the prime reasons businesses fail is undercapitalization. It is hard enough to make your profit goals, therefore do not start off with a deficit.

What are your financial goals?
It is important to distinguish between the salary you earn from your business and the rate of return on your investment, as illustrated by the following table.

Example: The business you are considering buying for $100,000 has the following simplified income statement.

Sales	$ 280,000
less cost of goods	– 155,000
Gross profit	$ 125,000
less operating expenses	– 93,000
Net profit	$ 32,000

If the profit is $32,000 and it is a proprietorship, any monies taken to pay the owner come out of that $32,000. If you are working full time at this business and you need to draw $25,000 per year for personal living expenses, that leaves only $7,000 available to pay back the investment. That translates into a 7 percent return on investment, which might not appeal to you. However, if you were to buy that same business as an investment without giving up your present earning capacity, you might be able to pay a manager $12,000 per year and make a $20,000 or 20 percent return on investment, which might be very appealing. The entrepreneur must be able to determine financial needs in contemplating the value of the business for sale. Too often businesses are bought on the premise of how much the new owner can improve the sales and profits of the firm. This all takes time as the new owner must first overcome the poor image and precedents of the previous owner. Bill and Rona thought they had all the answers when they purchased the Card and Party Shops.

In January of 1988 Bill and Rona formed a partnership for the purpose of buying a group of four card and gift shops for $140,000. Bill was a former greeting card salesperson and would manage the operation and Rona, a CPA, would be a silent partner, except for handling the financial aspects of the business. They managed to borrow $100,000 from the same bank with whom the seller had a high position. The total note was in excess of $150,000 including interest, and had a five-year maturity with annual payments of approximately $30,000 per year. The business had current annual sales of a little over $300,000 and showed a profit of approximately $40,000 annually. Admittedly the current profit was not high enough to pay Bill a salary and pay back the bank, but the partners felt confident they could raise sales immediately to $350,000. This would enable them to meet their bank obligations and pay Bill a reasonable salary.

In June of that year a fire destroyed the weakest store in the chain. From the insurance settlement they paid the bank $15,000, which reduced their annual bank obligation to $25,000. Remaining monies of the settlement were divided equally. Gross sales were now running at $250,000 and profits were still in the $40,000 range.

In early 1989, a large regional mall opened across from the number 1 store. Total sales dropped immediately to the $200,000 level, with net profit dropping to $30,000. Having trouble meeting their bank obligations and falling to 30 days past due to their suppliers, they sold their number 2 store. This enabled them to reduce their bank debt obligation to $20,000 per year, but their sales fell to the $140,000 range and profits were now at $23,000. In lieu of this they sought new opportunities and bought a toy store, borrowing more money. Their total debt including interest was now $115,000 with annual sales of $210,000 and a note payment of $27,000. The projected profits were now $32,000.

In early 1990 they opened a new card and gift shop. Additional borrowed monies kept their total debt at $115,000; however, annual bank payments rose to $35,000 as the bank refused to extend the maturity date. Sales were back to the $300,000 level and profits at $40,000. Table 2-1 lists the shop's financial obliga-

_____ Table 2-1 _____

Card and Party Shops' Financial Obligations

	Sales	Bank total debt	Bank annual debt	Profits
Jan. 1988	$300,000	$150,000	$30,000	$40,000
June 1988	250,000	120,000	25,000	40,000
Jan. 1989	200,000	107,500	25,000	30,000
June 1989	140,000	80,000	20,000	23,000
Oct. 1989	210,000	115,000	27,000	32,000
Jan. 1990	300,000	115,000	35,000	40,000

tions. As time went by the business had trouble meeting bank obligations and fell 60 and then 90 days behind with suppliers. The bank became concerned and demanded the note paid.

Eventually the partners found a buyer for the entire operation and managed to satisfy the bank. During this time the friendship dissolved. It is also of interest to note that during the three years of operation Rona was able to buy a new car, a new house, and live quite handsomely.

These entrepreneurs got themselves into trouble because of numerous mistakes made in evaluating the business for sale.

- Why was the owner, who was also a banker, willing to let go of this business? Probably because he had already seen the plans for the large shopping center; Rona and Bill could have discovered this with a little investigation.

- They counted on the old "We are going to do it better" theory in planning their profit projections. Although this premise can hold some merit—depending on experience, it normally takes time for sales volume to grow and should not be counted on for initial sales projections.

- Neither had any background for the toy store idea. Experience in the toy industry would have shown that although the sales potential in toys is great, it is a very price competitive retail industry with a low gross profit percentage.

- The cash flow problems were handled very poorly. In a later chapter, proper cash flow handling will be discussed in detail. It is sufficient to note that with the insurance claims and selling off one property there was cash available that, if used properly, could have made the difference. If you are wondering how Rona lived so handsomely you will learn later that by not paying her bills on time there was a false impression of extra capital available.

Hindsight certainly suggests the partners moved too quickly on the opportunity. Their overwhelming desire to own the business prohibited an in-depth investigation of all areas. If they had learned of the proposed new shopping mall it would have been a valuable tool to use in negotiating the selling price downward. Buying the business at a more reasonable price, applying more equity, and lessening the salary dependency might have resulted in a favorable investment.

What are you buying?
Thoroughly check out the physical facilities, inventory, and equipment. If the real estate is part of the package have the roof, plumbing, and all other physical aspects of the building checked out by a professional. Also, check with local zoning ordinances. People who go to great extremes in assuring that a house they might buy is in good condition are often careless in inspecting business property. If it is leased property, carefully have the lease reviewed for the landlord's responsibilities for upkeep.

The inventory should be evaluated at its *actual* value, not at its cost or retail value. It must be up to date. If you were to buy a ladies' fashion boutique you would not want to buy last year's fashions. If it is a manufacturing facility, the buyer must be assured all machinery is properly valued and in good working condition. Broken-down equipment results in shutdown time for a manufacturer, which is very expensive. Make sure replacement parts are available.

Are the terms and conditions fair?
Businesses are sold showing a list of assets on their balance sheet with assigned values. Often the term goodwill is shown with a value. This is an arbitrary assignment of a figure that the present owner believes she deserves for building, developing, or creating the business. It is, very simply, the profit they hope to receive from selling the firm. The buyer needs to ascertain its true worth, as it might be very exaggerated. This can be done by accurately figuring the rate of return from verified income statements.

An extensive buying situation is defined in marketing terms as one which requires much collecting of information. Of all the times a businessperson might need the services of a good accountant and attorney, this is the most important. There should be nothing taken for granted. A complete and thoroughly audit should be taken by an outside person, usually a CPA, and all terms and agreements must be reviewed by the buyer's own attorney.

Let's compare two similar opportunities: The prospective buyer is looking for a small department store or variety store for sale. He comes upon two opportunities.

- A 12,000-square-foot deluxe specialty department store located in a 55-store enclosed mall. Current sales are $650,000 with a net profit of $16,000 after all taxes and expenses. It is a corporation and the owner's salary of approximately $30,000 is included in the expenses. Total assets are $140,000, of which $60,000 is in up-to-date modern fixtures. The total rent including all shopping center charges is $84,000 per year. The store includes ladies' fashions, cards and gifts, a bridal boutique, a children's department, and a small cafe. It is the leading fashion store in a community of 40,000. Four years are remaining on its current lease.

- An old, established family owns a 20,000-square-foot store with two floors in a downtown area of a town of 12,000 people. Sales are $450,000 and holding. Profits are hard to establish because bookkeeping habits are rather sloppy. It is probably a breakeven situation; however, there is enough extra capital to pay an owner a $30,000 salary. Total assets are approximately $250,000, of which $225,000 is merchandise valued at cost. Total rent is $24,000 per year. The inventory consists of a large variety of everything from household goods to western wear. It is very poorly merchandised. The lease can be fixed for however long the new owner requests.

Both of these stores are priced at $250,000. Which one represents the better opportunity? There are numerous factors to consider in a situation such as this; however, some ideas come immediately to the surface.

- Store number 1 is certainly the eye-appealing store which appears to be well organized and ready for the new owner. Store number 2 is basically an eyesore which will require much work, leasehold improvements, and fixturing. Conservatively figure $25,000 to improve the appearance of the store.

- Using the profit figures available, store number 1 indicates a return on investment of 6 percent; store number 2 shows none. Neither appears a good investment if we stop there.

- Which holds the greatest future potential? Store number 1 is in a 15-year-old shopping center with two major anchor stores and appears to be solid for the time being. If a new center were to be built, there is the threat that the new competition could do substantial harm to the store. Greater sales potential will have to be generated by increasing inventory and offering a greater selection. Store number 2 has been in the same location for 50 years and is probably somewhat immune to the threat of a large shopping center in a town its size. Greater sales will have to come through renovating, better merchandising, and new merchandise.

- What assets are you getting for the money? Store number 1 has glamorous fixtures, $80,000 cost inventory, and probably a good reputation. Store number 2 with $225,000 of cost inventory has only $25,000 in fixturing and probably a worn-out reputation.

The potential for both stores lies in the fact that they are hovering around the breakeven point. The breakeven point is reached when the total revenues allow the firm to meet all financial obligations, i.e., cost of goods and all fixed and variable expenses. The excitement of doing business comes at this point because the profit percentage per unit sold rises dramatically after reaching this point. As long as the fixed cost of the business can remain constant, the variable cost should decline as a percentage of sales as sales volume grows. There will come a point that instead of achieving a 10 percent net profit on each dollar sold, that percent might rise to 30 or 40 percent for each dollar sold after reaching the breakeven point. So what one is the best investment? At first glance it might appear to be store number 1. Assuming this store is being properly managed, the new owner might be limited on increasing profits without increasing investment. To increase sales, at least $50,000 more in inventory will have to be purchased raising the investment to $300,000. Presume that the additional inventory could increase sales $200,000, profits should rise to the $45,000 level, because it has surpassed the breakeven point. Therefore, for $300,000 you will have a store generating $850,000 in sales and $45,000 in profits, which gives a rate of return of 15 percent.

Store number 2 might be approached in another manner. Immediately sell at cost $75,000 of obsolete merchandise. Use these monies for fixtures and improvements ($25,000) and new merchandise ($50,000). Presuming the new merchandise and the new look can add $125,000 in sales, the new owner will have a store which generates $575,000 in sales and possibly $50,000 in profits if he continues running a low overhead business. Since his investment is still at $250,000 he might be able to gain a rate of return of 20 percent in a more secure location.

Creating a business

There are a number of very good reasons an entrepreneur would venture out and start a business from the grass roots.

- You have developed a new product or service that has not been marketed before.

- You wish to avoid the dependence, interference, and policy-setting dictates of a franchise.

- The entrepreneur does not wish to assume the poor characteristics and precedents of an existing business.

- You have found what you consider to be an ideal location and have the support of bankers and suppliers. Creating your own business is the most challenging, exciting, and potentially rewarding situation the entrepreneur can enter. It takes the willingness to assume risks and a special ingredient of marketing savvy. The successful entrepreneur has that special gift of marketing her product in a manner different or better than anyone else in her marketing environment.

The inventor

Inventing your own product or service is the ultimate way of entering into entrepreneurship. No other method offers the unlimited potential that marketing a new product does. Whether it is the next Pet Rock or Hoola Hoop idea, or a break through in technology, hold on to your hat if it catches on. The inventor of the Pet Rock sold millions in just a few weeks.

Inventions occur in two ways. Either by accidental discovery or by deliberate research. Many tools have been invented by individuals at their work benches trying to figure out a better way of fixing something. Cooks have had ideas of brilliance while working in the kitchen. Someone invents a gag gift for a party like the Pet Rock. These are examples of ideas which can be turned into products and marketed for a profit. Many ideas never get by the thought due to the lack of entrepreneur spirit.

The other method by which inventions come about is through a deliberate search of the marketplace to determine unfulfilled needs. This requires surveys, laboratory work, and sometimes only the capital that the large businesses have available. Unfortunately, a great idea does not immediately turn into great profits. It must be designed, evaluated, tested, patented, and copyrighted.

Patents and copyrights

The first step in taking an invention to market is to find out if it is a unique idea. A patent attorney is a lawyer who spends time exclusively assisting would be inventors. The first work done for the inventor is to make a patent search. This is usually accomplished by a visit to the library of patents at the U.S. Patent Office in Washington, D.C. The patent attorney will research your idea and report back any similar patents already registered. In the event your idea is unique he might recommend that you apply for a design or a utility patent. The utility patent is the more comprehensive patent as it protects the inventor against all possible duplications of the intent and use of the product. The design patent is not as extensive, but does protect the invention against duplication of its general design. The other difference is the cost. Be prepared to spend $2000 to $3000 in legal costs and registration fees in an attempt to secure a utility patent. A design patent costs about one-third of that amount. It might take a number of years and a lot of haggling with government patent inspectors before a patent is granted. Once you have the patent you will enjoy patent protection for 17 years.

For considerably less expense and time, the creator might wish to have her work copyrighted. Copyrights apply to pieces of written work, design, or art. They assure the author, designer, or artist that his or her work cannot be duplicated in the exact manner as he or she has presented it. H & N Products did this with their baseball plaques so that, if nothing else, an imitator of their product will have to create a new format. This relatively simple procedure is inexpensive and can be done through a patent attorney or by the creator.

Before a great idea becomes a product there is production design work to be done. Questions such as how much will it cost, can it be produced, what will the final product look like, will be answered by producing a mock or sample product. This first unit will be very expensive. Once made there will be many further decisions. How should it be packaged? Who is the target market? How is it to be distributed? Having the idea is just the icebreaker. The real challenge is: Does the entrepreneur have the confidence in the product to undergo the expense, time, and effort to bring the product to market?

Developing a business opportunity

Most businesses are created because an individual believes she can do a better job of selling a product or service than those already in the marketplace. This belief should stem from the individual's educational background and work experience and not just from one's desires. Businesses fail for a number of reasons, one being a lack of preparedness of the entrepreneur for her new endeavor.

Writing down the entire business plan is a good start. Describe the idea and project the marketing, operational, and financial considerations. Discuss it with any interested parties: bankers, accountants, other entrepreneurs, friends, and relatives. Do not be shy about asking questions in the evaluation stage of an idea. Remember usually the best source of information comes from existing entrepreneurs and the vendors and suppliers of the products you are going to need.

Reputable business firms are a very valuable ally to the aspiring entrepreneur. The remainder of the book will discuss in detail and chronological order the necessary steps to be taken in opening a business. Figure 2-3 gives an indication of the steps and timing required before opening a retail operation.

New Store Checklist

To Do	Deadline before
Select store location	16 weeks
Select lawyer and accountant	16 weeks
Sign lease	16 weeks
Prepare floor plan-measure site	16 weeks
Plan dollar stock investment by resources	12 weeks
Purchase floor covering, wall paper, etc.	12 weeks
Plan store hours	12 weeks
Order cash register	12 weeks
Prepare stock control system	10 weeks
Order wrapping supplies, store stationery	10 weeks
Order pricing tickets	10 weeks
Place merchandise orders with resources	10 weeks
Plan bookkeeping system	8 weeks
Select store manager	8 weeks
Plan grand opening promotion	8 weeks
Conduct store management training program	8 weeks
Secure insurance	8 weeks
Notify utilities	4 weeks
Secure licenses	4 weeks
Buy fire extinguishers	4 weeks
Order cleaning equipment	4 weeks
Buy tools and stepladder	4 weeks
Order office equipment	4 weeks
Secure forms, job applications, W-4's, etc.	4 weeks
Make merchandising signs	4 weeks
Hire salespeople	2 weeks
Install telephone	2 weeks
Install shelving in stockroom	2 weeks
Install carpeting, wallpaper, paint	2 weeks
Prepare customer request book	2 weeks
Secure sales tax charts	2 weeks
Buy supplies	2 weeks
Open bank account	2 weeks
Receive and price merchandise	1 week
Set up fixtures and merchandise	1 week
Set up weekly schedule for salespeople	1 week
Place advertising for grand opening	1 week

Figure 2-3. New store checklist.

The entrepreneur spirit project—step 2

Equipped with your project preference you are ready to begin your search.

- Look for any opportunities for sale including franchise operations that interest you. Comb through the classifieds and visit at least one business broker. Even if you are convinced you wish to start your own business, this will be an educational step.

- Start to write out your business plan and ideas. Begin to search out answers to your marketing, operational, and financial questions. Set up appointments and visit with existing owners and managers of similar types of operations. Have these people direct you to wholesalers and manufacturers who can be of help to you.

- Make a list similar to the one in Fig. 2-3 to serve as a guide in planning the opening of the venture. With this information collected you are ready to start analyzing your prospective market.

3

The Part-Time Entrepreneur

For many the best way to enter the world of entrepreneurship is starting a business on a part-time basis. In 1990 there were over 7,000,000 part-time businesses operating in America and the number continues to grow. Often these businesses are started at home during weekends or after work hours.

Advantages of a part-time business

The goal of most part-time businesses is to build a market demand for a product or service until it reaches the point that the owner is forced to leave his or her full-time employment in order to fully develop the business. By doing this the entrepreneur is able to reduce the risk associated with starting a new business.

For those starting a business on a shoestring, it gives time to develop a business while continuing regular employment. It allows the entrepreneur to start a full-time self-employment endeavor with a customer base intact. The part-time business owner grooms customers for the full-time business. By doing this the entrepreneur will be able to come to work the first full-time day with an agenda filled with customers to see and orders to fill.

Operating a business on a part-time basis allows time to gain experience. Beginner's mistakes will not prove so costly when you are still on someone else's payroll.

Part-time businesses are often an outgrowth of hobbies or fields of interest. They are operated by people who enjoy what they are doing. If a hobby can turn into a business you will be guaranteed job satisfaction.

If the business is home-based there are numerous tax advantages. Providing that a certain portion of a residence is used solely for business purposes, the owner can deduct a certain portion of housing and utility costs as business expense from taxable income. Therefore operating from one's home not only saves the overhead of rent, it can be a tax saving. Also a home-based business is convenient and can be worked at the owner's discretion.

Disadvantages of a part-time business

By its very nature, being part-time implies secondary priority. Priority will be given to one's full-time occupation. Working after work hours or during normal leisure time can be tiring and will require discipline. You will sometimes feel that you are never off work. Motivation must be strong.

Family activities might suffer, particularly in the home-based operation. You will need the freedom to remove yourself from the demands of family living in order to pursue your goal. It is a good idea, when possible, to involve family members with the business. This will give them understanding of your goals and, in some cases, provide a unified team approach.

Ideas to consider

The following is a partial list of ideas that can be pursued on a part-time basis that might grow into a full-time occupation. They are for the most part not expensive to start, ranging from a few hundred dollars to $5000. Give some thought to ideas of your own not on the list and see if you can arrive at a list of five opportunities that would be feasible for you to consider.

1. *Mail order.* Build an inventory of an unusual product that is easy to send through the mail or delivery services. It might possibly be something that you invent or create. Research to find publications that appeal to your market. Inquire as to rates, publication dates, circulation, and other particulars. Check your library for the monthly publication of *Standard Rate & Data Service,* a guide to publications.

2. *Catalog sales.* Inquire to major mail-order catalog companies regarding the possibility of having them advertise your product in their catalogs. This can sometimes be done on a commission or flat-fee basis.

3. *Mailing service.* Address or label envelopes for local businesses or organizations.

4. *Free-lance writing.* Prepare articles on a subject that you are knowledgeable about. Send out to newspaper and magazine editors. Check *The Writer's Market,* a handbook and publication guide for writers, at your library.

5. *Desktop publishing.* This requires word processing and printing equipment. The most-requested service is directories for use by local businesses. Sell advertisements to insert in directories. Also newsletters to organization members are a good product.

6. *Garage sale service.* Make a commission on selling your neighbors' old stuff through regular garage sales.

7. *Flea market sales.* Rent a flea market booth on weekends to sell whatever unusual or inexpensive products you can find during the week. Collectibles sell well.

8. *Recycling.* Collect newspapers, aluminum cans, and glass bottles and sell them to your local recycling plant.

9. *Pet sitting.* Take care of people's pets at their home or yours while they are away.

10. *Child care.* Most states will allow you to care for as many as six children in your home without special licenses.

11. *Tutoring service.* Help struggling students after school and in evenings get through that tough course. If you have the talent, teach music or dance.

12. *Pamphlet distributing.* Place advertising pamphlets or flyers on door knobs or car windshields. This can be offered through monthly contracts.

13. *Paint house numbers.* Using stencils, paint house numbers on curbs, walkways, or driveways.

14. *Firewood service.* If you have a source, cut and sell firewood.

15. *House sitting.* Check on homes that are vacant during vacations. Check with realtors for need to watch homes for sale.

16. *Home safety and energy-saving devices.* Everything from smoke detectors to child-proofing cabinets. Check with manufacturers for wholesale prices. Sell door to door and drop off flyers.

17. *Novelty button making.* Purchase an inexpensive kit that allows you to produce tailor-made novelty buttons for organizations such as school booster clubs. See Appendix A.

18. *Handicrafts.* Make customized products to sell to retailers through flea markets, catalog houses, or mail order.

19. *Repair service.* Fix everything from bicycles to small engines. If you have the tools and expertise, market them to neighbors and let your reputation grow.

20. *Parking lot striping.* Someone paints all those yellow lines, why not you. This will take some equipment investment, but shop around for those who need this service.

21. *Janitorial service.* Clean offices and stores. Also house cleaning.

22. *Cake decorating/birthday services.* Make party and special occasion cakes, include party setting up service. Also consider making goodies for college students who are away from home by contacting their parents to arrange for delivery of birthday cakes or exam goodies.

23. *Lawn maintenance.* An old standby that keeps getting better as homeowners keep getting busier with other projects.

24. *Balloon delivery.*   A new craze, delivering and selling novelty balloons for special occasions.

25. *Pet grooming.*   Take pet grooming to pet owners' homes. Also consider pet breeding and sell the offspring to stores and individuals.

Some entrepreneurs will carry on more than one part-time business. It is easier to maintain more than one if they are associated to each other, such as a mail-order business that sells different products to different markets.

Getting started in a part-time business, as in any type of business, requires a business plan. The most difficult part for some is finding the product or service they wish to sell. This requires a review of your background and interest. Find a product or service that is easy for you to sell. Selling is easy when you believe in the product you sell. Ideas can be generated from areas that you are knowledgeable in. For example, if you are a good cook, sell your recipes, or if you know a better way to do something, sell the instructions.

You might want to try a grading exercise such as shown in Fig. 3-1. Add ideas of your own to the list and then go through and rate each of the three indicators on a scale of 0 (no interest) to 10 (maximum interest).

One suggestion for finding something to sell is to research what sold well 30 or 40 years ago and is now difficult to find. Products go in cycles and what was popular at one time might be popular again with possibly a new look. Look for a product you enjoyed in years gone by, find a resource for that product, give it a new look, maybe a new color or design feature, and bring it back to life. In this type of situation you might find the former popular product will be sold to you at a very substantial discount since its time has been perceived as past and the seller wishes to get rid of it.

Creativity can go a long way. Some crazy ideas have worked. For instance, one gentleman advertised in a fishing magazine that if you would send him an old fishing lure that no longer worked for you, and a dollar plus handling charges, he would send you a different lure to take its place in your tackle box. Basically he was just exchanging customers' inventory at no cost to him and he did quite well with the idea. Give some thought to any creative ideas which have crossed your mind in the past.

The business plan for the part-time operation must give particular attention to time management. Start by making a list of all current responsibilities and block off the necessary time to complete them. You must face any potential conflicts with your regular job and family obligations from the beginning or else the business can become a nightmare.

If it is home-based, address your home's suitability in the business plan. Will adjustments to present living arrangements be required? Can the business area be shut off from the rest of the house when working? Will you need a separate telephone line? Will you be in violation of any zoning ordinances? Will the changes planned require additional insurance coverage? Check with your insurance agent to make sure your inventory, equipment, or any other business assets can be properly insured if kept in the home.

Building a plan of action

Once your idea is in place, make an action plan similar to the new store checklist in Chapter 2. For most it will start with the following:

1. *Name your business operation.*   The main requirement of the name is that it tells what the business does. If you choose a name like Smith and Associates, make sure there is a logo or tag that tells what Smith and Associates does, that is, Smith and Associates, Bookkeeping Assistance for Small Businesses.

2. *Decide on a mailing address and phone number.*   Many owners of home-based businesses prefer to use a post office box versus a residential address. Post office boxes are inexpensive, they might give more credibility, and they give the business owner a reason to get out on a daily basis. Order a separate phone line if needed.

3. *Order business cards and stationery.*   This will give you immediate identification. Pass them out, let others know what you are up to.

4. *Organize your work.*   If you are doing business from your home, create a separate work space and office area. Buy necessary supplies and organize.

5. *Open a commercial checking account.*   Keep your personal expenses separate from the business entity.

6. *Set up a simple bookkeeping system.*   Visit your local office supply store and shop for a standardized bookkeeping system. Most can be tailored very easily to your particular business. They will include instructions on maintaining the system. You do not need an accountant.

7. *Check with your county or city for licensing requirements.*   If you are involved with a commercial enterprise it will be necessary to secure a business license. In most cases it will be expensive and in your hands within five days of filling out a simple form. Be careful of zoning regulations. Generally as long as clients do not come to your home to purchase your product or service, zoning restrictions will not impede what you wish to do.

8. *Identify the target market.*   Start to build a list of potential customers.

9. *Set the business into action.*   Do the mailouts, handouts, or classified advertising needed to attract customers.

10. *Arrange for a cost-effective system of distribution.*   Shop for the most inexpensive means of getting your product to the intended customer.

Once started, the part-time business must be monitored closely for signs of expansion. Remember, the idea is to build a market demand for your business. This might be done through expanding the product or services you offer. If you are selling something at a satisfactory level, look for products that complement your main product. Sell accessories or enhancement products. Hopefully the day will

	My Level of Interest	Personal Strength	Market Strength	Total Points
Personal services				
—house cleaning				
—babysitting				
—tutoring				
—secretarial				
—catering				
—direct mail				
Handicrafts				
—needlework				
—ceramics				
—jewelry design				
—upholstering				
Artistic work				
—painting				
—photography				
—prints				
—wire sculpture				
—engraving				
Repair services				
—small appliances				
—furniture				
—clothing				
—TV and radio				
—automotive				
Instruction skills				
—languages				
—math				

—**gourmet cooking**
—**music**
—**home repairs**
Mail-order ideas
—product sales
—repairs
—business service
Seasonal products
—foodstuffs
—clothing
—gift items
Party sales
—cookware
—plants
—plastic goods
—cosmetics
Your own ideas
For other ideas, check your local public library.

SCORING

0 to 10	Almost a sure loser.
11 to 15	Reconsider but proceed with caution.
16 to 20	Some potential here, worth further study.
21 to 25	Probably a winner, if you answered correctly.
26 to 30	How can you lose?

This checklist should give you a good idea of the kind of business that would suit you best and why.

Figure 3-1. A checklist for selecting a *part-time business*. (Small Business Administration, Publication MP15)

come when you outgrow your part-time working space and must find more time and space to accommodate the market demand.

The entrepreneur spirit project—step 3

Can your business idea be started on a part-time basis? If so,

- Write out your plan of action step by step.
- If it is home-based, write out a suitability description.
- Design a time log that allows you the necessary blocks of time to concentrate on developing the business.
- State the goal in terms of revenue needed before the business could be converted into a full-time operation.

4

Scanning
the Environment
for Opportunities

The small business sector dominated the retail industry for many years. The 1980s brought tumultuous times to the small independent retailer. The growing strength of mass merchandise discounters and national chains has threatened the hold of the entrepreneurs on this sector and has caused a dramatic shift to the new opportunities in the service industries. By 1990 the service industries dominated the list of growth opportunities for aspiring entrepreneurs.

Our society's concerns about the environment have brought a world of opportunities to entrepreneurs. The environmental movement has created businesses that are ideal for the entrepreneur to pursue. Recycling has become a household word. In many ways it is a case of the small businesses cleaning up after the big businesses. The clean world emphasis has extended into the nineties and will continue indefinitely. The start-up entrepreneur might wish to consider ideas related to this booming industry.

Recycling

More than one-third of our landfills will be full within the next two to three years. The Environmental Protection Agency has flagged source reduction as a top priority. Although the large companies are talking a lot about the measures they will be taking to assist in tackling this problem, small business owners are taking action and making profits.

Much emphasis has been placed on recycling paper as the most immediate method of alleviating the landfill problem and promoting a more ecologically aware generation. Paper accounts for 40 to 50 percent of landfill waste. There are not enough programs existing to collect and sort consumer-generated wastepaper for recycling at mills. This means opportunity to entrepreneurs.

The same holds true for the recycling of aluminum cans and plastic containers. The majority of our population is not involved with recycling mainly because we are not educated to its value and do not have the means to participate. However, more than 40 states have introduced legislation aimed at curbing the problem; therefore, we can expect the general populace to be more informed during the upcoming years.

Entrepreneurs are making money by finding cost-effective methods of collecting and sorting recyclables and selling them to material recovery facilities.

Others are making money by turning waste into resale products. For example, paper shredders can be used to produce packing materials. Shredded paper makes an excellent packing material because the loosely intertwined shreds do not allow the product to shift during shipping. Some have packaged shredded paper into confetti for resale.

Entrepreneurs have long been involved with the remanufacturing of products, particularly furniture. Remanufactured or recycled furniture is used furniture that has been made to look new. Once recycled, the furniture can sell at 50 percent off the new furniture price, thus creating an attractive market. One segment of entrepreneurs are brokers who do not remanufacture, they simply buy and sell the once junk furniture.

Industry happenings

The recycling market is one of constant change and innovation. Since the first Earth Day 20 years ago, entrepreneurs have continually found new avenues to explore.

An Ohio company makes plastic lumber. It turns recycled plastics into products such as picnic tables, mailbox posts, and speed bumps. Plastic lumber requires less maintenance, weighs less, and lasts longer.

Printers have increased their market by appealing to the ecology minded by offering recycled paper. Many take trade-ins of used white paper in exchange for credit on follow-up print orders.

Some entrepreneurs have approached hospitals to assist in the disposal of waste, particularly infectious waste which is hazardous if disposed through incineration. Hospitals are turning to local disposal companies to have their hazardous waste carted away.

Franchising has come to the recycling industry. A Minnesota company has begun franchising its operation of collecting and recycling aluminum cans, nonferrous metals, glass, plastic bottles, newspaper, cloth, and office paper. Their franchise package describes everything needed to set up and operate a recycling facility—a buyback center, a processing facility, and a network for marketing the recyclables.

There are thousands of small companies that do rador
mental Protection Agency has called radon one of the mos
health problems. One franchisor provides all the training nece
ing and remediation of radon.

There are also retailing opportunities available in the environmental indus..,
Retail outlets selling everything from remanufactured furniture to recycled paper
products are finding a market with environmentalists. One franchise, Wild Birds
Unlimited, has over 50 stores selling all kinds of supplies for birdwatching, including bird houses and feeders, customized blends of bird seed and a selection of gift
items.

Starting a recycling business

If the idea of entering the environmental industry has touched a nerve, your starting place will be research, research, research. Check with your library on the
availability of recent periodicals and government publications on the subject matter. There are two trade associations you might wish to contact.

Aluminum Recycling Association
1000 16th St., N.W.
Washington, DC 20036. (202)
    785-0951

Institute of Scrap Recycling
    Industries
1627 K St., N.W., Suite 700
Washington, DC 20006. (202)
    466-4050

Ernest Galyean started Recycle-It after six months of research. Ernest was
looking for an opportunity after suffering an industrial accident in his job as an
industrial maintenance supervisor. He received his initial stimulus from watching a
television documentary about environmental problems. Shortly thereafter he received an offer from the large disposal company that picked up his trash to do a
recycle pickup service for $33 per year. This sounded too expensive to Ernest, so
he set off to research the possibilities of forming his own company to pick up, sort,
and market recyclable household waste.

By calculating the national average per household of recycled waste, Ernest
was able to establish the potential income he could receive per household pickup.
Using conservative projections and forming a plan to keep investment and operating cost at a minimum, he offered his service at $12 per year for monthly pickup
service. After he was satisfied with his discoveries and feeling confident in his
idea, he formed Recycle-It and proceeded with his marketing plan. His initial
thrust was to distribute 2000 flyers to homeowners (see Fig. 4-1). The response
rate was 6 percent, giving him over 100 customers to start the company.

Working from a simple business plan, Ernest rents all necessary equipment.
He educates his customers as to their responsibilities of separating aluminum,
newspaper, and plastic and equips them with collection bags for each. On the
designated pickup day, he does curbside pickup and returns it to his warehouse
for further sorting and bailing. Parked outside the warehouse is a tractor trailer for
the eventual disposition of the waste. When the entire tractor trailer is filled, a re-

RECYCLE-IT CORPORATION

in cooperation with

CLAYTON CLEAN AND BEAUTIFUL

introduces curbside recycling pickup with

NO MONTHLY CHARGES

Beginning March 19XX, RECYCLE-IT Corporation, a local, privately owned and operated company will offer Clayton County homeowners an opportunity to recycle items without leaving their home. An annual service charge of twelve ($12) dollars will be required when the account is established. Pickup will be once a month for the following items:

CANS — NEWSPAPERS — PLASTIC CONTAINERS — GLASS

Labels need not be removed
No separation required
Newspapers should be bundled or in paper or plastic bags

RECYCLE-IT will continue to support Clayton Clean and Beautiful by donating a portion of the recyclable items to CCB.

HELP KEEP CLAYTON COUNTY
CLEAN AND BEAUTIFUL

TOMORROW'S SOLUTION — RECYCLING TODAY
for further information contact

RECYCLE-IT CORPORATION
Box 236
Jonesboro, GA 30237
or call
404-603-9393

25% SAVINGS on first year service if you establish
your account before March 15, 19XX

Figure 4-1. Sample advertising flyer.

cycle cartage company is called and arrangements are made for delivery and payment to Ernest for the recycled waste.

The company is only six months old, so it is premature to judge its degree of success. However, Ernest is quite optimistic considering that there are over 40,000 residences in his immediate market and little in the way of competition. He is also looking down the road at opportunities in neighboring counties. He has been most pleased with the acceptance given to him by municipal and county officials and is discovering that the industry is wide open for opportunities for environmental entrepreneurs.

The entrepreneur spirit project—step 4

If your interest lies here:

- Research the environmental market for opportunities.
- In addition to library and published research, contact your state's Department of Industry and Trade to inquire if there is a designated list of state experts in the field of waste management.
- Write out a description of the environmental service your company will serve and why you believe there is a market.

5

Analyzing
the Market

Who are your customers?

Equipped with a well-thought-out idea, the next step is to make sure that there is
a market for your product or service. A market is composed of potential customers
who have the purchasing power and unsatisfied needs for a particular product.
The real question may not be whether there are customers for your business, but
are there enough of them to constitute a profitable endeavor? In many cases the
magnitude of the number of people it takes to buy a relative low-priced product or
service in order to make a profit can easily discourage the would be entrepreneur.
The number of scoops of ice cream at 85 cents per scoop that must be sold to
reach a gross sales of $250,000 is an example of the requirement to be sur-
rounded by a large market. In order for the entrepreneur to make sure a suitable
market is available, it is necessary to launch a complete marketing research
project of the environment in which the business will operate. The starting place is
demographics—a study of the makeup of the population.

Doing market research

Market research follows these six steps:

1. Define the problem.
2. Determine needed information.
3. Collect information.
4. Analyze the information collected.

5. Implement the information to determine feasibility.

6. Evaluate the results to make the decision.

In this case we start with the problem of deciding if there is a profitable market available to sell a particular product or service. The entrepreneur must go to the available sources and ask questions. He or she should keep a file of all material related to the idea. It will become quite full if the research is thoroughly performed. Part of this search often requires attending seminars or classes relating to opening and operating a business. After the initial collection period is completed, it will be necessary to pull out the pertinent information. A test market should be run, or a hypothetical scenario created, to determine the feasibility of the project. As this process occurs, a story starts to unfold. By putting the story in a logical framework of events, a conclusion becomes apparent. Usually the entrepreneur will find alternatives to choose from along the way. These are the critical decisions that will be made. For those who are not definite as to the direction they wish to follow, separate searches and research should be done on each idea. The goal of the research is to find the right marketing mix of product, price, place, and promotion. The more information gathered and analyzed will mean less risk in the decision.

Demographics

The information available through population studies is invaluable. Not only does this information tell us the number of people in a given area, it also tells us all about them. A good demographic study tells the number of people in an area, the age of the population, the sex ratio, their level of income, level of education, their disposable income, how much they spend on food, lodging, entertainment, and how much they save. Once we have all of this information, it is then possible to tell how they live and what they like to do.

Putting this information together is not as mind boggling as it appears. There is a wealth of information easily available. Visit these three immediate sources.

The local Chamber of Commerce. One of the principal functions of the Chamber of Commerce is to lure new businesses into the area and help them get started. They should have at least a skeleton of the demographics of their area and will readily share this information.

The local library. If the local library does not have ample statistics concerning employment, sales by industry of the area, and other pertinent information, someone is not doing his or her job. All of this information is compiled by state resources, such as the department of revenue, and is made available to the public, usually by sending it directly to the local libraries.

Area colleges and universities. This may be the most satisfying of your visits. Many colleges and universities will have already put together a complete report for you. An ambitious professor's study of the area or a class project may be lying on a library shelf waiting for you. If not in the library, take a stroll across campus to the business school and ask around.

Once the information is collected, how is it put to work? To illustrate, let's investigate an area for a possible retail shoe store.

A quick review of this basic information assures us that in raw numbers there are enough people, with enough income, to support this business idea. We must carry it forward to ascertain whether or not there is a community need for the product or service. To be successful, there must be unsatisfied needs that your business can fulfill. To be discovered, the potential customer must be alerted to the existence of the product or service. This is target marketing.

The first step is to circle on a sectional map all areas which you are considering. This will give you an idea of the geographical considerations, including distances between areas. Look into the population figures, including projections for the future (Table 5-1). The vital statistics include number of people, the median age, age group percentages, minority percentage, education level, and the male-female ratio.

Check the income level and compare it to other areas. This will give you an idea of the affluence of the area. A look at the breakdown of sales by retail sectors tells how the population spends its money. Compare these with other areas in the state to get an idea as to whether products in your classification appear to be oversold as a percent of total sales or undersold, which may indicate a community need.

Let's apply this approach to opening a women's shoe store. If the idea represented an investment large enough that the store would need to draw from the entire surrounding community, the first consideration should be given to a centralized location in order to be accessible to the greatest number of people.

On the map, Fig. 5-1, this would include a choice from 12 communities. If the styles of shoes to be sold are to be fashionable and up-to-date, look for the youngest area. In this example, City A is the youngest. If the store was being de-

Table 5-1
County Population Estimates

1980	Community	1990	1995	2000	1990 people per H.H.	1990 estimate of households
46,536	A	51,960	55,000	61,000	2.59	21,753
18,560	B	38,768	48,000	65,000	2.65	15,915
5,078	C	7,984	10,000	13,000	2.66	3,068
1,118	D	1,696	3,500	5,000	2.52	689
1,004	E	1,000	1,000	1,000	2.56	287
77	F	152	300	6,000	2.26	68
2,843	G	3,100	3,100	3,100	—	—
9,163	H	10,527	11,300	12,000	2.93	3,812
5,967	I	7,518	8,500	9,600	2.67	3,064
2,883	J	3,323	3,400	3,600	2.52	1,399
2,713	K	3,787	3,500	3,900	2.57	1,405
34,610	Unincorporated	48,278	49,000	54,000	2.64	19,203
130,552	South County	178,083	196,600	231,900	2.54	70,663
96,653	Central County	116,260	125,300	146,900	2.54	59,148
43,653	North County	53,069	57,200	68,400	2.64	25,508
272,959	Total County	347,422	369,000	439,400	2.64	155,319

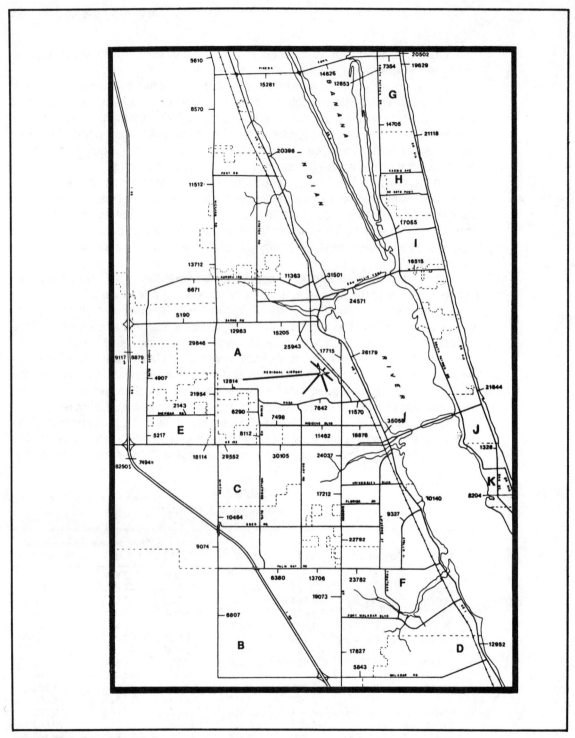

Figure 5-1. County map.

signed to feature shoes for the older woman, J or K would be considered since the population is 10 years older, indicating a lot of retirees (Table 5-2).

Turn your attention to the financial statistics. Community A has the second highest per capita annual pay in the state, approximately 12 percent higher than the state average (Table 5-3). Looking at the industry sales ledger (Table 5-4), it shows approximately $40.98 is spent on shoes per capita for the area. If by comparison it was discovered that $40.98 is below other areas, it would indicate the market is losing sales to neighboring communities and there may be community need.

At this point it is possible to draw a scenario. City A may be an excellent consideration for a fashionable women's shoe store, it has the largest and youngest population, it is also centrally located. The area has a high per capita income and there are indications, based on the sales, that there is a market need for the product.

This is a simple exercise using limited demographic information. It can become as complex and complete as the individual wishes. The main point is that in considering potential customers for starting a business, it is a worthwhile exercise that many individuals and companies do not utilize. In the following chapter choosing a specific location will be discussed, but first it is important to make sure there is a community need.

Target marketing

Target marketing means exactly what it says. Take the entire market that a product or service sells to and aim all the marketing efforts at the center of it. The market for a women's fashion store may be all women 16 to 80 years old. However, due to styles, sizes, price, etc., the overwhelming percentage of those who buy from that type of store are 25 to 40 years old. This is the store's target market.

It is very important to recognize the segment of your market that represents the highest percentage of sales. This should dictate the marketing activities, the layout of the business, the location, and the management activities of the business. Once the entrepreneur discovers the target market, she can then position her product to appeal to their interest. This can be achieved through a study of a population's psychographics, that is, its lifestyle. In addition to knowing how big the market potential is in terms of demographics, the entrepreneur's interest must also be directed toward where the target market is and who composes it.

Statistics on education level and occupational indexes are valuable tools in discovering the makeup of your customer. Equally important is the nonstatistical information of a community. Is it a resort area or blue-collar? Is it social (meaning are there a lot of country clubs and social organizations)? Who are the leaders, politically and socially? In other words, find out what the active organizations are, who is in them, how they interact, and whether their needs are being met. Then devise a plan to service them.

Marketing theorists point out the importance of opinion leaders. They are regarded as those who set the tempo and make decisions. Whether your business sells to manufacturers, wholesalers, retailers, or the general public, it is important that the businessperson be accessible to the opinion leaders. Their involvement

Table 5-2
County Age and Race Structure

Community	Median age	% white	% black	% Other		County age structure				Other breakdowns	
					Age group	Population	% of population		Age group	Population	% of population
A	32.9	87.5	10.9	1.6	0–19	78,541	28.7		16 years and up	215,775	79.1
B	32.1	91.9	6.1	2.0	20–24	24,154	8.8		18 years and up	204,925	75.1
C	34.5	98.7	.2	1.1	25–34	36,358	13.3		21 years and up	189,440	69.4
H	37.0	97.9	.7	1.4	35–44	31,689	11.6		60 years and up	50,850	18.6
					45–54	33,294	12.2		62 years and up	44,068	16.1
I	38.4	97.8	.8	1.4	55–64	34,257	12.6				
J	42.5	98.9	.1	1.0	65–74	23,877	8.7				
K	43.5	98.8	.1	1.1	75–	10,789	4.0				
County	34.1	89.8	8.7	1.5							

Table 5-3
State Average Annual Pay

Average annual pay in state	
County	**Average pay**
1.	$18,427
2. xxx Designated county	17,978
3.	17,565
4.	17,146
5.	16,969
6.	16,495
7.	16,495
8.	16,204
9.	15,858
10.	15,020

Where income is growing	
These 10 cities will lead the nation in business and income growth during this decade.	
City	**Income growth by 1990, %**
1.	38.8
2.	37.8
3.	37.8
4.	37.6
5.	37.0
6. City A	36.9
7.	36.8
8.	36.8
9.	36.7
10.	36.6

Per capita personal income			
	1990	**1995**	**2000**
County	$13,591	$15,101	$17,461

either as customers or suppliers will have a positive, snowballing effect on the operations of the business.

Discover who your customers are, where they live, what they do, and how you can best serve them. Research, ask questions, discuss your plans with others, and plot out a plan to discover your market.

Sales forecasting

Finding a starting point for predicting sales is a difficult assignment. Sales forecasting for a new product or service to be sold by an inexperienced entrepreneur involves a lot of intuition and guesswork. There are some guidelines to follow.

Defining your market is the starting place in terms of numbers and approach. The first step is determining the cost involved with doing business, and then dis-

Table 5-4
County Retail Sales

Gross sales in county

1989	$4,593,162,500*
1988	4,090,175,000
1987	3,523,300,000
1986	3,084,200,000
1985	2,925,000,000

Retail sales per household

	1985	1990
Total County	$12,275	$20,955

Annual sales potential

Store type	Total sales	Per capita sales	GLA†
Grocery	$1,038,734,000	$926.16	587,000
Department	74,311,000	496.08	697,000
Restaurants	58,377,000	389.71	12,175‡
Drug	27,562,000	184.00	196,000
Apparel	27,354,000	182.61	269,000
Furniture	13,465,000	89.89	251,000
Convenience	12,548,000	83.77	74,000
Liquor	10,719,000	71.56	58,000
Variety	6,380,000	42.59	128,000
Catalog	6,714,000	44.82	32,000
Shoe	6,138,000	40.98	46,000
Appliance	5,087,000	33.96	71,000
Jewelry	7,148,000	47.42	17,000

*Estimate
†Gross leasing area
‡Seats

covering how many units must be sold in order to make it a workable idea. In rough form this is a breakeven analysis—finding the volume of business which must be achieved in order to meet all fixed and variable costs involved with selling the product. The more information you gather, the less complex the procedure. At the beginning stage the objective is one of finding out if your idea is worth exploring. Let's look at two possibilities, one involves manufacturing and the other retailing.

H & N's baseball plaques required certain initial steps to determine if the idea had merit. The first step was to find the cost involved in manufacturing the product. The second step was to determine if the market was large enough to warrant marketing the product. A production analysis was run which indicated the production cost was $1 to $3 per unit, depending on the size of the production run. The first question was how many units and what price they needed to be sold at in order to cover the cost of producing, shipping, and handling of 1000 units. On that size run the unit cost was calculated to be $3, plus an additional $1.75 per unit for transportation and other overhead costs, for a total of $4750 (1000 units × $4.75).

By adding the marketing costs, in this instance advertising, the partners could calculate how much money had to be taken in to cover their costs. If the advertising cost was budgeted at $1250, the entrepreneurs could figure it would be necessary to charge $6 per unit to recapture the cost involved in an initial experimental production run of 1000 units ($4750 plus $1250).

Now the question turns to marketing to determine if there is a market of 1000 customers for the product. By using demographic studies and researching and testing the industry market, they could determine if there was ample space to sell x units of the product. If it is discovered that there is an opening in the market to sell many thousands of a product, a new cost standard can be used. In this example it was learned that a production run of 10,000 units brought the cost of goods down from $4.75 to $2, with the exception of marketing. Two steps follow. The first is a discovery step, used to gather information that will enable the enterprise to forecast sales of a new product. The second step is the go ahead stage. In this case the inventors produced 1000 units and advertised with the intent of not making a profit, but of securing market information. If successful at selling 1000 units in a limited marketing effort, the entrepreneurs will then have a basis for making a sales forecast for the new venture. If $1250 was spent on advertising for successfully selling 1000 units, they could multiply that figure by 10 in an attempt to sell 10,000 units.

If all statistical research was reviewed to make sure the initial advertising expenditure covered 10 percent of the market or less, the entrepreneurs may wish to take the plunge and invest the money to manufacture 10,000 units.

A retail venture, such as a shoe store, would follow a different path. Having completed a statistical analysis of the area and arriving at a profile description of the potential customer, how does the entrepreneur discover how many shoes she can sell to make a successful business? Since this is a venture into an established industry, the very best source of information will come from that industry. Do not be shy, at this stage, about approaching people in the business. Contact the sales representatives of the various companies whose shoes you are considering selling. If they are reputable companies they will become your strongest allies. They are allies because they want you to buy their product and be successful in order that they can sell you more products in the future. They will share industry and company information with you, such as per capita dollars spent on shoes and what percent of that figure is spent on their brand. In addition, they will be able to provide information related to the operating cost of a shoe store. Combining your research of the area with their information of the industry you will be able to make a rough attempt at doing some sales forecasting for the venture.

Presume the average sales per capita of a given area of 50,000 population for fashion shoes is $20. The market potential for this type of product would then be approximately $1,000,000 ($20 × 50,000). Using what you have discovered about the area, its affluence, the number of competitors, etc., it is possible for you to arrive at an estimate of what percent of market share is available for you. Your research may show that your area has a higher per capita income than average, a higher education level, and is younger. This would indicate a sales per capita potential of higher than $20, which means the $1,000,000 market potential could be low. Knowing the local competition mix of department stores and specialty stores, it might be possible for you to estimate a market share of perhaps 20 percent of $1,000,000 plus. This would indicate a sales projection range between $200,000 and $250,000. Equipped with this ballpark estimate, the entrepreneur is able to proceed with finding a suitable location that will have direct bearing on increasing or decreasing that projection.

The point to be emphasized at this stage is to ask questions of anyone remotely related to the business idea. We have mentioned company representatives, but also include established shoe store retailers. Visit store owners and managers in a neighboring community who do not represent competition—they may be glad to offer advice. Experience is important in the business arena and whenever possible use it.

Sales forecasting for the new venture is very risky. Once established, a business has history, trends, and experience to utilize in gaining very accurate short- and long-term sales projections. A sales projection at this point is a guideline only to help you make your decision. Later on we will equip you with the tools to make a long-term five-year plan. This is important because the hope for profits generally lie down the road. Very seldom should initial sales projections be made to achieve a profit. Usually a breakeven situation for the immediate future is a very substantial achievement.

A look at Bob and his expansion into the fine china business gives an idea of the pitfalls that may occur in sales forecasting.

The Cardinal room

Bob had enjoyed success in his retail and gift shop for seven years. He had enlarged the store from a basic card shop to a 4500-square-foot store filled with an exciting display of gifts for all occasions. The store was located in the major mall in a town of 30,000 people.

In seeking ideas to expand his offerings, Bob investigated the idea of adding a 500-square-foot fine china department in the rear of his store. In researching the competition he discovered only a local florist and jewelry store were selling fine china in the immediate community. There was more competition, including a number of large fashion department stores, in the neighboring town. However, they were 20 miles away. He decided all indications showed a community need. Armed with a demographic study of the area he met with Steve, a representative of the Cardinal China Company. The two of them could find no reason why a community of 30,000, medium per capita income, and good educational level, would not support the idea if done properly. The principal investment required approximately $8000, the wholesale cost of dinnerware, much of it in the form of five-piece display sets used as samples to sell special orders. Bob traveled to the main office of a major department store and met with the china buyer, whom he knew personally, to learn the techniques behind operating a successful fine china, bridal registry service.

The decision was finalized and in a few months a fine china department was set up with all the trimmings. In addition to the fine china, a silverplate flatware display was included, along with other ideas relating to the bridal customer. New carpet, chandeliers, and new fixturing all added up to a fine and complete look. The total investment was $15,000. The initial customer response was "How beautiful, this town needs something this classy."

Bob had made a rather extensive attempt at projecting sales for the department. After consulting with Steve, the Cardinal representative, and drawing from his own knowledge of the area and the gift business, he projected sales to be $50,000 the first year. This required selling merchandise at $100 per square foot (500 × $100) which was in line with the rest of the store.

First year sales were $18,000; the second year not much better. Eventually all merchandise was reduced, sold at below cost, and the department discontinued. Bob believed he had done his homework, but went back to find out where he had gone wrong.

The biggest error was made in his analysis of the demographics. A closer look would have revealed that the community was heavily populated with retirees. The number of marriage licenses had been decreasing each year for the past five years. This also showed up in a decreasing per capita income. Many potential sales were lost to the neighboring city's department stores, who were much more equipped to arrange installment credit purchases for young couples planning large purchases. There was also some question that a retail store with card and gift emphasis was not as ideally suited for the china business as the jewelry store or the florist shop who were both directly involved with wedding arrangements.

These are a few pitfalls encountered that serve as an example of mistakes that are made if the research does not cover all bases. Sales projecting for a new business or idea should be figured conservatively with a broad range of fluctuations.

The entrepreneur spirit project—step 5

Take the information you have received from this chapter and put it to work.

- Embark on a demographic study of the market you wish to serve. If it is retailing, research the communities you are considering. If it is manufacturing or wholesaling, research the industry for potential customers. Your goal is to get an estimate on the size of your potential market.

- Segment and target your particular market. Divide your potential market until you are satisfied with where the biggest and most productive target lies. Learn as much as possible about this customer. Ask questions, visit with industry sources, and use questionnaires if applicable. Write out a descriptive profile of your potential number one customer.

- Do a rough sales projection using industry and demographic information. Leave room for error. You are now ready to take this information out into the market place and begin a search for a suitable location for your business.

6

Location:
Where Do You
Set Up Shop?

There are many endeavors in which the location you select is the most important decision made in determining the ultimate success or failure of the business, regardless of how effectively the owner manages. There have been numerous businesses that have been doomed to failure, no matter how good the manager is, strictly because it was not accessible to the customer. Subconsciously consider your customers as stupid and lazy. Please don't tell them this, but if you operate under this philosophy you will service them much better.

By lazy, assume they will not lift a finger to go out of their way to buy your product or service. They will not cross a street, park a block away, not even open a closed door to do business with you. They will not travel to your plant, answer your letters, or return your phone calls. The entrepreneur must do everything he or she can possibly do to take the product to them.

By stupid, presume the customer is unable to find a way to buy from you. They are not intelligent enough to read a map, figure a discount, or understand an advertisement. The objective is to place the business in a location so obvious it cannot be overlooked, and to operate the business in a manner so that there is a minimum of decision-making on the part of the customer. Being in the right place at the right time is an important step.

What to look for

Start with three general considerations: location, transportation, and surroundings.

What town?

Is it really necessary to set up and possibly relocate to a busy, vibrant, large metropolitan area to enjoy success? It may be a serious temptation. If it requires starting cold, with no contacts, think twice. Contacts, particularly in the financial community, are important. Capital and credit requirements can serve as a prohibitive factor; stay close to your financial contacts if possible. In your hometown you know a banker and he knows something of your history and character. He will open the door to listen to you.

Friends are customers and potential investors and can give leads to future contacts. Some businesses start on the road to success with a small nucleus of people the entrepreneur knows, serving them as the first customers. The business begins with this nucleus, and from word-of-mouth advertising begins reaching out to other groups. A new hairstyling salon may start by doing a good job on 12 associates from a social circle or church group. They tell 12 others. Needless to say, if the operator burns the hair of these first loyal customers it will not matter where the business is located. Do not turn up your nose at your hometown. It is familiar to you and you are familiar to it. It is the logical choice if the demographic and psychographic factors support it.

Transportation

If the entrepreneur is considering a wholesaling or manufacturing business, there must be suitable means available to get your product to market. This requires that the area be serviced by truck lines, railroad, and airlines. The cost of transporting the products can be a major one and can be reduced substantially with a location accessible to transportation centers. Many communities have developed industrial park areas for light industry that are accessible to transportation arenas.

The surrounding environment

This is a particularly sensitive subject in retailing. A glamorous jewelry store selling high-priced merchandise must be surrounded by an environment that is conducive to attract those who can afford its product. Different businesses will have different environment requirements, some of which are not obvious and must be thought out. A restaurant is a good example.

Neighborhoods should be avoided if they harbor loafers, have unpleasant odors, or are noisy. Restaurants generally should not be located near funeral homes, hospitals, or cemeteries. Churches and schools are not good neighbors for a restaurant. They may affect liquor licenses and might cause sidewalk congestion, noise, and other disturbing factors.

Parking facilities must be taken into account. A water hydrant in the front of a restaurant prevents parking, handicaps food deliveries, and can be responsible for puddles of water near the entrance. However, an alley can be beneficial for assisting delivery.

The restaurant should be planned to suit the budget and the needs of the people who live and work around it, since they are the ones who will eventually decide its success. If located in a residential area, the owner must realize the luncheon trade will be light and should be more concerned with the evening trade. The nature of the neighborhood will determine whether customers will come in as family groups, couples, or singles.

A restaurant located in an industrial area will be dependent on the surrounding plants. It is necessary to know if the plants operate their own lunchrooms, how many people they employ, the hours they work, and the percentage of people who bring their own lunch, as well as the type of work they do, the wages they receive, and the type of food they prefer. In an industrial area, the objective is to serve large portions at reasonable prices.

A roadside restaurant should be on a main highway, preferably just on the outskirts of a city. There must be ample parking and the exterior must be attractive if it is going to catch the attention of the motorist. Except in such cases as outstanding dinner spots, people today want accessibility too. There must be a fit as to the type of business and the environment in which it operates.

Retail locations

There are three general classifications given to shopping centers: neighborhood, community, and regional. Each name is indicative of what market they serve.

Neighborhood shopping centers

The neighborhood shopping center (Fig. 6-1) is normally composed of fewer than 20 stores and is often anchored by a supermarket. It is intended to serve the immediate population that resides in its area. Its total gross leasable area (GLA) is usually less than 100,000 square feet, of which approximately 50 percent belongs to the supermarket. It is most suitable for businesses that sell convenience goods. Convenience goods are those products that are easily found and demand little effort or decision making by the customer. Everyday food items, cigarettes, film, or dry cleaners are examples of convenience goods or services. The rent costs are moderate, the stores are small, and the parking is limited. Usually the leases are relatively simple and the rent cost per square foot is comparatively low. Rent is always quoted as dollar per square foot on an annual basis. For example, a 1200-square-foot store (20 feet wide by 60 feet deep) that rents for $8 per square foot would cost $9600 per year ($8 × 1200) or $800 per month.

Community shopping centers

Community shopping centers are capable of attracting shoppers from the entire community in which they are located. Considerably larger than the neighborhood centers, they generally have one or two anchor department stores with approximately 40 other smaller tenants. There may be more than one in a community since the community may be large enough to shop numerous centers. The total GLA may be as much as 400,000 square feet and the cost may be quite a bit higher than the neighborhood center in square foot costs and other additional

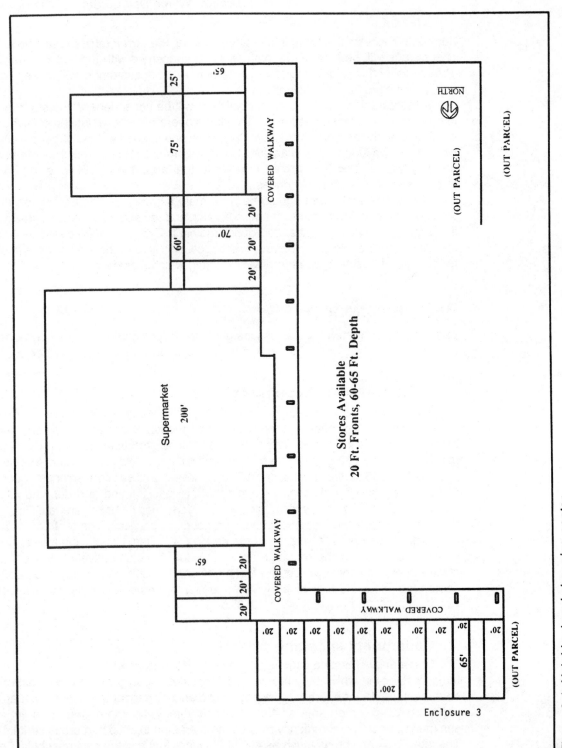

Figure 6-1. Neighborhood shopping center.

64

charges. The rent will be higher per square foot plus there most likely will be additional charges for:

1. *Merchants' association dues.* Most shopping centers this size have formed an advertising and promotion association which collects dues from tenants which are used to promote shopping at the center. These associations advertise and plan special promotions such as car shows, entertainers, and community events. The dues might range from $1 to $2 per square foot and the merchant might be required to advertise a minimum number of times per year. They are also responsible for setting the business hours of the shopping center.

2. *Common area maintenance.* Referred to as CAM, this charge is levied on shopping center tenants to help pay the costs involved with keeping the shopping center and parking lot in good condition. This includes the costs of janitorial and maintenance personnel hired by the landlord. The fee generally ranges from $.75 to $1 per square foot per year.

3. *Heating, ventilation, and air conditioning.* Termed HVAC, this is an additional expense paid by tenants of an enclosed mall to pay the utility charges incurred for heating and cooling the shopping center. It may include just the mall itself or in some instances the individual stores are also cooled and heated by the shopping center. This charge generally ranges from $1.50 per square foot on up depending on what is included.

4. *Real estate tax assessment.* Most leases are written using a pro rata real estate tax clause for the purpose of assessing annual real estate taxes. The landlord assesses each tenant a percentage of the real estate taxes, corresponding to the percent of the GLA leased.

As you can see, the tenant is paying for almost all the costs involved with owning and operating a shopping center. Sometimes referred to as triple net leases, they are very prevalent in community and regional size shopping centers and are very expensive propositions to the tenant. To quote a base rent cost of $8 per square foot can be very misleading. If the merchant's association dues adds $1 per square foot, CAM $1 per square foot, HVAC $1.50 per square foot, the true rent is $11.50 per square foot plus additional assessments for real estate taxes. In a 2000-square-foot store this translates into a cost of $23,000 per year, of which $7000 or 44 percent of base rent is for extra charges incurred.

Regional shopping centers

These are the big ones that are dominating the retail industry. They are glamorous, exciting, and very expensive. They have a minimum of three department stores, 500,000 to 2,000,000 square feet of gross leasable area, and are capable of attracting customers from a radius of 100 miles. They are usually developed by one of a handful of large national development companies such as the Edward J. DeBartolo Company of Youngstown, Ohio. They are all very similar in design (see Fig. 6-2) and tenant mix. This is because 80 to 90 percent of the GLA goes to

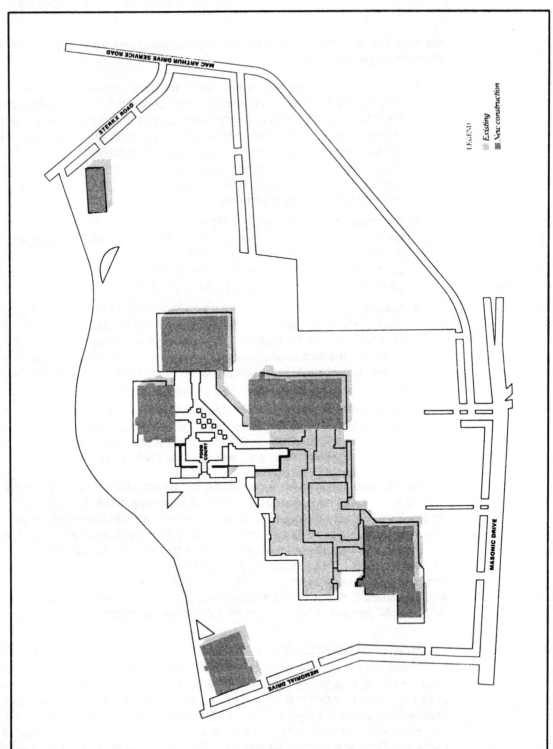

Figure 6-2. Regional shopping mall.

national chain tenants, who are usually the only ones who can afford to operate successfully at this level. Base rents are very high per square foot, in addition to the many charges we discussed for the community center. A moderate-size regional shopping center may charge a 2000-square-foot store $25 per square foot base rent, with additional charges of $10 per square foot, which totals $70,000 per year annual expense to the landlord. Since the tenant bears the cost of all leasehold improvements (carpeting, ceiling, electrical, etc.) in these centers, the risk factor is very high for the new entrepreneur. For this reason the developer feels much more comfortable with leases signed by large national concerns with a triple A credit rating. The developer also uses signed leases as collateral in borrowing money to build the center. Many of the large companies will commit to a number of leases at one time for proposed shopping centers to ensure being represented. Therefore, it is not only risky but also difficult for the new merchant to secure a lease in one of these mammoth ventures.

The type of product or service and the amount of money you are able to risk will determine the type of shopping center you may wish to investigate. A high-volume, highly impulsive store such as a Hallmark card shop or a Baskin-Robbins ice cream outlet will require the merchant to be in a high traffic center. A highly specialized jewelry store or bridal shop will be less dependent on pedestrian traffic and may not have to consider such an expensive location. As an entrepreneur, you must have your market properly targeted and locate where your customers will shop.

If you do decide on a shopping center location, then it must be decided where in the center your store belongs. Locating beside one of the leading anchor stores is going to cost more than being located along the entrance way from the parking lot. Also the more space leased, the lower the rent charge per square foot. The merchant is concerned with what type of shopping area, where within that area, and how much space is affordable.

Different shopping centers, although in the same classification, may be quite different in terms of tenant mix and layout, making one preferable to another. Look at this example of two competing centers.

Sears mall versus the J.C. Penney mall

Within the same community of 35,000 people there are two community-size malls. Shopping mall A is anchored by Sears Roebuck; shopping mall B has two anchor stores, J.C. Penney and Belk Lindsey department stores.

Each has a leading national drug store, a national variety store, and approximately 30 other stores. Shopping mall A only has the one department store, Sears, the biggest, and a leading grocery store at the other end. Mall B has the two anchors, one at each end, but no grocery store. Mall A leases at $5 per square foot, mall B at $8 per square foot. What center would be preferable for a 2000-square-foot card and gift shop?

Shopping mall B is a much better opportunity in this instance. Although the tenant must pay an additional $6000 per year rent ($3 extra × 2000), the pedestrian traffic is 2:1 B over A. If that means double the sales volume, i.e., $150,000 to $75,000, the $6000 is easy to make up. The reason for the large difference is that mall A is very poorly designed. By placing Sears at one end of the shopping center and the grocery store at the other, the developer eliminated the cross flow of traffic between anchor stores which is essential to small impulse retail stores. There are two reasons a grocery store will not serve this function in a mall location. Number one is that you can't leave ice cream in the car after grocery shopping and then shop for clothes. Number two, who has money left to shop after finishing grocery shopping? Good cross flow traffic is what the small tenant is paying for in a shopping mall this size. In a strip shopping center the grocery store is a good anchor as it allows exposure of the small tenants while parking at the grocery store.

One other point on shopping centers before moving on. They have life cycles. Marketing students learn that products, including shopping centers, have life cycles. A product starts at the introductory stage, moves through the growth stage into maturity, and eventually into a decline stage. All products go through this cycle, some just stay in certain stages longer than others. Shopping centers cycle also, as someday each center is replaced with a newer and more up-to-date center.

Generally shopping centers can stay strong for a period of 20 to 25 years. After that the anchor store leases will expire and they will be available to move to newer and bigger centers. Before deciding on what center, study its history and project its future. If the merchant still has three years remaining on a lease when the large stores leave, he may have a lot of problems.

Other alternatives

If the entrepreneur's business idea is not fully developed, or if there is no need to require the large amount of pedestrian traffic a shopping center will bring, there are other types of locations to investigate.

Downtowns   Often deserted and dilapidated due to the outflux of families to suburban areas, there are still some viable locations for businesses, particularly if they relate to the business community. Although in most communities they are no longer the prime shopping area, due to decadence and crime, they are still usually the hub of the business community. If the business caters to the business community and can survive on the shortened hours that business people shop, there is opportunity at less expense in the downtown areas. The principal handicaps are lack of parking, age of the buildings, and the surrounding image. If the customer must drive around the block to find parking, it can spell doom to the business because it will not be accessible. If the building is old and decrepit, the money saved on rent will go quickly on the expenses of fixing up the space. If the new business is situated between a vacant, gutted out store and the Salvation Army mission, it will be impossible to overcome the image presented.

Downtown situations must be looked upon separately, as some can be very profitable. The downtown area of Bartlesville, Oklahoma, surrounds the headquarter operations of Phillips Petroleum Company. A very high percentage of this one-company town of 30,000 people work in the downtown area and have a long lunch hour. During these lunch hours and immediately after work there is more than ample pedestrian traffic to support almost any type of retail activity. Many downtown areas, where there are enough business employees, have very vibrant shopping activity between 11 a.m. to 2 p.m. and 4 p.m. to 6 p.m. five days per week.

Another development that is receiving a lot of publicity is the renovation of downtown areas. Many communities are giving their downtowns a face-lift in order to attract shoppers. Wider sidewalks, landscaping, and creating pedestrian malls by blocking out automobile traffic, are ideas being used to inspire property owners to renovate their buildings in order to attract customers. The idea sounds great and has proved successful in cities such as Savannah, Georgia; Charleston, South Carolina; and New Hope, Pennsylvania. Keep in mind that in order to compete against the convenient and modern shopping center, the downtown has to be able to offer more than just nostalgia and cuteness. It must offer an exciting and practical tenant mix. The new-look downtowns have not usually been successful at doing this on a consistent basis and many will fail. One tenant of a newly renovated downtown area was asked to comment on how successful was the reopening of the area. "During the week of the reopening event, the mayor was cutting ribbons, the bands were playing and there was so much publicity, my business did fine. However, one week after all the hoopla the customers were back at the shopping centers and my sales were right back to their previous level."

The downtowns should be considered highly speculative for most businesses. There is no doubt the overhead will be less; however, you generally get what you pay for.

Standing Alone   Many businesses can be successful through exposure from automobile traffic. Good restaurants particularly will be successful as long as people can find them and there is ample parking. For businesses which can help make their own traffic, a building located on a well-traveled street can be ideal. Normally the rent factor is but a fraction of the shopping center and there are also property ownership possibilities. A nice-looking facility with ample parking and good access from the street can flourish. Most of the large discount operations were originally located in buildings not associated with shopping centers. The real estate costs were considerably less, and due to the small profit margin they operate on, it was considered the best method of reducing overhead. It proved successful because they were able to generate their own traffic with their price discounting. Recently, many of these stores are becoming associated with shopping centers of their own since other tenants wish to take advantage of the traffic they generate.

One big advantage to the entrepreneur in staying away from shopping centers is that he may be able to purchase the property as opposed to leasing it. This should serve to enhance the investment, since real estate generally appreciates. A merchant in a shopping center for ten years may pay out $500,000 in rent expenses and have nothing to show for it at the end of the lease term. That $500,000 will buy or build a pretty nice facility which can be sold at a later time for a nice profit.

Locations for manufacturers, wholesalers, and professional services

Location considerations for nonretailers are also centered around convenience, but in a different light. Convenience to manufacturers and wholesalers means being close to transportation facilities that allow fast and efficient shipment of goods to their customers. Convenient transportation facilities cut down freight costs and save time. Given a choice, the receiving customer will choose the supplier who is able to deliver the quickest at the least cost. Geographically, supplier businesses should be centrally located to those they ship to. This will allow easier access, at less cost, to make personal sales and customer service calls.

Many manufacturers and wholesalers locate in industrial parks. Industrial parks are parcels of land set aside by county and municipal governments for the use of industrial companies. These parks are accessible to transportation companies and generally are occupied by small and medium-size light industry companies. Quite often they offer a location used by similar businesses that will sometimes use each others' services. The improvement cost of industrial parks is often subsidized by the government entity in order to entice businesses to locate in their communities.

Also available in many communities are incubators. Incubators are locations that house numerous businesses under one roof in order to share in the cost of some of the operating overhead of a business. Such common expenses as utilities, receptionist salary, fax and copy machine costs, and maintenance expenses are shared on a pro rata basis. Incubators are often subsidized by government agencies as well in order to attract and help develop small businesses.

Professional services must be aware that their clients are also heavily influenced by the convenience factor. If clients must hunt for a service, they will forgo it. It is also important that the professional service locate in an area that enhances the professional image. A professional service must build credibility to survive. A nice office with a professional image in a convenient location will add to the credibility of the service.

Leasing

The subject of contemporary leasing is a far cry from a signed one-page statement and a handshake of years gone by. The modern commercial lease is often a long and complex legal instrument which requires much thought and consultation before signing. A typical shopping center lease may be thirty pages long and ties the tenant in so tight that the only way out if the business fails may be bankruptcy.

Types of leases

As discussed, most leases are written in terms of a stated base rent charge per square foot, plus added charges, computed on an annual basis and billed by monthly installments.

This is only the basic terms. The full terms of the lease spell out everything from the insurance the tenant will carry, what restrictions are placed on what she is allowed to sell, and what hours the business will operate. In signing and negotiating a lease, it is suggested the new entrepreneur consult with an attorney. The sample first page of a lease (Fig. 6-3) is shown to give some insight into the terminology used.

As the illustration shows, there may be a percentage rent clause included that rewards the landlord for all the hard work of the tenant. This says that if you really do well the landlord is entitled to a higher rent. Based on sales volume, it says, in this particular instance, that if the business has sales in excess of $146,000 per year, the tenant shall pay 6 percent of gross sales to the landlord instead of the agreed upon base rent. In other words, the base rent is $8748 per year ($729 × 12), but if sales exceed $146,000 it will be more. If the merchant does a great job and boosts sales to $250,000 per year, his new rent is $8748 plus 6 percent of the $104,000 overage, $6240, for a total rent of $14,988 per year.

The landlord will tell you that it is his reward for creating such a conducive shopping environment, the tenant may think of it as being gouged. There are some rare instances where tenants pay strictly a percentage of sales with no guaranteed rental amount. This can be to the tenant's advantage if the percentage is reasonable, since it directly involves the landlord with the success of the enterprise. This is very rare and occurs only when the landlord is desperate for tenants.

Other parts of the lease specify what the landlord will physically do to the premises to be leased. This can vary from offering nothing except the outlined floor space to totally outfitting the interior of the leased space. When the landlord is willing to pay for all floor coverings, wall preparation, lighting, bathrooms, partitions, etc., it is called a turnkey lease. When the tenant receives the key to the space, it will be ready for him to move in. A word of caution is that these costs are generally recaptured in the form of higher rent. However, this form of lease can be quite helpful to a new business owner with limited monies, it saves thousands of dollars of immediate out-of-pocket expenditures.

The lease also specifies the time duration of the lease and should include an option to renew. Leases can be written for any period of time but are most commonly stated for three- or five-year terms or longer. It is important to have an option to renew. This gives the tenant the right to continue operations for a specified period of time after the initial lease term, at a previously agreed upon cost. This is for the benefit of the tenant because it protects him from having his business terminated at the wish of the landlord. It, of course, does not require the tenant to stay. It is normally written to include a cost-of-living increase on the initial rent, but may be negotiated downward if business conditions have deteriorated.

All of this is important to know because it is all negotiable. Renting is very elastic in terms of supply and demand. If the landlord is having trouble securing leases, or if your particular business would be an asset to his existing tenant mix, then many of the terms can be negotiated. Too many inexperienced entrepreneurs fall victim to signing the lease as offered. Remember, this contract is a debt obligation just as a bank note would be. If the rent is $3000 per month for five

This lease, entered into this _____ day of _____ , 19_____ , between the Landlord and the Tenant hereinafter named.

ARTICLE 1. Definitions and Certain Basic Provisions. 1.1

(a)   "Landlord":   Smith Development Co. _____

(b)   Landlord's address ___ 120 Main Street _____
Springfield, Ill. 22573 _____

(c)   "Tenant": ____ Mr. John Doe DBA Gard Town _____

(d)   Tenant's mailing address: 32 Washington Ave. _____
Springfield, Ill 22513 _____

(e)   Tenant's trade name: _____

(f)   Tenant's address in Shopping Center   A-8 _____

(g)   "Demised Premises": approximately _____1200_____ square feet in Building   A   (computed from measurements to the exterior of outside walls of the building and to the center of interior walls) having approximate dimensions of _25_ feet x _50_ feet such premises being shown and outlined on the plan attached hereto as Exhibit A, and being part of the Shopping Center situated upon the property described in Exhibit B attached hereto. "Shopping Center" shall refer to the property described in Exhibit B, together with such additions and other changes as Landlord may from time to time designate as included within the Shopping Center.

(h)   Lease term: Commencing on the "Commencement Date" as hereinafter defined and ending   Thirty Six (36)   months thereafter except that in the event the Commencement Date is a date other than the first day of a calendar month, said term shall extend for said number of days in addition to the remainder of the calendar month following the Commencement Date.

(i)   "Estimated Completion Date": day of _____October 15, 19XX_____

(j)   Minimum Guaranteed Rental: $ _729.17_* per month, payable in advance.

(k)   Percentage Rental: _____6_____ % of gross sales in excess of $ _146,000.00_ per month during the calendar year, payable on or before the 10th day of each following month subject to Article IV, Section 4.3 below.

(l)   Initial Common Area Maintenance charge per month: $ _____52.08_____

(m)   Initial Insurance Escrow Payment per month: $ _____10.42_____

(n)   Initial Tax Escrow Payment per month: $ _____62.50_____

(o)   "Security Deposit" _$1,793.76_ , refundable upon expiration of term less any damages for unusual wear and tear or charges necessary to restore the Demised Premises to satisfactory condition.

(p)   Permitted use: _Hallmark store — retail sale of cards and gifts_ _____

1.2   The sum of:
Minimum Guaranteed Rental as set forth in Article I, Section 1.1 (j); and 729.17*

Initial Common Area Maintenance charge, as set forth in Article I, Section 1.1 (l); and 52.08

Initial Insurance Escrow Payment as set forth in Article I, Section 1.1 (m) 10.42

Initial Tax Escrow Payment as set forth in Article I, Section 1.1 (n) 62.50

Initial Base Sales Tax Payment as set forth in Article I, Section 1.3 . . . .   42.71

MONTHLY PAYMENT TOTAL 896.88

1.3   In addition to its obligation to pay the Monthly Payment Total, adjusted from time to time as provided herein, Tenant shall pay simultaneously therewith any sales tax, tax on rentals and any other charges, taxes and/or impositions now in existence or hereafter imposed by any governmental authority based upon the privilege of renting the Demised Premises or upon the amount of rent collected thereof. All payments provided for herein shall be in lawful (legal tender for public or private debt) money for the United States of America.

Figure 6-3. Standard shopping center lease.

years it is a $180,000 total obligation. If you are able to negotiate one dollar off per square foot, a lower percentage rent factor, or more landlord-paid leasehold improvements, you could save thousands of dollars toward this obligation. Ignorance of leasing considerations can cost money as Jack learned in his tobacco store.

Jack opened a tobacco shop in a shopping mall at what he thought was a fair rent. What he failed to learn was the intricacies of a percentage rent clause. His sales volume boomed mainly due to selling cigarettes by the carton at near the cost paid for them. This generated store traffic and cash flow, but at the same time pushed his sales volume over the percentage rent point. He was selling products for little or no gross profit and was forced to pay additional rent to do so. If he increased his sales $100,000 by selling cigarettes at cost he was increasing his rent $6000 at the same time. He eventually realized this, stopped selling his cigarettes at cost, but lost his store traffic and later closed his store.

Leasing is a bargaining confrontation between lessor and lessee. The following is an interview with a former retailer who now acts as a leasing agent for community size shopping centers.

What are the major determinants used in site selection of a shopping center?
The main considerations are competition and land costs, which includes the cost to develop the land. The objective is to locate as close to the population area as possible. We do not want locations where a competing shopping center could be built between ours and the population area, thereby cutting us off from our market. The cost of the land is important; however, we are not interested if there are problems such as no utilities or other complications that will drive up the cost to build. We use market research to gather demographic information and try to find out if any anchor store tenants would like to locate in the area. We share the demographic information with all potential tenants.

How are rent charges determined?
Rent charges are determined by the total cost of the site, the construction costs, and the cost of financing. The developer needs to show the bank a projected income statement showing that he can pay loans back based on projected rental fees. The final rent is determined in consideration of recovering costs, rent studies of area shopping centers, and a desired rate of return on investment. It is, of course, decided in the end by supply and demand. The anchor tenants are major determinants of rents, since they will contribute to the demand for the space. Excess competition will drive the price down. Keep in mind, however, the shopping center developer has made a financing contract with the lender that he will receive x dollars per square foot of space, and anything too far removed from this figure will raise the lenders eyebrows. There is a point in negotiations regardless of market supply and demand at which the developer is better off to carry a vacancy than to rent at reduced rates for an extended period of time.

How do you find tenants and what do you look for?
We want tenants that complement the shopping center. We do not want to put an auto supply store in an exclusive specialty store center. The great majority of my time is spent canvassing existing merchants in the general area to

alert them to our project. We prefer established businesses to the new business owner. An established owner can show us a track record and we will know what to expect. We really like established businesses that advertise a lot as they contribute to a more vibrant shopping center. We screen new business owners closely. We request financial information and detailed plans for the proposed operation. We like to see a source of outside income in the event initial plans do not work. In the event the tenant has absolutely no experience, we might attempt to direct him to a franchise. If there is not an abundance of capital and little experience, we will back away from leasing to that individual. New businesses usually will call us in response to a sign on the property or as a result of an announcement of our project seen in the newspaper.

The landlord is sometimes considered an adversary of the tenant as opposed to an ally. Having been on both sides, would you comment?
The landlord is a businessperson just as the tenant. He or she has the same objective—to make a profit. I have found the industry to be very ethical. The developer is very concerned with the tenant's success as it ultimately determines his future success. Landlords are not villains in black hats, they are legitimate business people with fair objectives. Although it is not as strictly regulated as the residential real estate market, it is for the most part a very professionally run industry. However, in commercial real estate I would recommend "Caveat emptor," let the buyer beware, as a guideline for the inexperienced entrepreneur.

The entrepreneur spirit project—step 6

- Based on the knowledge gained from the analysis of your market choose the city and the area of the city you wish to locate.

- List all potential locations available and analyze their pluses and minuses in terms of sales volume and accessibility.

- Discuss with the property owner of your chosen location all specifics in regard to leasing or buying of physical facilities and terms of the agreement.

- Write out all arguments for choosing that location.

- Review any potential lease or purchase opportunities with an attorney.

7

Financing and Organization: The Money Tree

The idea is formed, the market is analyzed, the location has been chosen—now where is the money? This missing piece of the puzzle is usually the hardest one to find and represents the greatest inhibitor to the aspiring entrepreneur. The entrepreneur knows she has a great idea, but unless she is blessed with abundant capital, she must be able to sell the idea to others. Let's look at this in ascending order of the most preferable path to follow in securing capital.

Capital sources

Savings account and personal holdings

Take a complete inventory of your liquid assets. Add up the cash values of your savings, your company profit plan, and any securities you own that you are willing to commit to your idea. Do not be shy about how much you are willing to invest, because if the idea is not sound enough to take risks with your own resources, you will have trouble convincing others to part with their monies. See how far short you fall in having the estimated capital needed and how much help you may need. Make a list of other sources you can consider, starting usually with your immediate family.

Blood is thicker than water, which means family is often more understanding than bankers or investors. Explain your idea to dad, brother, sister, or aunt to see if it generates any excitement. Express your dreams instead of asking for money. Hopefully the result will be an offer to help rather than an obligatory, "If you can't find it anyplace else I may be able to help." The best relative help comes in the form of long-term low-interest loans. Less preferable is giving up stock or ownership in your idea and adding additional voices in management.

Where there is no relative support available, you may wish to look for a supportive friend. There is some truth, however, to the thinking that business relationships can kill friendships. It takes a special type of relationship for this to work. Once again, approach this in terms of showing enough excitement in your idea that your friend volunteers support, rather than your making a plea for it. Unless there is an unconditional offer of help, friendship borrowing is not advisable.

Banks

Contrary to the ads you read and see on television, bankers are not always smiling people waiting to help you whenever possible. The banker is not a risk taker, the entrepreneur is; therefore there is a conflict. The bank is willing to help only if it is well covered in the event things do not go according to plan. Do not expect to present your idea to the bank and have it loan you the money to get started simply because you have a good idea. They will normally agree with your idea and then they will ask how you plan to secure the loan. By the time you have pledged every asset you own as collateral in case of loan default, you will realize the bank has taken absolutely no gamble.

Very seldom will inventory have a collateral value since the bank has no desire to assume ownership of something you have not been able to sell. Banks can be valuable allies in securing short-term monies to operate with after you have opened your business; however, they are usually a limited avenue in securing seed money for the new venture.

Trade credit and equipment loans

Depending on the business activity, there may be substantial aid available from the industry itself. Your suppliers and vendors will often be willing to sell to you on short-term credit arrangements. Trade credit can range from thirty days to much longer, depending on the industry. Normally extended strictly to product purchases, credit is intended to give the business owner time to sell the product before paying for it. It is granted after a review of financial statements and normally has a limit on it. This will assist the entrepreneur in the short run, but it should not be considered as seed money.

Equipment or fixture loans are very common within an industry. Generally they are tied into product purchases and are offers from vendors to allow you to use their equipment with generous purchase terms as long as you sell their products. In retailing, a vendor will often sell you the display cases for their products on extended low-interest terms in order to secure your business. Also any equipment such as cash registers, machinery, or furniture has a collateral value; therefore, a bank will loan you a certain percent of that value for purchase.

There are many variations of credit extended through franchise agreements. The parent company is often willing to enter financing arrangement on a long-term basis with their franchisees. This is only done, however, after certain minimum capital requirements have already been met.

How much money you need and where it comes from may be best illustrated by a chronological discussion of the avenues available and the steps to be taken. Familiarity with the industry projections and a knowledge of how large a market is available, how much the location will cost, and how much profit is needed to survive will draw a rough financial needs picture.

Industry sources may state that up to 10 percent of gross income can be spent on rent or mortgage payments in a marginally successful operation. If the preferred location will cost $25,000 per year, the sales volume must be in the neighborhood of $250,000 to be successful. Therefore, the entrepreneur must find out what is needed in terms of equipment, fixtures, and products in order to reach this figure.

For a particular retail activity, industry sources may tell you that the product turns over, or sells through, an average of five times a year. Using this as a guideline, it will be necessary to sell $50,000 of retail inventory five times per year to reach $250,000. Because the average retail markup in the industry is 50 percent of the selling price, it is necessary to have $25,000 of cost merchandise available to sell your customers at all times. Since you would never wish to sell out of all of your merchandise, you should have a base inventory equal to the amount that you are constantly turning. To find the inventory needed in this situation you would simply figure $25,000 invested for base inventory plus $25,000 for rotating inventory equals a total planned inventory purchase of $50,000. There is a little more to it if it is a seasonal type of business; however, this is the general rule of thumb.

Knowing that you will need $50,000 of cost inventory, you are now able to project what is needed to house and sell this inventory. By breaking down the $50,000 into how many x type units and how many y type units, etc., you can arrive at a list of the type and the amount of fixtures, furniture, and equipment needed and how much they will cost. By drawing a floor layout (see Chapter 8) a total cost picture of all that is needed can be calculated. If this figure were $50,000 also, the total initial capital investment of this hypothetical business would be $100,000.

If the business is one that will carry on accounts receivable, monies should be put aside to cover the average outstanding accounts receivable. The accounts receivable fund represents, in most businesses, monies that will always be outstanding until the business is sold or closed. This can be calculated by finding the average collection time of the industry and multiplying that percentage of the year times the projected annual sales volume. If it is 37 days, divide 37 by 365 days per year, which equals approximately 10 percent, and put 10 percent of $250,000 aside as monies always outstanding.

Monies need to be budgeted for one-time opening expenses plus an operating cash surplus to carry you through while the business is getting established. One-time opening costs such as grand opening advertising expenditures may be budgeted at $5000 and a three-month operating cost reserve may be projected at $20,000. The total capital needed for this business would total as follows:

Inventory	$ 50,000
Fixtures, equipment	50,000
Accounts receivables	25,000
Operating account	25,000
Total	$150,000

If the entrepreneur's total personal assets available are $75,000, he is $75,000 short of what is needed. Don't despair, start investigating ways to secure the missing monies.

- A relative is able to advance a $10,000 long-term loan. The deficit is now $65,000.

- Fifty percent ($25,000) of the monies needed for furniture, fixtures, and equipment is available through long-term financing arrangements with the suppliers. The deficit is now $40,000.

- By purchasing the initial $25,000 base inventory with cash in advance you should have no problem establishing trade credit for the $25,000 ordered as replacement merchandise that will be arriving after the business is open. The deficit is now $15,000.

- Now that you have your entire cost program laid out you are able to go to the bank with a short-term credit-line request of $15,000. Since this really represents operating capital reserve, it is possible it may not be needed, but it should be lined up in advance, just in case. If your presentation is complete and you have a good association with your bank, a $15,000 request for a short-term (less than one-year) loan should be favorably considered.

Aspiring entrepreneurs often want to know how much equity is needed. Financial institutions like to see a 2:1 ratio of assets to liabilities; however, much of it depends on the idea, the owner, and the plan.

The key is to be honest with your projections. There is a natural tendency to make an idea that you really want to succeed look good. If the needed sales volume is $250,000 you may try too hard to make sure that your projection comes to $250,000. Or the entrepreneur may decide that although the supplier's sales representative suggested a sales turn of five times per year, she is sure she can do six. Using a pessimistic approach, try using a sales turn of four, if told five, and see if it still works. Remember you are inexperienced and the sales representative may be overselling the product. If the entrepreneur can figure a way to make it work by planning pessimistically, it will give credence to the idea.

Extras, whether they are in the form of leasehold improvements, inventory, or advertising, are sometimes better planned for after the business is established. An example: new electronic cash registers may cost $2000 per unit; standard used cash registers can be found for $200. The old ones serve the same purpose without the glamour. They seldom break down, while the new ones require a maintenance agreement to guard against the many possible problems they can have. The new business can open with the old standard models and purchase the newer ones at a later date. A new business is like a young child, who must mature before new toys can be appreciated. The idea is to keep that initial investment reasonable or else the bank will balk at your presentation and the money will be put where it least belongs.

Small business administration loans

If the bank says no, don't despair, there is another avenue to follow—SBA loans. There are two types of SBA loans—direct and guaranteed.

Direct   Direct SBA loans are loans made directly from the government at very low interest rates; however, it is very difficult to qualify for one. These loans are intended to assist minority-owned and veteran-owned businesses that principally serve a disadvantaged or public-sector market. A very small percentage of SBA loan activity is in this limited market. However, if you think it might apply to your business activity, by all means inquire of the closest SBA office.

Guaranteed   Almost all SBA lending is done through the guaranteed loan program. The guaranteed loan program is available to those whose loan applications have been turned down by banks. If the applicant can qualify under SBA requirements, the SBA will participate with a bank in granting a loan that would be guaranteed for up to 90 percent of the outstanding balance by the SBA. In other words, the SBA helps secure loans. It must be pointed out, however, that qualifying for an SBA loan is almost as difficult as qualifying for a bank loan. There is a little more leeway in regard to collateral required, and more merit is given to the business plan. Therefore if you believe that you came close to getting a bank loan, an SBA loan is certainly a consideration. The other advantage to an SBA loan is more time to pay out a loan. Loans for property and equipment purchase often run 15 years, sometimes more, and working capital loans will usually have up to seven years to pay off.

It is sometimes a slow process and has its share of government regulation and red tape, but for those who qualify SBA loans might be the answer to the financial puzzle. In 1990 the SBA guaranteed more than $3 billion in loans.

Venture capitalist

You will hear much about venture capitalists and joint ventures. Venture capitalists are individuals, or groups of individuals, that use their financial resources to finance businesses in return for a share of the business's success. Since these people have accumulated the wealth necessary to be able to do this through successful navigation of the business world, they are normally quite astute in evaluating a business's potential. They are not interested in routine small business endeavors. They back companies that have the potential for developing sizable profits through innovative ideas. This would include inventors or companies on the verge of a product breakthrough if the capital were available. Venture capitalists are most interested in projects requiring a minimum investment of $500,000 that are willing to sacrifice some of the ownership for the investment.

The type of organization and its relationship to financing

There are basically three types of organization structures to choose from: the sole proprietorship, the partnership, and the corporation. The type of organization structure you choose will have an impact on your ability to raise capital.

Sole proprietorship

The sole proprietorship is exactly what it says. There is only one person responsible for the profits or losses of the business. It is the simplest type of ownership. There are no applications or forms to fill out, no special registration fees, and no charters or restrictions on what you are permitted to do. It just requires the will to do it yourself. It has severe limitations, however, in terms of raising capital. All capital investments and borrowings are done on the basis of one person's assets. All loan contracts will require the individual's personal guarantee. This means that if there is trouble, the lending institution will not only have the right to foreclose on the business assets but also can go after the individual's personal assets as well. This includes practically everything with the possible exception of the individual's home, which is protected by law in most states.

There are, however, some real advantages to the sole proprietorship. The prime one is that there will be no interference from partners or stockholders in the way the individual runs the business. This, of course, puts more responsibility on the owner.

Another real plus may be the income tax situation for the new business. There is a minimum of paperwork placed on the sole proprietor concerning tax reporting. At the end of the calendar year the owner simply attaches a profit and loss statement to her personal 1040 tax form and declares the profit or loss on form 1040. This can be of real value to the new entrepreneur as it may allow a few years of not having to pay personal income tax since a new business is usually rather marginal as far as showing any true net profit. Any monies taken out by the owner of the business are considered a draw against the capital of the business and not a salary. What is reported to the government is the net profit, not the draw against the business. Since a new business generally has a lot of depreciation costs, the owner can conceivably take considerable draws against the business to live on and still not declare a net profit.

For example, Randy opens a retail business requiring a $60,000 investment in fixtures, furniture, equipment, and leasehold improvements. This $60,000 is depreciable in varying degrees from $6000 to maybe $20,000 per year depending on the depreciation schedule used.

Randy may draw $20,000 per year out of the business for living expenses and not pay taxes since the business shows no profit. He will be using his depreciation allowance to live on.

An individual may be able to go a number of years without declaring net profits while taking enough money from the business to feed the family. Of course the day will come when depreciation allowances will run out and taxes will have to be paid on the profits. When this time comes, it may be time to change to a corporation whose tax advantages will be discussed shortly. Most small one-person leadership businesses should start as sole proprietorships.

Partnership

Taking in a partner or partners is a big decision that requires much contemplation. There are times when it is a necessity. A partner can bring added expertise and added borrowing power. A partner can also bring added headaches and disagreements. A partnership is when two or more people join together for the purpose of engaging in a business enterprise. There are variations, such as silent partners and limited partners, which can be investigated, but these still fall under the same formation as the general partnership.

The only reason a partner should be taken on is when there is a legitimate need for either added capital or brain power. Do not take a partner just for company, because it may backfire on you in terms of a broken relationship. No matter how well two people get along socially, the business world is a different environment. Many situations will occur that have not been expected, that will require confrontation, and this is not easy for friends or relatives. This is the severe limitation of a partnership.

Sue opened a fashion boutique with her best friend Sheila. Everything went well between the two of them, but when Sheila's husband became involved a serious problem developed. All of a sudden Sue was being asked to defend her business decisions to Sheila's husband. These constant inquiries eventually turned Sue sour on the business and damaged her relationship with Sheila.

If there is a need, often a partnership can be the best way to operate a business. The business s borrowing power is enhanced with the addition of added personal assets to pledge for borrowing. The adage "two heads are better than one" takes on importance. This is particularly true if the recruited partner adds technical expertise to complement marketing expertise or vice versa. It also lightens the burden of one person operating the entire business and assures the continuation of the business in the event of death or incapacity of one of the principles.

By forming a partnership, a more complex arrangement is entered into. There is more paperwork, expense, and tax work to be done. The partnership must be registered with all taxing authorities and a partnership agreement should be drawn up. This agreement is important and should spell out as much as possible all considerations that should be taken into account in order to assure the most efficient running of the operation. It acts as the referee in case of disharmony or dissolution of the partnership relationship.

The following items should be covered in the articles of partnership.

- Date of the formation of the partnership.

- Names and addresses of all partners.

- Statement of the business purpose.

- The amount and type of capital invested by each partner.

- The sharing ratios of all profits and losses, including any salary arrangements for working versus nonworking partners.

- Provision for the distribution of assets at the time of dissolution. This should be set on an equal basis as to the amount invested. Any personal considerations (such as property on loans from any partner) should be listed separately.

- The specific responsibilities of each partner.

- Any preset conditions to be followed by the partners. This would include any restraints, such as any disbursements, checks, or notes that must be endorsed by all partners.

- A provision for the voluntary or involuntary premature withdrawal of any partner. This should specify the responsibilities of the partnership to any partner who wishes to drop out to pursue other interests or the responsibilities involved with terminating a partner.

- Settlement provisions in the event of the death or disability of any partner. This should include a buy-sell agreement, normally funded with business life insurance, in amounts equal to the interest of each partner. This assures the survivorship of the business and satisfies the demands of the deceased's estate. Ideally, the agreement should be drawn up by an attorney, signed by all parties, and put in a place for safekeeping.

The tax considerations of a partnership are the same as a proprietorship, except all profits or losses are divided in proportion to ownership. Profits or losses are distributed to the owners to declare on their 1040 form. In the event there is a working partner and a non-working partner or partners, there may be a salary arrangement worked out which would be declared as an operating expense. The working partner would be treated as an employee and would receive a W-2 statement as any other employee. There is more paperwork for the partnership because it is necessary to complete a partnership income tax form which requires reporting all activities, assets, and liabilities of the partnership. All partners' profits or losses are reported on this form as well as on their 1040s.

Corporation

There are a number of factors to consider before deciding on a corporate form of ownership. It is much more cumbersome, entails additional expense, and may not be advisable for the new business, unless it has liability risks.

The most significant advantage is limited liability. By definition, a corporation is a legal entity by itself, operating in a business environment under the direction of a board of directors. It can own property, sell property, sue and be sued. It is really a clone of the entrepreneur. John Smith owns all the stock in Smith, Inc. All of John's business dealings are done in the name of Smith, Inc., a totally separate person from John. Strictly speaking, John is an employee of his corporation.

In the event the business fails, Smith, Inc., takes all the losses, not John. Creditors are only allowed to pursue the assets of the corporation, not of its owners and directors. In the event of an accident which results in a suit and judgment against the corporation, John will be glad he is incorporated. If the corporation defaults on a bank loan, the bank theoretically only will have the right to assume the assets of the corporation, not John's. It must be pointed out that most banks will require a personal guarantee to be signed by John since he is a small corporation. This, of course, opens John up personally for suit and limits this legal advantage of a corporation.

The other advantage John may enjoy as a corporation is that he can raise capital by selling some of his stock. Most stocks are issued with a stated dollar value called par value. It is a meaningless figure that has nothing to do with the actual value of the stock. The stock is worth whatever someone will pay for it. Just as on the national exchanges, stock is sold on the basis of demand. If you are able to show the potential of increased earnings for your corporation, the value of the stock will rise. In the past par value did relate to the original value of the stock; now stock certificates are generally written with a $1 par value or in some cases no par value.

You might decide to offer two classes of stock, common and preferred. Preferred stock is stock in which the stockholder has no voice in the management of the corporation. In exchange for not having a say, preferred stockholders are in line before the common stockholders in rights to assets. They are entitled to receive dividends first and have first claim to liquidated assets in the event the company fails.

The number of shares of stock a corporation can sell is specified in its original charter. The maximum is called authorized stock. The amount actually sold is the issued stock, the remaining is the unissued stock. New corporations normally sell only a small portion of their authorized stock, keeping the unissued in reserve. In the event all authorized stock is ever sold, the corporation must apply to the state for more authorized stock.

There are some situations in which starting with corporate ownership is a good idea. If your business idea is involved quite heavily with contracts and exposed to many liabilities, by all means consider incorporating. Industries such as construction, food processing, and high-technology manufacturing need the limited liability protection a corporation offers. If the use or consumption of your product or service could harm someone due to a mistake, the possible legal judgments could be far greater than an individual could afford.

There also can be tax advantages and disadvantages to incorporating. All profits are taxed at the corporate rate, which is sometimes lower than the individual rate. All monies paid to the owner are treated as salary and must be declared on a W-2 statement. However, all depreciation expenses belong to the corporation; therefore, in a loss year the individual will pay taxes on his salary regardless. The best arrangement is usually to be a proprietorship or partnership until profits rise to the point where you can take advantage of the corporate tax advantages. There is one other possibility that may represent the best of two worlds. A Subchapter S corporation has been designed for the benefit of the small corporation to give the owners the advantages of limited liability, while at the same time being taxed on the same basis as a proprietorship and partnership. This is only available to the small corporation and has certain restrictions on the buying and selling of stock.

Whether it is a Subchapter S or a full corporation, a corporate charter and application must be registered with the state and this does incur some costs. A corporation charter specifies the following:

- The name of the corporation and the date of incorporation.
- A formal statement of its formation.
- The type of business activity.
- The location of its principal office.
- Its intended duration.
- The classifications of types of stock.
- The number and par value of shares of each class of stock authorized.
- The voting privileges of each class of stock.
- The names and addresses of all incorporators and directors.
- A listing of all subscribers to capital stock and their addresses.
- A statement of limited liability of stockholders. Although the filing fee for corporations may be only $150, the legal costs of preparing all the documentation may be five times that amount. Being a corporation requires additional expense and more regulations. A small, closely held corporation should also prepare a stockholders' agreement to be signed by all stockholders. Similar to articles of partnership, it should specify agreed-upon conditions and responsibilities of the stockholders and directors. The business does not have to be large to be incorporated in terms of assets, but must have a registered board of directors and follow procedures as requested by the state in which it resides. The advantages and disadvantages to being incorporated should be well thought out before moving ahead.

The entrepreneur spirit project—step 7

- Prepare a complete list of all personal assets you are willing to risk on an entrepreneurial venture.
- List all sources available to possibly assist in securing capital.

- Prepare a capital needs statement for your proposed venture.
- Draw your plan of attack for financing. Discuss it with a banker.
- Choose the avenue of ownership that best suits your business. Discuss this with a qualified attorney or accountant. List the pros and cons of each.

8

Designing the Business: Setting Up Shop

The most exciting part of opening a new business often is designing the image to go with the idea. Starting with a pad of paper, the entrepreneur uses her creative abilities to begin to create a business enterprise that represents her individual personality and business philosophy. A rough drawing will become, when finished, a functioning business enterprise. This is often when that super flair—that ability to do it differently and better than anyone else—comes into being. Not everyone can be an inventor with a totally new idea; most must settle with trying an old idea and attempting to do it better.

The considerations at first seem endless. The retailer is concerned with customer traffic flow, color schemes, fixtures, display merchandising, signing, and all other space-use ideas that will help the business flourish. The manufacturer is concerned with production safety, efficient assembly, loading docks, storage, employee break areas, and administrative offices. A multitude of decisions must be made, but it is exciting. Remember you are now the boss; this is what you wanted. The business that is designed is the entrepreneur's product. It is her declaration of independence.

Environmental merchandising

Design the environment to fit the product or service that you are selling. This is called environmental merchandising. Create a theme that tells a story. If you are selling elegance—the environment must be elegant. If you are selling fun—the environment must be fun. A bridal salon requires chandeliers and elaborate dressing rooms to make a statement. A Shakey's Pizza Parlor requires games and characters to tell the story that it is fun for the whole family. The objective is to create an environment that is conducive to buy in. The consumer that is visiting your business has a need—by creating a conducive environment, you will be able to satisfy that need with a sale.

The steps of designing a business layout can be illustrated by using the following example of a card and gift shop. A normal size card and gift shop would be approximately 2000 square feet, possibly 40 feet wide by 50 feet deep. Start by drawing out to scale the shell of the store. In this instance the scale would normally be 4 feet to an inch. Proceed through the following steps:

- Identify the most important areas of the store (Fig. 8-1). The front is more important than the rear, and the front right is more important than the front left. For security purposes, cash register areas must be positioned so that the entire store can be seen. Storage areas should not exceed 15 percent of the rented space. These types of factors are important to know because the store must be designed to encourage the customer traffic flow to move smoothly and throughout the entire store.

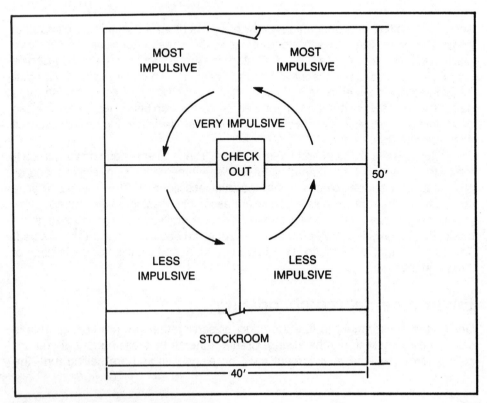

Figure 8-1. Store traffic flow layout.

- By utilizing our knowledge of preferred areas, place the most exciting and important products in the front, impulsive products near the checkout area, and the more specialized products in the rear. A card and gift shop carries product classifications of everyday greeting cards, gift wrap, seasonal cards and gifts, party supplies, puzzles, albums, stationery, and gifts. Since the greeting cards are the major source of revenue and identification, they are placed in the front of the store. The newest promotional or seasonal cards may go front right, since this is the direction most customers enter the store. Greeting cards in the front allow immediate exposure to the customer of the main theme behind the store—remember someone with a card.

The more specialized the product, the further back it will be placed in a store. In a card and gift store you would likely find candles and party goods, items which are less impulsive, toward the back.

Highly impulsive, small carryout items should be placed at the checkout area. This is typically where the consumer is exposed to point-of-purchase displays and a multitude of pick-me-up items. Take a look at the grocery store checkout lanes. The reason—this is where the merchant has you with money in your hands. It is very simple to suggest spending an extra dollar while the customer is reaching into his billfold. Since the customer has already decided to spend money, why not try for a little more? These extra, last-minute sales can add up to significant revenue over a year's period of time. Therefore, the checkout area must be properly located and planned.

Putting these thoughts to work, follow along the store layout example shown in Fig. 8-2.

Figure 8-2 identifies the four major product classifications and the checkout area. (1) Everyday, seasonal, and promotional greeting cards; (2) gift lines; (3) stationery products; (4) party supplies and candles; and (5) the checkout area.

Knowing the size of the fixtures available, in this case 2 feet by 4 feet, all product presentations can be depicted. It is important in this type of store to leave adequate and ample aisle space (3 feet to 4 feet). Proper aisle space allows for ease of traffic flow. Wide aisle space in a retail store enhances the appeal of comfortable shopping.

Permanent display space is designated. Displays are important, as discussed later, and should be planned in advance. Too many stores mistakenly use leftover space for displays, cutting down considerably on their effectiveness.

This particular example of the card and gift shop shows the same reasoning for any retailing venture. The next time you are in a large department store, notice the product layout. The first thing to hit you as you enter the ground floor will most likely be cosmetics, jewelry, and women's clothing. These products acknowledge the store's most important customer, the woman. Upstairs you will find the less impulsive, more planned purchases such as furnishings, china, and bridal departments.

Be careful not to confuse the customer. In keeping with our stupid and lazy customer philosophy, it is very easy to confuse him. Clear signing and accessibility will help, as will some more subtle suggestions. When applicable, merchandise products by color. Bathroom accessories, clothing, party supplies, home dec-

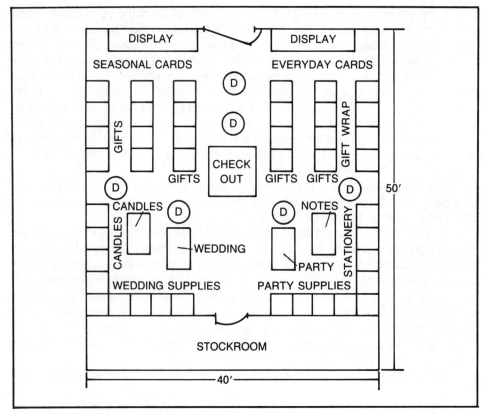

Figure 8-2. Store layout.

orations, and candles are examples of products that can be effectively displayed by coordinated colors. This enables customers to easily make a mental image of what they are selecting. Also, don't make them walk from one area to another to buy a related product. The tops of outfits need to be displayed with the bottoms.

Related products need to be together. If customers have to look too hard or walk too far you will lose their interest. Many retail customers are hesitant to request help from salespeople; therefore, if it is not convenient for them to find the article they want and pick it up, they will not buy. It is surprising the number of regular customers, even in a small retail store, who out of habit always go immediately to the same section of the store and are never exposed to other parts of the store. They might never realize that your store carries a particular line of merchandise unless it is made so obvious to them that they trip over it. Customers often wear blinders which prevent them from seeing sideways, up, or down. Place merchandise as much as possible at eye level and within easy reach.

In a finished layout, the blueprint will include wall and ceiling decor ideas, all needed electrical outlets, restrooms, and stockroom considerations. The stockroom must be planned to assure a workable and efficient method of getting stock to the sales floor. Be sure that any permanent physical obstacles, such as structural columns or posts, are taken into consideration.

Check all measurements very carefully, since the fixtures will be ordered from the final layout. If something is incorrectly measured or not taken into account, the fixtures will not fit and fixtures are very expensive. After the physical arrangement of merchandise and fixtures is completed, turn your creative eye to environmental merchandising. Remember, environmental merchandising is creating an environment conducive to buying. Pull out your targeted model customer profile and think in terms of what will make that customer feel good. Colors, decor, and fixturing should be designed to please this customer. If the customer feels good while visiting your business, the more she is likely to buy. The better the decor is thought out, the better the merchandise will appear. In the retail sector, imagination can run rampant and ideas can change quickly. A few years ago retailers were convinced that wild colors attracted attention. A multitude of stores opened showing lime green, turquoise, and other vibrant colors, in the belief that the customer would notice and be attracted by color to the store. Entire shopping malls were finished using colors such as oranges and pinks in their carpeting and corridors.

Later, the thinking changed to neutral and nondescript colors because the leading merchandisers were afraid the wild colors were distracting attention from the merchandise being sold. Therefore, the pendulum swung toward simplicity. Often, whatever the fashion industry is showing in colors is the determinant in color selection. The proper method of color selection is determined by considering the type of product sold and its type of customer. Certainly a record shop catering to a target market of 12- to 16-year-olds should consider different colors than the high-brow ladies' ready-to-wear boutique.

Color selection is tied into theme, which is tied into image. The use of decor has the same reasoning. Should the entrepreneur create nostalgia or the future as a theme to better sell a product? Should he mass merchandise his products or boutique them. Many fashion and specialty stores use boutiquing as a merchandising tool. Boutiquing is grouping like products together to show complete selection and tying together purchases.

Creating distinctive areas for certain groups of products in the merchandise mix creates a look of completeness for that product line. The customer feels totally surrounded by selection. If boutiquing is to be used it should be drawn into the floor plan and labeled.

Making the customer feel warm, secure, and comfortable is a psychological tool. It generates buying and creates goodwill. The image that the business casts is a reflection of how much the entrepreneur cares about his business.

The same considerations discussed here are employed in designing office, wholesaling, or small manufacturing businesses. The idea is the same—make the customer want to buy. A realtor's office must suggest confidence, a wholesaler's warehouse suggests completeness, and a manufacturer's must show efficiency. All are designed to assure maximum production and efficiency. Some large organizations have personnel who spend all their time designing and redesigning office and manufacturing layouts to improve operations. As a small businessperson, you will find yourself constantly trying to improve your efficiency by rearranging the business layout.

Naming the business

The name you choose for your business enterprise has two functions—it identifies and it displays an image. It should not be an ego trip. Therefore, there is no reasoning behind such names as Joe's Place, Sandy's, or Murphy's. A business name is an advertisement. It should identify the product or service sold. It can be cute or catchy as it will be retained easier and longer in the consumer's mind. The Clothes Tree, The Tobacco Patch, The Pub are all examples of good catchy names that also identify. When possible, use a recognizable brand name (i.e., Mary's Hallmark). If you wish to identify your name with the business, use it as a preface to the identity, such as Sam's Toggery, Murphy's Luncheonette, Jeanette's Hair Styling. Only the very established businesses are able to be identified on name only, like Macy's.

Regardless of the name chosen, in some states the owner must register this information in legal form on a fictitious name statement. This is then advertised in the newspaper with the intent of officially informing the public of who is legally responsible for the actions of the business. Since the name of the business is an advertisement, the best way of advertising it is in the sign selected for the business.

Good exterior signs are expensive, but considering that they represent location and product identification, they are worth the added expense. It is particularly important to be well represented by a sign if the chosen location is on a major artery and is dependent on drive-by traffic. It is also worth the added cost for proper illumination in order to be noticed.

If the business is clustered around other businesses, as in a downtown area or a shopping center, it is important to stand out in the crowd. A creative name, set off with creative signing, will enhance your ability to attract walk-by traffic. The extra $1000 invested in a proper sign will be quickly repaid in extra sales. All signs need to be strategically placed to assure being seen.

The same considerations apply to inside sign identification, particularly in retailing. Interior signing directs traffic flow and at the same time identifies product selection. Once again it casts an image and can be an important goodwill builder for the business.

One other factor that needs to be taken into consideration as the entrepreneur designs the business layout—the future. Without being overly optimistic, think through what your plans may be after you have achieved your initial objectives. Is there a plan or room to expand? Sometimes this requires additional space. However, it can often be accomplished through space redesign. A retailer may be able to use walls better by adding an additional shelf to each additional wall fixture. This simple idea may increase wall display by 20 percent without adding to rent cost. Possibly you can earmark a particular wall to be moved or torn down at a later date to enlarge the sales area, even though reducing storage. Creative negotiating of your lease may guarantee the use of the space next door when it becomes available at a later date. Another idea that manufacturers, wholesalers, and retailers may consider is the possibility of adding a second floor if the roof line is high enough. Expansion will be discussed in Chapter 21, but the possibilities should not be ignored at the time of the initial planning.

The entrepreneur spirit project—step 8

- Lay out the interior design of your business operation using the steps discussed.

- Visit with floorcovering firms, wallpaper stores, etc., in order to budget the cost of outfitting the business.

- Draw up the initial fixture, furniture, and equipment order and adjust to budget.

- Double check your estimate of the percentage of each product line that you will be stocking to make sure it meets the guidelines of the industry.

PART TWO

Understanding Your Customer

9

The Amazing Consumer

The successful entrepreneur must have an understanding of the psychological makeup of the consumer. What makes them want to buy? What are their needs? How can you motivate them to buy? In order to arrive at some answers it is helpful to draw a consumer profile.

It is the entrepreneur's goal to create motivations to fulfill a need. Motivations are the goal-directed forces within us that organize and give direction to the tensions caused by unsatisfied needs. We cannot create the needs, but we can create and offer motivations to the customer. If the entrepreneur can provide a reason to purchase, it may stimulate a motive. If the consumer is reminded of an upcoming friend or relative's birthday, a motivation to fulfill an unsatisfied need has been created. The only way of fulfilling this need, and lessening the tension created, is by acknowledging the birthday or rationalizing a reason not to. Filling the need requires buying a gift, sending a greeting card, ordering flowers, or making a phone call. All require spending money for a product or service; therefore, the competition begins.

Maslow's hierarchy of needs

The noted psychologist, Dr. A. H. Maslow, created the theory of a hierarchy of needs. Since the publication of his work there have been many refinements and spin-off theories, but the nucleus of his work remains intact. Individuals carry five different levels of need satisfaction in the following order:

Physiological needs. These represent the survival needs of food, water, etc.

Safety needs.   Protection needs such as shelter, clothing, etc.

Love and belonging needs.   This is the social need for friends, groups, organizations.

Self-esteem needs.   The need to achieve status and recognition in the eyes of others. Also the need for self-respect.

Self-actualization needs.   The need to feel accomplishment, achievement, and fulfillment of personal capabilities.

Everyone possesses these needs in different degrees. The physiological and safety needs are basic and consistent with all of us. The social, self-esteem, and self-actualization needs, however, will vary greatly depending on personality, values, and cultural backgrounds. The entrepreneur must be aware of what need his product or service appeals to. This information will help develop the direction taken in advertising, promotion, the business layout, and customer relations. Let's trace this thinking in the card and gift shop example.

The store is designed to maximize the exposure of greeting cards. The walk-by traffic sees the card display and is reminded of an occasion which calls for a greeting card. A need has been recognized and tension has been developed. By using effective merchandising, the entrepreneur is attempting to motivate the potential buyer to satisfy the need with a card and a gift as opposed to flowers or a phone call. If successful, the individual will enter the store as a potential customer with a need. Depending on the strength of the need and the makeup of the individual in terms of values, personality, and attitudes, a wide range of purchase opportunities and motivations become possible. Whether the purchase is an expensive card; a card plus a gift; or a card, a gift, and gift wrap paper will depend on the attitude of the individual. An attitude is a feeling toward an object or a situation, organized around knowledge which directs human behavior.

An obligatory purchase for a relative is not on the same level of the need scale as a gift to impress a new boss or lover. The purchase for a relative is an answer to a basic social need and may be an inexpensive card. The purchase for the boss or lover may be an expensive card plus a nice gift, that is nicely wrapped, which might answer a self-esteem need.

This thought process will prevail whether it is for a greeting card, a dress, or a piece of machinery. The consumer's need directs the motivation for the purchase.

Specialty clothing stores have long been in the business of selling to self-esteem needs by either selling for a special occasion (i.e., a Christmas party) or selling a new outfit to someone who just needs a perk-up from a depressing day. Automobiles are often bought to fulfill self-actualization needs. A new car may represent a self-actualization need as the owner is expressing her status or success. Need identification is an interesting and complex maze which needs to be understood, if you are to successfully sell your product.

Gear your marketing program to stimulate the motivations of your customers and beware of inhibitors. An inhibitor is an unplanned obstacle which prevents a sale and can come from many sources. The card shop customer may leave her potential purchase on the counter if treated rudely by a sales clerk. The machinery salesperson with bad breath might cause a negative reaction from the buyer.

Inhibitors can be dangerous to the health of the business, so be alert to their existence. They are capable of destroying all the efforts that you have placed into selling a product.

Another thing we know about consumers is that they have a need for utility satisfaction. Utility means the satisfaction expected from the product or service in exchange for what is given. There is a desire to know the purchase decision made was a correct one. The greeting card purchaser is hoping the receiver of the card will call to say how much he enjoyed the card. The automobile purchaser is hoping for looks of envy from his friends. The entrepreneur should be the first one to offer utility satisfaction. The sales clerk of the greeting cards should comment on how nice the card is. The automobile salesperson should reinforce the purchase decision by offering some complimentary statements on the car chosen. This allows immediate feedback to the customer and gives confidence in the purchase.

Consumer power

Contrary to our hidden marketing philosophy of considering the customer as stupid, in reality she has never been smarter, nor had as much power. The consumer of the 1990s is very well informed. Through the tremendous exposure of mass media and the growth of product choices the consumer has learned a great deal. No longer does she have only three television networks to choose from, instead she may have sixty. She is exposed to much more information about many more products, therefore she is much educated in her product selection. She also has more disposable income.

These two elements, education and income, have created an upsurge in consumer decision-making power. No longer does the consumer buy strictly on the basis of brand loyalty. Brand loyalty in the past served as the confidence builder for the decision maker. This is being gradually replaced by product education. Generic name products are now making their presence felt in the market due to the well-informed customer.

This increased product wisdom can work to the advantage of the small entrepreneur. He can now place his product alongside the established brand names, and if it is a better product the consumer might react. Ralph Nader's consumer crusade of the sixties has worked and has opened the minds of the consumer.

Lifestyles of the consumer

In Chapter 5, psychographics was discussed as a factor in considering where to locate a business. It is an important ingredient to understanding how to market to the consumer. The basic unit of buying behavior is the household. Table 9-1 gives an overview of the life-cycle stages and buying behavior of most households as they pass through those stages.

_____ **Table 9-1** _____
Consumer Life Cycle

Stage in life cycle	Buying behavior pattern
Bachelor stage	Few financial burdens. Fashion leaders, recreation oriented.
Newly marrieds, no children	Highest purchase rate. Cars, refrigerators, furniture.
Full nest I: youngest under 6	Home purchasing at peak. Baby needs, washers, dryers, etc.
Full nest II: youngest child over 6	Financial position better. Many wives working. Buy large packages.
Full nest III: older couples with dependent children	Financial position still better. Hard to influence with advertising.
Empty nest I: older couples, no children at home	Home ownership at peak. Not interested in new products.
Empty nest II: older couples	Drop in income. Stay home, buy medical care products.
Solitary survivor, in labor force	Income good, but likely to stay home.
Solitary survivor, retired	Drop in income, medical needs.

In addition to gathering information through the information media the consumer will also rely on personal contacts, or reference groups, in making purchase decisions. This is particularly true in considering a new or different purchase. If you are marketing a fashion item, perhaps a new look in ladies' sweaters, you would be wise to consider the five consumer classifications of innovators, early adopters, early majority, late majority, and laggards.

Betty arrives at her social circle gathering wearing a brand new look in sweaters. She is considered an innovator and if the sweater receives favorable attention she will start a cycle. At the next get-together two or three other ladies will be wearing similar sweaters; they are the early adopters. The third meeting has many of the group wearing the new look; this is the early majority. By the fourth gathering most of the women are wearing the new look, the late majority.

At the fifth meeting Betty shows up wearing another new look while some of the ladies are just wearing what is now the old look; they are the laggards. To successfully market a new or different product it is important to get the attention of the innovators. They are the pacesetters. On a large marketing scale they are the Jackie Kennedy's or Princess Di's. In your local community they might be the Betty's, the popular high school student, or the mayor of the town.

Repeat sales

Once the business is set up and operating, the single most important factor in determining its future success is repeat sales. This is true for every business that is expecting long-term survival. Even undertakers must work to please the family of the deceased or else the family will use a competitor for their next funeral arrangements. A good business will make every effort to assure the return of the customer. This is the total customer concept. It is the obligation of every entrepreneur to go as far as possible to guarantee satisfaction. Unfortunately, to satisfy every customer is virtually impossible. There will be times when the line must be drawn, or the long-run profitability of the business will be hurt.

The total customer concept requires you to view your customers with regard to their total lifetime value to the business. If the average customer spends $75 per year and you are in business for twenty years, that customer represents $1500. Do not lose $1500 over a misunderstanding concerning a $10 sale. By winning the argument for the $10, you have gained a gross profit of possibly $5 and lost a gross income of $1500. In order to properly operate a total customer concept, the entrepreneur must have clearly defined and well-thought-out customer relations policies.

Policy setting is a real bureaucratic mess in the large businesses. The small business holds a very strong advantage in that it has greater flexibility and less red tape in setting its policies. It has the flexibility to change a policy if necessary to please a customer. There is no need for time-consuming committee meetings and reports; the boss of the small business can make a decision on the spot. This is one key reason the small business sector survives, because it is able to offer personalized service to the customer. It is often worth the added cost to the customer to deal with a business that can react quickly to her needs. This is customer relations—two very important words. To the entrepreneur it means how do his customers feel about him? He needs to know how very important it is for him to be highly regarded and must constantly seek to maintain and improve his image. The objective is to do as much as possible for the consumer in order to assure his satisfaction, without sacrificing long-term profits.

Services can be offered without necessarily driving up costs. Employees can do more while on the payroll. Whether it is giftwrapping packages in a retail store or washing the cars for all service customers at a car dealership—these types of services can be performed by personnel already on the job. They are mainly labor-oriented jobs that require little investment in product; therefore, they represent only small additional expense which will be regained many times in future repeat sales. Good customer relations mean repeat sales that result in added profits. There is a great need for diplomacy and tact when dealing with the public.

Diane is confronted with an irritated Sharon, one of her best customers, as she enters her clothing store. "Diane, I think you owe me a $40 refund. You reduced the price on the other $200 dresses like the one I bought here, by $40, and I haven't had an opportunity to even wear it yet." Diane recognized the dress as one which had been on the rack for well over the three-month selling period that her clothes were sold at full price before being reduced.

She always tried to prevent reducing any style dress sold to a regular customer, until she was sure there would be no problems. "I am sorry Sharon, let me see what can be done." By checking the receipt, Diane quickly found the problem.

Sharon had originally put the dress on layaway for over two months, long past the thirty-day layaway policy. When she had finally paid in full for the dress, she had requested additional alterations, requiring another five days. Because she had tied up the dress for over sixty days, she now believed she had paid $200 for a dress she could have bought for $160. Diane recognized she had a serious problem as she could not give Sharon $40 without setting a precedent for all customers to request refunds for items purchased before being put on sale. "Sharon, I understand why you are upset. Please understand that sales are a necessary part of our business. I am not able to give you $40 in this particular instance, due to the layaway situation. Allow me to offer you a 20 percent discount on your next purchase to compensate." This was agreeable to Sharon and a problem situation was solved without losing a valued customer. Diane had utilized the flexibility given to her as a small business woman to please a customer. The customer comes to a business with a need to be fulfilled. It is the responsibility of that business to do its very best to fill that need.

Customer relations reach past the individual customer to the community. A successful business must be recognized by the community as one to put trust and confidence into. In addition to pleasing the customer, it is the entrepreneur's responsibility to put something back into the community from which she derives her existence. There are numerous requests to the business community to support nonprofit organizations.

It is not possible to support all requests, but there is a definite moral responsibility to do one's share. The successful entrepreneur is involved in her community. She may serve the chamber of commerce, the YMCA, the March of Dimes, or whatever organizations that she can fit into her busy schedule. A portion of advertising expenditures should be directed toward high school newspapers, benefit programs, and other charitable media to show support for the community. The time, effort, and dollars spent on behalf of these types of organizations will not show up immediately on the profit and loss statement, but will add to the community support of the business. It will result in future customers for the business and in the long run will show a handsome return on investment.

There is one customer situation to approach with caution. Dependency on one or a small group of customers can cause catastrophic problems. For example, the small paint manufacturer who sells to Sears Roebuck. The original purchase order may be for 250,000 gallons of paint at $5 per gallon. Upon receiving the contract the entrepreneur makes the necessary capital equipment purchases to produce the increased volume. In order to assure completion of the order for Sears, he is forced to turn down requests from smaller customers. Although he is delighted in receiving the Sears order, he has had to cut his profit margin per unit to receive the contract. He produces paint for Sears for two years, then loses the contract to a lower bidder. The end result is an abundance of capital equipment, which he is most likely still paying off, and he has lost his nucleus of small customers. Similar situations can happen in any small business—retail, wholesale, or manufacturer. The best policy to apply is to treat all customers, regardless of size, the same in determining price and terms of sale.

The entrepreneur spirit project—step 9

- Write out a written description of your target customer in terms of need satisfaction. List ideas of how to appeal to those needs.

- Describe your customer relations policies in respect to how you wish your employees to treat customers.

- Outline a community involvement program which would be of interest to you and to the betterment of your organization.

10

Advertising and Promotion

The function of advertising is very simple—to draw attention to a product or service. If consumers don't know what you sell, or where you sell it, it is impossible to make a sale.

The advertising spiral

When, where, and how much to spend is the difficult question for the small businessperson. Without good planning, advertising becomes the most unproductive and inefficient expense incurred by the business. The most important rule to follow is consistency. Advertising is not effective when a business jumps from one medium to another without a calendar or purpose. Any advertising must be clearly defined and planned in advance. It must have a specific objective.

How much money to be spent will depend to a large extent on where the business and its product falls on what is referred to as the advertising spiral (Fig. 10-1). The advertising spiral can be thought of as a graphic representation depicting the competitive market the business finds itself in.

As a business moves through these various stages, the objectives of its advertising program will change. A new business will be in the pioneering stage with the objective of becoming established. Its advertising terminology will emphasize *new, just opened, under new management,* and other expressions attempting to arouse attention to its existence. This stage may last a year or longer, depending on the market it is entering.

As the business grows it will have to change its advertising appeal to recognize its competition. It will have to take on the established members of its industry and be prepared to encounter new entries into its market. Advertisements in the

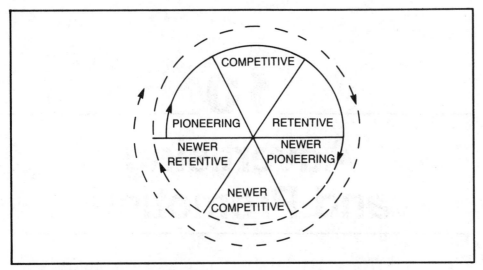

Figure 10-1. The advertising spiral.

competitive stage will emphasize better than, more durable, less expensive, or an endless list of product advantages. The theme and content of this advertising will be directed by what the competition is doing. The business philosophy has changed its objective from new market entry to gaining market share (Fig. 10-2).

Eventually, with experience, time, and success, the enterprise will gain maturity. Market share will be gained, competition met, and the advertising strategy will change. The objective will be to hold market share while continuing to achieve

Figure 10-2. Competitive ad copy.

a natural growth. Up to this point, most of the advertising has fallen into the classification of product advertising.

Product advertising is aimed strictly at drawing attention to the existence and advantages of a product or service. In the retentive stage, there is more room to use the other classification of advertising called institutional advertising. Institutional advertising is aimed at drawing attention to the business enterprise. It emphasizes doing business with a particular organization and why. Key words such as established since, the industry leader, put your trust in, are used to suggest image, stability, and create confidence. The advertiser does not abandon product advertising at this stage, but also toots his horn about a very important competitive advantage.

Depending on the marketing strategy, it is very possible for the business product to continually cycle throughout the spiral. A simple change in target market or a slight change in the product itself may take the advertiser from the retentive stage back to the competitive stage or from the competitive to the pioneering stage.

Johnson's Baby Shampoo changed its target market from babies to adults with the advent of an advertising campaign utilizing pro football player Fran Tarkenton to demonstrate an appeal to the adult market. It left the baby appeal in the retentive stage and entered the pioneering stage of a new market. Arm and Hammer Baking Soda placed its product back into the pioneering stage when it advertised its usefulness as a freezer deodorant to the homemaker. Many other products have changed places in the advertising spiral by adding a new feature or benefit to an existing product. The advertising spiral is an ongoing cycle depending on the marketing appeal and form the advertiser is aiming for. Where the business falls in relation to the nature of its competitive market has a lot of influence on its objectives and how much money is allocated for advertising and promotion.

The small businessperson's goal is to establish a consistent advertising program with well-defined objectives that are set in consideration of the marketing environment. It demands a calendar be laid out with a controlled budget. For the new business the initial budget can be derived from the industry standards. This is usually based on a certain percentage of projected annual sales volume. It may be 2 percent, 10 percent, or higher in an extremely promotional business. Since a new business is in the pioneering stage, a larger-than-standard percentage of sales may be desirable while becoming established. There are many strategies to choose from.

The business may choose a snowballing strategy by designing the advertising program to peak in a crescendo effect at a certain point in time. Or the entrepreneur may choose a big-early, little-late strategy of promoting initially with a boom and then tapering off as time goes by. The strategy will vary depending on the type of product or service sold. Gaining market share is very expensive.

Consistency refers to the planning, not necessarily to the expenditure. An advertising calendar for a department store is laid out well in advance to show advertising events. Certainly much more money goes into December as opposed to January; however, January is still planned. The annual January white sale and winter clearance promotions are consistently planned even though not as elaborate, nor as expensive, as a Christmas program. As in any budget, there must be some flexibility allowed for change of plans. There will be times when certain unplanned events and situations arise that demand advertising expenditures.

Creating copy

Creating the copy is a very simple process because the whole idea is to keep it simple. Remember our philosophy of considering the customer as stupid—use it in your advertising copy ideas. The more information you try to disperse, the more confusion will occur. Simple messages receive attention and are more easily retained.

To create effective copy post the letters AIDA (*Attention, Interest, Desire, Action*) on the top of your worksheet. See the box on the following page for a complete explanation.

By listing AIDA on your worksheet and following through with simplicity, an effective advertisement will be produced. It does not require an ad agency or an expert, just good practical and concise thinking. Figure 10-3 shows a diagram of an ad.

The communication channel

Advertising communicates a message to the receiver. It is extremely hard to accomplish because of the difficulties encountered in the communications channel. All communications start with a message sender. This individual forms the message in the sender's mind and attempts to deliver it to the receiver through the following steps (see Fig. 10-4).

Encoding refers to how the sender sees the message to send. It is our mental picture of the best way to express an idea. The sender then picks out what he considers the best vehicle or method available to send that message. In advertising, he determines which media to be used. In receiving the message the receiver deciphers, or decodes, the information into how he understands it.

This can be a stumbling block because we often interpret a message differently from how the sender envisioned it. Anyone who has ever played the game of whispering a message around a circle of people to see how it ends up has witnessed the difficulty in encoding and decoding.

Once the receiver has decoded the message, the sender awaits the feedback—in advertising, hopefully, a purchase or inquiry. Further complicating the process is the influx of noise, the *x*'s in the diagram, that surrounds each step in the process. Noise represents all the obstacles that get in the way of proper communications.

A simple example of this as it relates to the small business would be a radio commercial intended to reach the attention of a young mother. The advertiser has carefully created the message, picked the proper medium, and has paid to have the commercial broadcast during the afternoon drive time, when mothers are picking up children from school. The potential customer is listening to the radio as she

AIDA

A—Attention. The most important goal of the ad is to receive attention. Without attention the rest of the copy will not be noticed. In a survey covering 32 newspapers and 6400 personal interviews conducted by the Starch marketing reporting service, it was found that only the following percent of newspaper readers even noticed an advertisement:

Size of Ad	Women		Men	
	Noted	Read Most	Noted	Read Most
1 page or more	48%	19%	34%	11%
3/4 to 1 page	43%	13%	30%	8%
1/2 to 3/4	36%	10%	31%	9%
1/4 to 1/2	29%	10%	22%	7%
1/8 to 1/4	28%	10%	20%	7%
under 1/8	15%	5%	13%	5%
All ads	31%	11%	24%	7%

Advertising is extremely competitive. Whether TV, newspaper, radio, or billboards, the media is filled with many advertisers with the same objective of getting attention. The small business is further hampered by a small budget which limits the amount of space purchased and the number of times an ad will run. Therefore, whether it is the headline of a newsprint copy or the lead in of a radio commercial, it is crucial for the advertisement to stand out in content and presentation in order to be noticed.

I—Interest. The advertisement must generate sufficient interest if it is to keep the consumer's attention. Failure to do so will void the intent of the copy. Proper use of the sub headline and body of the ad will stimulate the audience to read on.

D—Desire. This represents the desire that is hoped to be gained for the product. Having aroused attention and created interest, there must follow a device that will instill a motivation in the consumer's mind. In the earlier discussion of needs, it was stated that creating a need causes a tension which can be relieved by action. By developing the desire, the ad should motivate to the action.

A—Action. The action is the request that you buy the product or service. This is accomplished with the use of terminology such as ''buy now,'' followed with where it is available. An advertisement is not complete without a call for action.

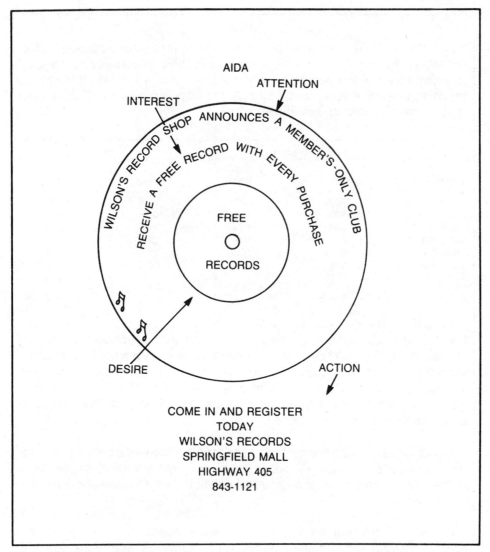

Figure 10-3. Diagram of an ad.

sits in her car waiting for the children. The commercial comes on and she raises her attention to the message. Just when she has riveted her attention to the message the car door opens and five noisy children jump into the car, obliterating the remainder of the ad. Therefore, no action and no feedback from the potential customer. Advertisers recognize that certain noise factors are out of their control. This is one reason advertisements are repeated many times. Particularly clever advertisements help reduce the noise factor.

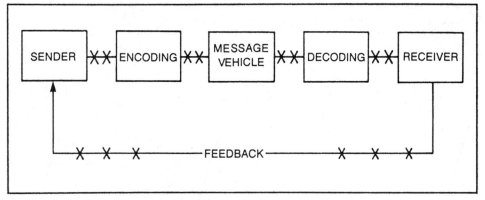

Figure 10-4. The communication channel.

Direct-mail advertising

The most effective means of circumventing the noise factors of the communication channel is presenting the advertising message in a one-on-one situation. This can be done by using the mail.

As we have seen it is very difficult to get the attention of the potential buyer, because of the competition of other advertisers trying to do the same. This is particularly true for the small business whose advertising budget does not allow full-page newspaper advertisements or prime-time television commercials. The small business must fall back on its strength of being more personal than the large business to compete for attention. What is more personal than a letter?

If properly done a mailing to customers can far outperform media advertising at a fraction of the cost. The key to effectiveness is personalization. This means no mailing to occupant or using computerized labels. The best direct-mail method is handwritten envelopes and personalized salutations to the receiver. Think about it. What letters do you open first when you get home? The ones that are hand-addressed. Why? Because there is always the question, Who is this letter from? An old friend perhaps? Computerized addresses get opened last, if at all. Another cost-saving technique for mailing is to send handwritten postal service postcards. These prestamped cards save time and money over envelope mailing and can be effective for a quick announcement such as a new product arrival or a special sale. The small business must make sure that its mailing stands out. Therefore the handwritten address acts as the attention-getter and the well-thought-out message inside, in which you have got the reader one-on-one, serves as the interest, desire, and action of the ad.

If you send a flyer or a brochure through the mail make sure a letter is attached. The letter should be to the individual, not a Dear Sir or Madam approach, as illustrated in Fig. 10-5. The flyer or brochure must follow the format of a good advertisement.

The effectiveness of a mailing program will be dependent on the validity of the mailing list and the effectiveness of the follow-up. When possible, a mailing list

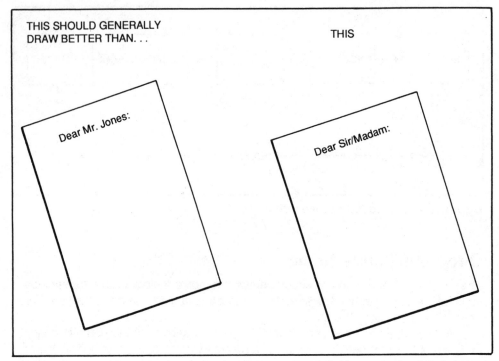

Figure 10-5. A letter accompanying a direct-mail advertisement should always be addressed to the individual.

should be made up of current and past customers and prospective customers identified by your target market. Advertising to your customer base is a very effective means of reinforcing your name to them and at the same time promoting word of mouth, or referral, advertising. Your customers carry your message to others. By informing them of current happenings and offerings in your business they will tell others. New businesses must sometimes use rented mailing lists. This should be temporary for most businesses until the time they can build up their own list.

Effective follow-up means telemarketing. Telemarketing procedures are discussed in Chapter 11. It is most important that whenever possible, a direct mailing be followed up within a week with a telephone call to inquire if the recipient has received the correspondence and if there is any other information you can provide. It is a courtesy call which allows the business the opportunity to make a personal contact with the client.

Calculating advertising cost

All advertising rates are based on the number of people the particular media reaches. Advertising media companies live in a very competitive world of constantly trying to out do the other. Evidence of increased viewership, readership, or listenership allows them to increase their rates, thereby increasing profits. It is an industry which continuously puts itself under the scrutiny of surveys and questionnaires.

Television

Nielsen ratings are often used as a survey source to determine television viewership. Originally sample TV viewers were asked to fill out periodic forms which indicated what programs they watched. Now the sample audience is equipped with an electronic device attached to their TV sets that instantly monitors their viewing habits. The results of the Nielsen ratings weigh very heavily on deciding the advertising rates for a particular show. A plus or minus of one-tenth of a point on a national scale will mean a big difference to the network in terms of advertising demand and revenue.

The same thing is done on the local level. Your eleven o'clock news programs compete with each other for rating points. Whatever station shows the largest audience will charge the highest rate.

Many small businesses use cable channels. They are not as expensive as the major networks since they do not have as large a viewership; however, they may have programs that appeal to your target market. A sporting goods store that advertises on Saturday morning wrestling or Friday evening high school football might do very well for less than the cost of newspaper advertising. One note of caution: when you discuss advertising rates with the television station sales representative make sure you have a clear understanding of the production costs involved. This is not part of the cost per spot charge and can be a considerable expense.

Radio stations

Radio surveys and ratings are often performed by a company called Arbitron. Through random surveys Arbitron is able to give the various local radio stations ratings of listenership for different times of the day on a quarter-hour basis. To calculate a rating divide the estimated number of listeners by the area population to discover what percent of the population was listening. They will also report the share of audience by dividing the total listening audience by the number of listeners tuned into a particular station. If you know the average number of listeners of a station at a particular time you are able to figure the cost per thousand (CPM) of reaching your market. Take the average number of listeners times the number of spots run to get the number of gross impressions your ad is making. When you divide the cost of a spot schedule by the number of gross impressions, you get the cost per thousand. The formula is

$$CPM = cost\ (\ \times\ 1{,}000) \div total\ listeners$$

Using this formula, if you ran a spot plan of 12 commercials between 6 a.m. and 10 a.m. and reached 9000 listeners, you will generate 108,000 gross impressions (12 × 9000). If each spot cost $18 then the total cost for the formula would be

$$12 \times \$18,\ or\ (\$216 \times 1{,}000).$$

The CPM of that schedule would be:

$$CPM = 216,000 \div 108,000 = \$2 \text{ per thousand}$$

The information gained from the Arbitron surveys is useful for comparative purposes; however, keep in mind that if a particular station is not reaching your target market it doesn't matter what its ratings are.

Newspapers

Newspaper advertisements are sold by the column-inch. This rate is determined by the amount of circulation. Column-inches refer to the width of the newspaper measured in terms of columns. Most newspapers are laid out in an eight-column format. The depth is measured by lines, of which there are fourteen to an inch. Therefore if an ad is a 4 × 4 column-inch ad, it would be four columns wide by four inches (56 lines) deep. If the rate were $14 per column-inch, the cost of the ad would be $224 (4 × 4) or 16 times $14.

All media companies offer discount packages depending on the amount of advertising contracted for. Radio and TV offer discounts depending on the number of spots you contract for over a given period of time; newspapers by the number of column inches you agree to. TV charges more for prime time viewing, radio for drive time, and newspapers for Sunday readership. As you get involved with media packages you will be exposed to a seemingly endless number of surveys, plans, and features of the various companies.

Evaluating the results

Evaluating the results of an ad is not simply looking at the immediate sales result. Proper advertising serves a long-term interest as well. A $200 newspaper ad featuring a $10 item would have to sell 40 additional units just to cover the cost of the ad and the product, assuming the product carried a 50 percent retail markup. This may be very difficult to do, particularly since a $200 ad in most newspapers would not be very large. However, the ad serves other objectives. It has brought attention and recognition to the business. It will sell other products to the customer who comes in for the $10 product. It will expose the business to new customers who will come back in the future. If the advertiser looks only at the immediate increase in revenue generated, he is naive to the other functions of advertising. The real success of an advertising campaign must be evaluated from a longer-term viewpoint. Comparing the sales period to a year earlier will give a better analysis.

Gary opened a retail business with a $3000 grand opening expenditure. He was convinced that he had overspent in this promotion until he compared his sales figures a year later. He discovered that his comparative sales for the same month a year later were down considerably from the previous year. At that point he realized that the advertising had indeed generated additional revenues, in addition to exposing his new business to the public. Therefore, the advertising program was deemed a success.

The greatest mistake the small businessperson makes when planning advertising is overreaching her prospective market. This sometimes comes from the ego of imagining the business is stronger than it actually is. A single retail outlet in suburban Philadelphia that advertises its offerings in the full circulation of the *Philadelphia Inquirer* is paying to reach people who are not geographically potential customers. Television, radio, and newspaper all base their advertising rates on the potential number of viewers, listeners, or readers in their market area. A television station which beams its broadcast 100 miles to a million viewers is charging the advertiser as much for the viewer 100 miles away, as the one 3 miles from the business. Unless the business has branch facilities throughout the area, or is strong enough to attract customers from a far distance, it is better off to concentrate on more local media. There are many avenues open to accomplish this. Large newspapers will offer zoned edition advertising. This means the advertiser can choose to have his advertisement appear only in newspapers that are circulated in his region of distribution. There are also newsprint media available that service only the local areas. Weekly papers, shoppers (newspapers which carry only advertisements), and mailing services all concentrate on smaller areas. The expense of advertising demands that the business pay only to reach the market which it can service.

The same strategy applies for radio and television. Pick radio stations by the life-style of your target market. Country and western stations are great for selling western wear and farm equipment, but not suitable if your market is gourmet cookware. Look at local television stations or cable stations before tying into the major networks at a much higher price. Concentrate on your target market.

Grand opening

The most important advertising campaign a business will run is its grand opening. It must spend money to inform customers of its existence. If the business relies solely on word-of-mouth advertising, it will spend a long time in the pioneering stage. Word-of-mouth advertising is very important, but seldom is it enough to generate the volume of sales a business needs. A grand-opening campaign must be well thought out and properly planned financially. The budget for this one-time event should be in addition to the normal advertising budget. Customers love a grand opening and will respond enthusiastically, if it is properly planned. A grand opening means new products, excitement, and usually savings, and customers love all three.

Businesses that appeal to the general public serve a social function. Informed retailers realize that shopping is a social experience. Shoppers go to shopping centers not only out of need but also out of the desire to be around people and see what is new. A large portion of the population is lonely and bored, and shopping is a place to go to meet people as well as spend money. A grand opening says, "Come and join the fun and save money." Be creative. Have entertainment, a ribbon cutting, refreshments, giveaways—any idea which adds to the fun. This is the entrepreneur's opportunity to show her stuff, attract customers, and make a good first impression. Don't be shy, be a creative marketing genius.

For some reason many businesses fail to take advantage of this special occasion. Many wait a month or more after opening to stage the grand opening. They use the excuse that they need time to get the kinks out of the operation. By doing this they are losing revenues and diluting the excitement of the event. If the business is not ready to operate at full capacity upon opening, it is not ready to open. Customers respond to newness and a business is not new after being open a month or longer.

Advertising too far ahead of an event is another common mistake. In consideration of the competitiveness of advertising, do not expect customers to remember your ad of a few days ago. Whether it is a grand opening or a sales event, ask for immediate action, because the ad will be forgotten by the next day.

A grand opening is not necessarily a one-day event. Although stretching it out too long will cut into its immediate impact, it can continue over a weekend or even a week. Give the customers who are not able to be present on opening day an opportunity to share in the fun and savings. Therefore, advertise more than once. If it runs three days, advertise each day, plus a day in advance to draw attention to the event.

Promotions

Promotions are fun. Promoting is part of the advertising scheme with a slightly different purpose. The advertisement draws attention to the business and the product or service being sold. A promotion is the act of putting emphasis on a particular feature of the product. Promotions are fun because they require involvement on the part of the owner, employees, and the customer.

Promoting is marketing with a flair. The objective of promotions is to generate interest, cash flow, and goodwill. Promotions entertain, with the idea of producing revenues. Whether it is a fashion show at a ladies' boutique, a clown at a local fast food restaurant, or a professional baseball player signing autographs at a car dealership, they all serve the same function of making shopping fun. A businessperson who sells to the general public is in the entertainment business. Whatever you can do to make shopping in your business enjoyable will bring in extra dollars. Promotions do not have to be expensive. A simple count-the-jellybean contest for a prize costs very little, but adds an element of fun to the business. Fun creates goodwill.

Wholesalers and manufacturers can add excitement to their businesses through product promotions. By offering rebates, a free gift with purchase, or contests, it livens up the routine buying situations. There are marketing companies that do nothing but assist with promotions. They may sell you calendars, pens, address books, or many other ideas with your business name on them for giveaway. Any time you are emphasizing in an unusual and appealing manner the purchase of products from your business, you are engaged in the adventure of promoting. The business that goes the extra mile to please the customer is normally the winner.

Publicity is the best form of advertising because it does not cost. A newspaper article about the uniqueness of your business is worth thousands of dollars of advertising. Be aggressive in searching for publicity. If the business has an unusual twist, the newspaper will want to know about it. There is always a need for news and your business may make an excellent article. If you can't get a news article about the business, the owner can get publicity for various contributions and involvements with community groups. Contrary to Hollywood thinking, bad publicity is not good publicity. Any publicity must be in keeping with the goodwill and image objectives of the business.

The entrepreneur spirit project—step 10

- Plan a first-year advertising and promotion calendar for your business.
- Draw up the copy for the grand-opening campaign, including the budget.
- Contact and investigate all possible media choices for your venture. Make a file of all rate schedules and special programs available of each medium.
- Make a list of promotional and publicity ideas.
- If direct-mail advertising applies to your type of business, design a sample brochure, flyer, or letter.

11

Salesmanship: Dale Carnegie, Where Are You?

The lifeblood of any business is its ability to sell. No matter how well organized, designed, or merchandised, the organization will only succeed if it operates under a proper selling philosophy.

Can selling be taught? Does successful selling come from the organization structure? Can sales motivation be sustained over long periods of time? The answer to all three of these questions is yes, if management understands salesmanship.

Sales training

There are many excellent selling courses and textbooks devoted to the proper training of sales personnel. Many will differ in their approach and need to be studied to make sure they fit the objectives of your business. Dale Carnegie courses are considered the leader, but even its approach may not fit the personality of a particular business. There is a correlation between the personality of a business and its sales personnel and the success of sales training. Sales training cannot work miracles. It cannot transform the highly technical introvert into a dynamic extroverted sales person. It must have as a basis a person who is motivated to become a salesperson. There is a definite link between personality and sales ability. A good sales course or training manual will help discover and bring out the individual's sales ability and personality. They will teach proven sales techniques and emphasize the difference between order-taking and order-getting.

Anyone who can fill out an order form is capable of taking an order. However, not everyone knows how to get an order. As an entrepreneur it is important for you and your associates to learn how to get an order. Sales courses and instruction manuals will help, but first there must be a clear understanding of the sales objectives and philosophy of the business.

The sales philosophy of the enterprise must be designed to fit the clientele. Certainly automobile selling is different from food service selling. Different types of customers respond to different tactics. Retail selling is easier than door-to-door selling. In retailing, the customer comes to you, as opposed to the door-to-door approach to the customer. Hard sell works for some, soft sell is appropriate for others. It is imperative that the salesperson be able to determine *needs* and then motivate to be effective. In retailing, needs and motivations can be created through visual displays. In one-on-one selling, needs are determined through learning about the potential customer.

The better you know the customer, the better you can sense what about the product or service will appeal to him. Once again, it is important that you have properly identified and target marketed the customer. The businessperson must create the proper marketing mix for his product. The marketing mix refers to the entire marketing scheme of the product, the four Ps—product, price, place (how the product is distributed), and promotion. A good selling program comes from the proper integration of these four elements. Thoroughly know your product, have it properly priced, develop the most efficient system of getting your product to the customer, and recognize the product's most promotional aspects before attempting to sell it.

Knowing the product means knowing its FAB—its features, advantages, and benefits. Successful selling is determining needs and then skillfully relating your product's FAB to show how the product will fulfill the customer's needs. Understand the buyer's situation. He will first have to recognize his needs, then he will want to collect and evaluate necessary information before he can decide to buy. After that he will determine if the purchase will satisfy the need. These steps will vary depending on the complexity and the amount of investment required. It is the salesperson's job to guide and assist him through this process. You and your sales organization must be able to accomplish this mission.

Good salespeople are persuasive. They have the ability to change a person's belief, attitude, and course of action. The better a person communicates, the greater his chances are at being a successful persuader. To sell successfully, the individual must be able to generate feedback in the form of questions, be understanding and patient, keep things simple, create mutual trust, be able to listen, generate enthusiasm, and be able to back up statements with proof. There must be knowledge if there is to be confidence between the buyer and seller.

Know the product and also know your company—its policies, facilities, and its capabilities. Backing up the sales organization with advertising and promotion helps get the foot in the door.

Where do you get customers? In retailing they come through advertising and location, in other sectors they come through prospecting. Prospecting starts with leads, which are names and contacts. Leads come from acquaintances, mailing lists, people who know other people, newspapers, and telephone books. A lead must be qualified. Qualified means a potential customer with a need that has the financial resources available to buy.

Do not waste time on customers who do not have the authority or ability to buy your product. Prospecting methods are numerous—direct mail, telemarketing, cold calls, public demonstrations, referrals, and any other creative methods your mind can conjure up. The best method is the one that best fits the product and image of the business.

Armed with a list of potential customers, the entrepreneur must devise the proper overall sales strategy that fits her sales philosophy. This includes the approach and presentation. Since the first impression is critical, the approach must be well thought out. This requires an understanding and knowledge of the environment the salesperson is working in.

The approach is intended to get attention, stimulate interest, and provide a transition into a sales presentation. Depending on the product, this may best be accomplished by opening with a statement concerning a benefit of the product, a demonstration of the product, or a question designed to uncover a need or problem. This will evolve into a presentation that will discuss the FAB of the product thereby creating a desire, developing a positive attitude, and instilling a belief and conviction in what you are selling. A good presentation will persuade, build trust, ask for participation, and prove statements. It will SELL—S—show features, E—explain advantages, L—lead into benefits, L—let the customer talk.

The good salesperson must be able to handle objections. By properly anticipating objections the salesperson can turn them into a question that will give reason to buy. It is important to recognize the objection (sometimes they are hidden) as to whether the person is stalling, has no need, or has no money. Money is often a hidden objection to purchase. Objections must be handled as they arise and then make sure they have been adequately answered by using a trial close before moving on with the presentation.

No matter how well the salesperson has handled the approach, made the presentation, and handled the objections, he must be able to properly close a sale in order to get the order. Closing should be thought of as helping customers make a decision that will benefit them. At the conclusion of the presentation or after handling an objection, test the waters with a question or a statement intended to make sure the customer is still with you. If you pass this trial close, you are ready to ask for the order and close the sale. There are many closing techniques. However, use the one that best fits the personality of the salesperson. It is important to emphasize that the salesperson ask for the order regardless of how many objections or how difficult the presentation. Remember, nothing ventured, nothing gained.

As your sales grow, and your organization matures, there will be just as much emphasis placed on keeping customers as on developing new ones. Make sure your sales philosophy includes generating goodwill at the conclusion of the selling effort, whether it has been successful or not. You must be welcomed back. Good selling requires thinking ahead to the next opportunity. Good salespersons are masters at leaving a good impression in the customer's mind through the use of compliments or other satisfiers.

Telemarketing

The telephone has become a sales tool for many small businesses. Although not suitable for businesses selling tangible products that must be seen and touched, many small service businesses have enjoyed success using telemarketing techniques. The advantages are the large number of people who can be contacted at a relatively inexpensive cost. The disadvantage is the largely negative image telemarketing has received from companies not following rules of etiquette.

If your company is one that can make effective use of telemarketing be sure the sales personnel have the following characteristics:

Pleasant personality with good articulation.

Intelligent and knowledgeable regarding the product or service being offered.

A voice with good tone and sound level.

Naturally enthusiastic.

Calling lists can come from rented mailing and calling lists, telephone directories, and existing customer list. The sales message follows the same format just discussed. Figure 11-1 is a suggested telemarketing procedure.

Preparing Your Telemarketing Script

1. Identify yourself, your company, and why you're calling (briefly). Call your customer/client by name.
2. Identify decision maker or influencer.
3. Pause. Find out if this is a convenient time. If inconvenient, find out a better time and call back.
4. GET THEIR INTEREST! Opening statement. Tell the benefits and reasons to buy your product/service.
5. Determine if prospect qualifies (if appropriate)—fact-finding.
6. Overcome objections (find out why he or she is not buying).
7. Sell benefits.
8. Trial close.
9. Close.
10. Summarize and confirm.
11. Thanks.
12. Follow-up method or date.

Figure 11-1. These guidelines will help telemarketing sales personnel prepare a pleasant and knowledgeable sales message.

Telemarketing is also used as a follow-up to direct mail as discussed in Chapter 10. When it is used as a follow-up it is suggested that the approach, presentation, and close be tied into the mailing or quite possibly used solely as a means of making personal contact and setting up a person-to-person meeting.

Displays

An important selling tool, particularly to the retailer, is the display (Fig. 11-2). A good display can be as effective as a salesperson and much less expensive. Creative displays can transform an ordinary store into a great store. A proper display makes a statement, a presentation, handles objections by showing how used, and, with proper signing, will ask for a purchase. The ingredients of a good display are:

It must be fresh and new.   It should use the newest and most exciting merchandise and be changed frequently. The length of time of a display will vary

Figure 11-2. An effective display.

with the circumstances. It may be seasonal, which would last for the duration of the season, or it might be a fashion showing of a week or less. You might show an item display indefinitely by periodically changing its location in the store.

It tells a single story. Display one coordinated group of items; more than one will cause confusion. Most customers do not stop to study a display; therefore it must be kept simple. The biggest mistake store owners make with their displays is overcrowding the contents and the idea.

Make it pertinent. There must be a reason for its existence. It should be timely, such as a seasonal item.

It is creative. The display is competing for attention, therefore utilize your imagination.

It is neat and clean. A good display must be well-lighted and well-maintained.

It has proper signing. The signing should show FAB, the price, and ask for action.

The entrepreneur as the customer

As a small businessperson you are not only selling, but you are also being sold to. It is important for you to understand the sales representatives who will be calling on you. Knowing their objectives will enable you to be a more efficient buyer. Large sales organizations usually take on the structure of the XYZ company illustrated as follows.

Sales objectives normally start at the top and are passed down in a snowballing effect. The president of the company meets with the vice president of sales in order to congratulate her on a job well done and to set the objectives for the upcoming year. If the previous year showed a 5 percent sales increase, the president may ask for a 7 percent increase for the upcoming year. This allows the president to report a commitment of a 6 percent increase to the board of directors, thus giving an extra 1 percent for miscalculation. The vice president, who must always be optimistic replies, "No problem J.B., we can get it." She then proceeds to meet with her national sales manager and reports the president is hoping for an 8 percent increase for the new year. The national sales manager commits and goes out to the field where he informs the regional sales managers the objective for the coming year is a 9 percent increase. They in turn pass on a 10 percent increase objective to the district sales managers, who in turn pass on an 11 percent increase to the individual sales representatives. As you can see, by everyone covering themselves for error, the original objective has almost doubled by the time it gets passed down to the area sales representative. No one wants to disappoint the next level up; therefore the lowest level has the most difficult assignment. The added increases will mean that not everyone will make his objective, but, hopefully, the team as a whole will. The sales representative who is not meeting his objectives will probably be okay as long as the district he works in makes its objectives. If the district fails, the district manager must answer to the regional manager, who can make life miserable for her, particularly if the region misses its objectives. You as the customer are important to your sales representative's objectives and the sales techniques used on you may vary, depending on how well the district's sales program is progressing. By understanding this, you will be better prepared to deal with your salesperson. It enables you to understand her problems better and to be on the lookout for overly aggressive selling.

Some organizations will attempt to set their objectives the proper way—from the bottom up. This means starting by asking the sales representative for an honest sales forecast. Using this information, objectives are passed upward in a more realistic manner. Unfortunately, many organizations will give lip service to this idea, but the pressure to exceed the previous year's totals will destroy the plan. However, you as a small businessperson should utilize this approach.

Set your sales objectives after consulting with those who sell for you. They are often in a better position than you in predicting market changes, since they may be in closer contact with the customer. A retailer needs to discuss the future with his sales clerks to find out customer whims and desires. The manufacturer and wholesaler need to talk to their field salespeople to find out what the competition is doing, and what needs are not being met. Listen to these people and others in the environment before setting sales objectives for your business.

Compensation and evaluation for sales personnel

Compensation for sales personnel can take many forms, straight salary, straight commission, salary plus commission on all sales, or salary plus commission on sales over quota. Most successful sales programs will use a commission incentive of some kind. The expectancy of reward based upon performance will direct salespeople to use their time wisely and to perform at maximum capacity. Their own abilities will determine their earning potential. It gives them the feeling of being in business for themselves.

The base salary plus a commission on sales, or a commission on sales over quota, usually combines the best of two worlds for the company and the salesperson. To the salesperson it gives a feeling of security and belonging. Too often straight commission plans do not build loyalty to the company. The salesperson feels unattached and lives under a cloud of fear, of not making sales through no fault of her own. Combination salary-commission plans may be devised to offer 80 percent straight salary and 20 percent incentive, 70/30, 60/40, or whatever split best suits the objectives of the firm.

In the event a straight salary plan is employed, it can be effectively backed up by a good bonus system. Many businesses, particularly some types of retail, have trouble designing commission structures that tie directly into performance. For these it is beneficial to utilize bonus incentives for superb performance. Bonuses might be in the form of extra pay or prizes. The objective is to make sure the bonus qualifications are clearly understood.

Evaluating a salesperson's performance should be done by his immediate sales supervisor. The proper evaluation should be based on quota standards, territory management effectiveness, leadership abilities, selling skills, new customers obtained, and customer satisfaction. Too many companies lose the meaning of the word representative in evaluating sales representatives. They are overly concerned with evaluating strictly in terms of meeting sales quotas. This gives the salesperson the feeling of being paid only for how much product he unloads in a given period of time. The company and the salesperson then become negligent of customer satisfaction and company image. The era of mass production has been accused of making the product first and then seeking out the customer to unload the products. Good salespeople have a greater responsibility than just selling— they are the standard bearers of your business. Evaluate their total performance. Discover how their customers feel about them and design your reward system to recognize more than just sales quota standards.

The entrepreneur spirit project—step 11

- Research the various sales training programs to find one that complements your type of business.

- Write out a sales philosophy that you believe will produce effective results for your business.

- Draw a sales organization chart. Make sure it allows for setting objectives from the bottom up.

- Learn as much as possible about the sales organizations that you will be dealing with concerning how they sell.

- Design a compensation and evaluation system that is comprehensive for the total salesperson's responsibilities.

PART THREE

Managing for Success

12

Pricing: How Much Is Too Much?

Placing the proper price on a product or service is important to the profitability of the business. However, it is also a very important customer relations tool.

Poor pricing strategy will be a major inhibitor to securing repeat sales. Effective pricing will assure you of customer satisfaction and a fair profit margin. It will also be a major promotional device, particularly with regard to word-of-mouth advertising.

The total pricing concept

Just as we emphasized the total customer concept, we must emphasize the total pricing concept. The price of the product must accomplish the following:

- Cover the total cost to the entrepreneur of what he is selling. This includes all shipping charges related to getting the product to the market.
- Cover all operating and overhead expenses needed to sell the product.
- Make a contribution to the long-run stability of the enterprise. This takes the form of retained earnings—monies available to reinvest in the growth of the business.
- Give the owner a fair profit for the effort expended. This sounds very basic, but it is often badly abused, usually in the form of underpricing. Look at the following simple example.

Most small retailers need to receive a gross profit of 50 percent of the retail price of merchandise. A normal retail cost breakdown might run: cost of goods 50 percent, freight 4 percent, rent 8 percent, payroll 10 percent (excluding the owner), advertising 2 percent, utilities 2 percent, other operating expenses (supplies, depreciation, insurance, miscellaneous) 10 percent, a total of 86 percent for a profit of 14 percent. A $100 sale would break down as follows:

Sale	$100
less cost of goods	−50
less freight	−4
Gross profit	$ 46
less operating expenses	−32
Net profit	$ 14

The $14 goes to the owner, bank debt, and reinvestment for the future. This 14 cents on each dollar is not much and is hard to get. The small businessperson must protect her profit margin at all cost. Most of the expenses she incurs are relatively fixed. Advertising and payroll can be trimmed a bit, but the rest of the costs are always there. All too often the small business makes the mistake of trying to compete with the large businesses in terms of price. This is a no-win situation since the big companies live under a different set of rules. Their objective is to please stockholders and this is often done by showing a 2 percent net profit on a sales volume of millions of dollars. The entrepreneur's objective is to feed her family, and 14 percent of sales of, say, $300,000, will barely enable her to do that, particularly if she is paying bank debts and reinvesting monies for the future. If she reduces her prices 20 percent in order to compete, she has taken away her 14 percent, plus some, and is doomed to failure. Therefore, in setting pricing policy, the total pricing concept of today and the future must be taken into consideration.

The intelligent entrepreneur is a realist in setting prices. He is reasonable in his expectations and knowledgeable of supply-and-demand factors in his market. Pricing policy must be constantly reevaluated depending on the product, the market conditions, the competition, and the goals of the enterprise. A 50 percent markup on retail goods may be acceptable; however, there are also times when 40 percent is more realistic and times when 60 percent is suitable. Use common sense. An everyday item should carry a consistent markup acceptable to customer expectations, and in line with competition. An unusual item, which the dealer has searched out specially, may carry a higher markup. A product whose appeal is not what the dealer had in mind may have to sell for less. Be realistic, consistent, and honest, but protect that profit margin. Profit is not a dirty word. To the small businessperson, profit is synonymous with salary.

Markup and markdown

Figuring markup and markdown percentages is initially difficult to get a handle on. Over a period of time it becomes second nature to the experienced entrepreneur. The following formulas can be used as guidelines:

Markup is the difference between the cost or wholesale price of a product and its retail price. It can be expressed in dollars or as a percent. If an item costs $5 and sells for $10, the markup is $5 or 50 percent of the retail price. When expressed as a percent it should be expressed as a percent of the retail not the cost.

$5.00 cost

$10.00 retail or 5/10 or 50 percent markup

When you know the cost and want to calculate the retail, and you know that you want a 50 percent markup, you divide the cost by the reciprocal of the markup. The reciprocal of a 50 percent markup is 50 percent, the reciprocal of a 40 percent markup is 60 percent, and the reciprocal of a 45 percent markup is 55 percent. In other words, to get the reciprocal of the markup, subtract the markup percent from 100. In this case, the reciprocal of 50 percent markup is 100 − 50, or 50 percent. So you divide the cost of $5.00 by 50 percent and get the $10.00 retail. If the cost had been $6.00 and the markup 40 percent, you would divide the $6.00 by the reciprocal of 40 percent, or 60 percent.

$6.00 cost

40 percent markup (reciprocal of 40 percent is .60)

$6.00/60 percent = $10.00 retail

When you know the retail price and want to know the cost, and you know the markup percent, you multiply the retail price by the markup, and subtract the answer from the retail price. If the retail is $10.00 and the markup is 50 percent, $10.00 times .50 percent equals $5.00 and $10.00 minus $5.00 equals the $5.00 cost.

When you know the cost and the retail, and want to know the markup percentage, you subtract the cost from the retail price and divide the difference by the retail price. The cost is $5.00 and the retail is $10.00. To find the markup, subtract $5.00 from $10.00. Divide the difference of $5.00 by the retail price of $10.00 and the answer is .50 or 50 percent markup.

This gives you some background on how markup works, the rest you will learn as you grow. Manufacturing, wholesaling, and mail-order businesses can apply the same formulas once it is determined how much gross profit margin is needed. The pricing margin varies with each industry and activity. The grocery store chain may only have a gross margin of 10 to 15 percent above cost, but do well because of the tremendous volume of sales. The mail-order business may have to sell at a 500 percent markup of the original cost of manufacturing the product in order to adequately cover all marketing, manufacturing, and handling costs.

There must be built into the final price a provision for taking markdowns. It is an essential part of any business to clear out excessive and obsolete inventory by utilizing markdown strategies.

Markdowns need to be taken for a variety of reasons:

Inventory is soiled or damaged. Damaged merchandise should never be sold at the regular price. If an item is slightly damaged, pass it on to the consumer with a savings. If it is greatly damaged, do not attempt to sell it.

Inventory is old or obsolete. If a product is out of style or out of season, or has been around too long, reduce the price. It is important to clear out slow-turning items in order to raise the money needed to purchase newer and better-selling inventory. Most retail stores will operate under a shelf-life philosophy. If a product group is taking up valuable shelf space and it is not selling, it makes economic sense to get rid of that item to make shelf room for new merchandise.

Broken assortments and odds and ends. If you have the top to an apparel outfit but not the bottom, you have decreased its salability. Reduce the price of the top.

Special promotions. Customers look forward to periodic sales or price cutting. In addition to raising capital, these promotional events are a way of increasing goodwill to your customers. Retail outlets will normally have a yearly calendar of markdown and special sale promotion events.

Meet the competitor's prices. If your small business competition takes a markdown, you must attempt to match him or offer an advantage to buying from you.

How much of a markdown you take depends on how badly damaged an item is, how old, how out of season, or how much in demand. It is a matter of judgment and experience. The idea is to sell it quickly. Sometimes 10 percent is enough, other times it takes 50 percent. When to take markdowns? Take them as soon as possible after the need is recognized. There is no reason to delay since inventory is only worth what it will sell for. The only reason for holding back is when you are waiting for a special event.

Learn the best markdown method for your business. Plan markdowns and do a thorough job. Make the best use of this pricing tool.

Arriving at a price. The retailer's price is greatly determined by competition and what the market will bear. The manufacturer, however, is a bit more complicated as he needs to run a breakeven analysis to determine his ultimate price. Aware of all his fixed cost, he can graph a chart indicating where price points should fall for his operation, as in Fig. 12-1.

Pricing strategies and techniques

The pricing strategy eventually decided upon will assist in mapping out the sales plan for the product or service. Different strategies can be applied depending on the long-run objectives.

A profit-oriented strategy allows the highest of gross profit margins. It is often used with a short-selling-cycle product in order to "make hay while the sun

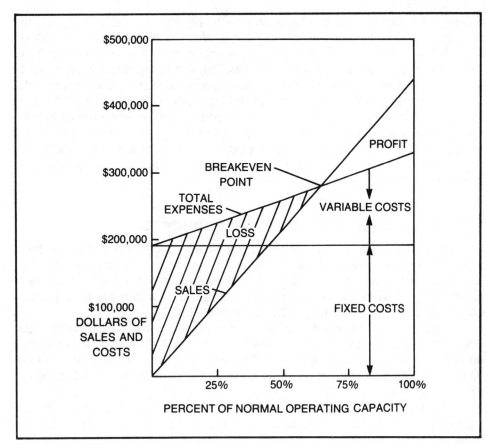

Figure 12-1. Breakeven chart.

shines." Fad products, such as the Pet Rock, that have a very short selling cycle need to sell quickly and get out. They will ask for the extra profit margin to help offset the high-risk speculation.

By selecting a strategy of selling at the lowest possible gross profit margin, the entrepreneur is operating under a sales-oriented pricing strategy. This is often done to attract attention upon entering the market. Often it is tied to the philosophy of gaining market share and then raising the price slowly to gain profits.

Most small businesses will eventually enter into a status quo pricing strategy. Once the entry into the market has been achieved, competition and the customer will direct pricing strategy. As the business matures, you will want to make sure it holds on to its market share and so price products accordingly. By allowing market conditions to dictate pricing strategy, the entrepreneur will remain status quo until a situation arises to warrant a change of pricing strategy.

Loss leading is a very valid pricing technique. For some reason, many consumers do not believe that businesses ever sell products for less than they cost.

However, in retailing, it is done quite often with very sound reasoning. By selling one particular item or group of items at a loss, the retailer is counting on selling enough of an associated product to more than make up for the loss incurred. The idea is to generate traffic and sell more units. The retail customer will often see it at drug store chains or the major discounters, particularly at Christmas time with toys. Large retailers, such as Sears, know how important it is to get customers inside their store during a big purchasing season and will sacrifice profits in one area to receive additional profits in another. Loss leading is an effective attention-getting device that when well planned can lead to greater profits. It is a more difficult and riskier strategy for the smaller stores as it requires a tremendous increase in traffic and inventory investment.

The discounter versus the independent

Jeff and Sheila discussed an interesting idea over coffee before opening their women's ready-to-wear boutique for the day. "We are getting killed by the discounters," Jeff noted, "and we seem helpless to do anything about it. They used to offer only off-name brands or their own brands, but now they are selling practically everything in the industry at 20 to 30 percent off."

"You don't need to tell me about it," commented Sheila, "I am losing regular customers everyday and I can't always blame them. They can save $25 on an outfit by going five minutes out of their way. It scares me to death. We finally start getting on our feet and now we can't compete. What are we going to do?"

"I'm worried too, Sheila. Maybe if we can't beat them, we have to join them. I am going to work out the figures to see what happens if we go discount and lower our prices 20 percent."

Jeff went to work on the idea and pulled out a summary statement of the past twelve months.

Sales	$500,000
less cost of goods	−260,000
Gross profit	$240,000
less operating expense	−220,000
Net profit	$ 20,000

His goal was to find the sales volume point, selling at 20 percent off, he needed to increase his profits. His first assumption was that a 20 percent discount would realize a 20 percent increase in the number of units sold, as in the calculation below. He figured his average unit sale to be $100 in his present operation, which translated into 5000 units sold at $100 equals $500,000. Therefore, with the 20 percent discount, his unit sales would rise to 6000 (5000 plus 20 percent) but the average unit sale would drop to $80 ($100 minus 20 percent). Buying the extra units would drive up his cost of goods 20 percent and he would incur higher operating costs due to extra personnel needed to sell extra units and the increased advertising expenditures to announce the change.

Sales	$480,000	(6000 units × $80)
less cost of goods	−312,000	(6000 × $50 plus freight)
Gross profit	168,000	
less operating expense	−240,000	(additional costs)
Net loss	$ (72,000)	

Now Jeff started to realize the idea behind discounting. Sell a tremendous number of units if you are to survive. Therefore, he worked his scale up to a 100 percent increase in units sold, if sold at a 20 percent discount.

Sales	$800,000	(10,000 units at $80)
less cost of goods	−520,000	(10,000 × $50 plus freight)
Gross profit	280,000	
less operating expense	−280,000	(additional costs)
Net profit	-0-	

100% increase at a 20% discount

"My God," thought Jeff, "we would have to double our unit sales, add additional payroll, significantly increase our inventory, and run a complete advertising campaign just to arrive at zero. Granted we may receive a slight discount on goods due to volume purchases, but it would not be enough to make that much difference. I never realized the effect of discounting prices has on the financial statement of a retail store." Before conferring with Sheila, Jeff ran one more projection using a 400 percent unit increase factor.

Sales	$1,600,000	(20,000 units × $80)
less cost of goods	−1,040,000	(20,000 × $50 plus freight)
Gross profit	$ 560,000	
less operating expense	−320,000	(additional costs)
Net profit	$ 240,000	

400% increase at a 20% discount

Now it finally made sense. How could their store in its present size and location handle that much volume? Where would the money come from to buy the necessary inventory? It all sounded too risky to Jeff.

Distribution

One of the main ingredients of price setting for the manufacturer is the cost of distributing the product. There are four basic channels of distribution to choose from.

The longer the distribution channel, the more cost to the final consumer. Theoretically, it should be less expensive to buy directly from the manufacturer. As the product passes through a channel, its price must increase at each stop in order to pay the intermediaries. The simplest—the manufacturer to the consumer—is seen predominantly in the mail-order business. The manufacturer to retailer to consumer channel is often seen in franchise operations. The most common channel is the manufacturer to wholesaler to retailer to consumer, which involves three markups to cover three different intermediaries' costs and profit margins in moving the product to market. The fourth channel, which includes an agent, is used by manufacturers who want nothing to do with marketing their product. They turn over all marketing activities to a marketing agent who sets up the distribution channel.

Often, the reverse can be true and the product with the longest distribution channel can be sold at the lowest price. This is because the more people involved with selling means more unit sales, thus driving down the unit production costs. The small mail-order manufacturer might be able to cut the unit cost by 75 percent or more if he increases his production run 1000 percent. This savings might be more than the total cost of distribution. The choice of method of distribution will be a major determinant of the price a manufacturer assigns to his product as it will direct the quantities to be produced and the cost of getting the product to the market. A manufacturer must be certain that the final price offered to the consumer is acceptable.

The entrepreneur spirit project—step 12

- Research your industry for pricing strategies.
- Choose the pricing strategy that makes the most sense for your business. Survey the competition.
- Chart out in graphic form your breakeven analysis.
- If you are a potential manufacturer or wholesaler, investigate channel of distribution possibilities and consider their effect on your pricing strategy.

13

Securing the Proper Personnel: How Do You Keep the Key People?

How the small business competes for the good people is a challenging dilemma for the entrepreneur. Normally she is straddled with such a tight payroll budget that it is impossible to compete dollar for dollar with the larger companies. There is most likely no room for pension plans, stock options, country club memberships, or company cars. She will be fortunate if the company can afford a group medical insurance plan.

Why would anyone work for the small business if he can make more money and have more benefits with the larger companies? For the same reason you started the business—the challenge and excitement of being part of something they can identify with. Going back to Maslow's hierarchy of needs, we mentioned the need to belong, the need to be part of something. A small business can instill the fulfillment of that need much better than the large corporation. There are many capable people who are more interested in belonging to something they believe in than what is in the weekly paycheck. In searching for the best people, the entrepreneur needs to appeal to that need.

Tools to use

The best tool available for this is honesty. If you need a particular person to work for you, tell them how much they are needed. Do not try to appeal to their financial needs and do not overglamorize the job, it will backfire. Tell them that they are needed to fill a particular role. Explain that opportunities, and, hopefully, financial rewards, will develop as the business grows. Describe your philosophy on doing business and see if they agree. Share your personal value system—it may appeal to them. Show them that the work environment will not be one of red tape and bureaucratic hassles. They will join a work force of people who will share common goals and build a camaraderie that will never be found in a large company. In recruiting personnel, you have one big advantage—the human advantage. The small organization can react to fulfill an individual employee's needs in a much more personal way.

All of these intangibles are nice and they can help persuade, but there must be reasonable monetary rewards as well. The pay must be fair, particularly in consideration of the lack of benefits. The work environment must be comfortable. There cannot be a million policies governing everything from coffee breaks to creating look-busy work. The employee must be a direct participant in designing his job responsibilities. Let employees do what they do best. Build on their strengths and not their weaknesses. Listen to your employees, give them freedom, give them challenge, give them opportunity. When possible, allow them to structure their job around their personal life. That's one of the reasons you left the big company, so give them as much consideration as possible. If an employee needs a Friday off to take a trip, the entrepreneur should try her best to comply with that request. You can't pay more, but you can give more, and some of what you are able to give can be very tangible.

All of this will work if the entrepreneur follows one rule. Hire people you like. You must like them because it is imperative that they like you. Running a small business is a very personal experience. You will expose a lot of yourself to the people who work for you and they must be understanding of you. This requires trust, cooperation, and, most of all, some genuine caring. When you hire someone, place them on a probationary status for a certain period of time. This enables you to evaluate their performance and personality, and allows them to evaluate their job. At the conclusion of this period of time, no matter how good their performance, fire them if you don't like them.

If you don't like them, they probably do not like you, which eliminates the necessary trust and caring. As a small business you will normally not be involved with union regulations and grievance procedures, therefore feel free to terminate an employee if you feel they do not fit. The small business must be cohesive to function at maximum efficiency.

Where to find employees

There are many places to look for potential employees. You must take the initiative in recruiting good people. The more applicants you have to consider, the more selective you can be. Your goal is to obtain the cream of the crop. The following list gives sources available to the entrepreneur in locating personnel:

- Help-wanted advertising either through a sign in the window or a classified section of the newspaper. Although advertising allows no screening, it is effective in creating large numbers of applicants.

- Employee referrals might provide excellent prospects. A good employee will not recommend someone of inferior ability.

- Employment agencies, either public or private, will have a list of potential employees. The private agencies will screen applicants for you to find the qualifications you desire; however, either you or the applicant will be required to pay a fee for their services.

- High schools, community colleges, universities, and vocational schools can be an excellent source for employees. This is particularly true for part-time employees if you are able to work their schedule around their school responsibilities. Many colleges and vocational schools will have placement offices to help graduates find full-time work after graduation.

There will also be a number of unsolicited applicants, either through the mail or walk-ins. Even if you have no immediate needs, take the time to interview these people and keep their applications on file for future needs. It is a good idea to keep an active applicant file.

Job interviews should be well planned. Determine your questions in advance and listen attentively. Conduct the interviews in a quiet atmosphere, try to put the applicant at ease, and observe closely. You are trying to discover in a few minutes whether the applicant possesses the qualifications you need to fill a position. Poor hiring is expensive, since you cannot afford to spend the time and money to train someone who does not have the correct credentials for the job. Training takes time and time costs money.

Most training in the small business sector comes through on-the-job training. Seldom does the small business have the budget to supplement job training with university residential programs or expensive seminars. On-the-job training available through the small business can be very effective since it will be very closely observed. It is important that the owner assure the new employee that he will be fully supported in the learning process and that the boss's door is always open for questions.

Some of the biggest problems the entrepreneur will encounter will be personnel problems. Recruiting is difficult, sustaining motivation and good employee morale is an ongoing problem, and losing key people can be a crisis. Some people will be lost, no matter what you could have done, just because people need change.

The good entrepreneur will not become too dependent on one person or a small group of people. By always keeping on top of all functions of the business, the owner will always be able to step in and fill a void. By being aware of the dangers of losing personnel, the successful entrepreneur will have groomed replacements to step in and assume new responsibilities.

You as the boss

What type of entrepreneur makes the best boss? The one who leads through participation. Remember you will not be working in an ivory tower with all kinds of specialized help to handle every task. The entrepreneur and his staff does it all. Everyone, including the boss, is involved with doing anything that makes it work. The entrepreneur sets the policies and also sets the standards, by showing how the job is properly done.

The reason it is important for the boss to pitch in is that it is the number one way of instilling loyalty among employees. Working side by side with people creates camaraderie. Camaraderie instills loyalty, which creates trust, trust creates honesty. The statistics you read concerning the tremendous amount of employee theft are unfortunately true. By working closely with your employees and getting to know them, you will build trust, and you will be less likely to be a victim of internal theft. Another by-product of this is that in the event someone is dishonest, another employee may find out and report the individual to you.

The ideal manager in the small business is not the overly aggressive, nail-spitting, order-giving theory X type of manager. He is the individual who is strong on fair policies, participation-oriented, appreciates effort expended, and operates in a theory Y mode.

What should the entrepreneur expect to receive in return? 100 percent and nothing less. Employees of small businesses work harder and are more conscientious. They work hard because they are involved. They are less prone to be clockwatchers. Their goal is not to see what they can get out of doing. They know if the business fails, they will be out of a job. Presuming that they like their boss, their working environment, and are treated fairly, they will have a very keen interest in the success of the enterprise. This will be particularly true if it is made clear that if the business does well, the rewards will be generous. All jobs are generally considered as line jobs, directly involved with the production and sales of the product or service. There are usually no staff positions, such as a personnel director. From the boss on down everyone is directly involved with the direct activity of the business.

Compensation

How does the new business decide on what is fair compensation? Start with the industry standards. If the industry is composed of principally minimum wage earners, so should your business, at least for starters. If the industry standards suggest commission pay, so should your business. Be competitive, not lower and not higher. There will be time to reward personnel financially after the business is established and on its feet. Sell the job on the merits of the job and the company.

There are some legitimate benefits which may be affordable to offer. Vacation pay, sick pay, and group medical plans that the employer can help contribute to are reasonable. Another program to investigate is a Keogh plan. Keogh plans are employer-subsidized pension plans that are designed with the small business in mind. They can be set up to reward loyalty and seniority by the employer. The employer makes periodic deposits into a tax-exempt, interest-earning account that is to be shared by him and selected employees who have met the standards set for eligibility.

Keeping your employees requires that the entrepreneur stay on top with ways to increase earnings without pay raises. Employee discounts on the company's products might be a way of increasing take-home pay, bonuses to reward superlative effort, contests to win prizes—these are all ideas that keep the payroll budget in line and are appreciated by the employees. Any time you can reward with short-term rewards versus long-term commitments, the better for the business. Only do what the business can afford. Customs such as annual raises do not have to be awarded if the money is not there in the small business.

The entrepreneur spirit project—step 13

- Write out job descriptions for possible positions in your business. If one person can do two jobs, eliminate the position.

- Draw an organization chart showing all positions considered and the reporting function of each.

- Determine pay scales and what benefits the projected budget will allow.

- Describe in general terms a basic on-the-job training program that will fit your business.

14

Cash Flow:
What Do You Do
With All That Money?

There are many businesses which survive for years without showing a net profit. These marginally profitable operations are very astute at making cash flow work for them. Although it is much preferable to have extra capital available through healthy net profits, using cash flow properly may hold the business together until that time comes. Rona, the woman with the Card and Party Shops in Chapter 2, survived for four years on cash flow. If she had handled the cash flow to the advantage of the business, as opposed to using it for personal monies, her business may have eventually turned a nice profit.

In many types of businesses there is usually cash generated on a daily or weekly basis that is available until the bills become due. This cash can be used wisely to make or save monies for the business.

Using cash wisely

A retail store, which during most of the year grosses an average of $20,000 per month, takes in $100,000 between Thanksgiving and Christmas. The owner may have an additional $80,000 to use for a short period of time before paying her bills the latter part of January. She needs to develop a plan to make the best use of this extra income that she has for approximately 45 days. She may wish to use it to pay some bills early, thereby receiving an extra discount for early payment. Depending on the industry, many vendors will offer early payment discounts of between 2 and 8 percent of invoice amount. These discounts as accumulated will give the business owner a healthy decrease in cost of goods sold. If she is a gambler, the owner could utilize the extra income for outside short-term investments. Placing $80,000 in a 10 percent interest-paying account for 45 days will earn $800. The proper plan is to map out a cash flow plan for a year in order to predict when extra cash is available for the owner's use. Let's do this for a $200,000 retail business.

Start with a projected income statement as shown in Fig. 14-1.

From this you can project the net cash flow by adding depreciation to profits and subtracting out loan debt reduction and inventory buildup, as demonstrated by the following calculation:

Projected profit	$ 10,580
plus depreciation	+5,000
less bank note reduction	−10,000
less inventory buildup	−900
Projected net cash flow	$ 4,680

This means that during the coming year the owner will have an additional cash surplus floating around of $4680. Now, make a monthly cash flow plan to determine at what times these monies will be available.

Figure 14-2 shows when there will be a surplus or shortage of funds and for how long. It can identify temporary or long-term needs. A very common reaction of a business that finds itself short of cash is to pay its bills as late as possible. This is done at a high cost, since you will be forfeiting any possible discounts. A 2 percent discount, if taken every month, is the equivalent to borrowing monies at an annual interest of 36 percent. Many times it is wiser to borrow monies to protect the discount savings and at the same time protect your credit standing.

With this information you are now capable of working out a daily cash flow diagram (Fig. 14-3) allowing you to comfortably plan for all payment obligations during the current month. If you miss the sales projection for a given day, adjust your plan accordingly for the rest of the month. There are computer programs available to make this process simple; otherwise do it manually—it will keep you on top of things. This gives the entrepreneur forewarning on any potential cash problems that are likely to occur during the month.

This is really a cash budget, and as with all budgets there must be flexibility built into it, by being conservative with the daily sales projections, planning on paying bills early, or adding miscellaneous expenses to the plan. By taking some precautions you hopefully will have a few more dollars in the bank than you originally planned. Use a form such as the one shown in Fig. 14-4 to calculate your projected cash flow.

Hopefully, there will be many times when there is extra cash available for unplanned purchases; there will also be times when a cash deficit will appear. You will have to act accordingly. A minor deficit for a day or two will most likely be covered in your checking account by check processing and mailing time. If you anticipate being slightly overdrawn at the bank, call your bank contact and advise him of a potential problem. As long as it does not occur too often they

PROJECTED INCOME STATEMENT
FOR THE YEAR ENDING DECEMBER 31, 19XY

	19XX Actual Year-End Results	% of Sales	19XY Projected Results	% of Sales
SALES	$200,000	100.0%	$220,000**	100.0%*
COST OF GOODS SOLD	114,000	57.0	121,000	55.0
GROSS MARGIN	86,000	43.0	99,000	45.0
OPERATING EXPENSES				
Payroll	31,000	15.5	32,000	14.5 *
Rent	20,000	10.0	22,000	10.0 *
Operating Supplies	4,200	2.1	4,620	2.1 *
Utilities	3,800	1.9	4,400	2.0 *
Other	14,000	7.0	15,400	7.0 *
Total Cash Operating Exp.	73,000	36.5	78,420	35.6
Depreciation	5,000	2.5	5,000	2.3
Interest	6,000	3.0	5,000	2.3
Total Operating Expenses	84,000	42.0	88,420	40.2
PRE-TAX PROFIT	$ 2,000	1.0%	$ 10,580	4.8%

*Items Used for Cash Flow Projection.

**Forecasted 10% Increase in Sales.

Expenses were combined for Presentation

Figure 14-1. Projected income statement.

will most likely oblige you by paying the overdrawn checks, although they may credit your account with a service charge. If you do not get the word to the bank, checks may be returned to the depositor marked NSF, nonsufficient funds. Don't panic, call the depositor and explain that you encountered a problem and have them redeposit the check and assure them that it will be covered

MONTHLY CASH FLOW FORECAST

19XY

CASH FLOW ITEMS	JANUARY	FEBRUARY	MARCH	APRIL	MAY	JUNE	JULY	AUGUST	SEPTEMBER	OCTOBER	NOVEMBER	DECEMBER	TOTAL
Beginning Cash Balance	$28,000	$4,805	$1,865	$2,610	($1,260)	$385	($990)	($2,220)	($950)	($2,515)	($6,470)	$3,840	
CASH INFLOW													
Sales	$10,320	$16,060	$14,125	$13,880	$18,700	$16,190	$12,255	$14,280	$12,740	$14,540	$21,870	$55,050	$220,000
% of Total Sales	4.7%	7.3%	6.4%	6.3%	8.5%	7.4%	5.6%	6.5%	5.8%	6.6%	9.9%	25.0%	100.0%
Total Inflow	$10,320	$16,060	$14,125	$13,880	$18,700	$16,190	$12,255	$14,280	$12,740	$12,740	$21,870	$55,040	$220,000
CASH OUTFLOW													
Purchases	26,685	11,275	6,250	10,105	9,290	10,155	6,315	6,300	7,450	11,925	4,225	11,655	121,900
Payroll	2,080	2,880	2,240	3,040	3,040	2,560	2,400	1,920	2,240	1,920	2,560	5,120	32,000
Rent	1,500	1,500	1,500	1,500	1,500	1,500	1,500	1,500	1,500	1,500	1,500	5,500	22,000
Operating Supplies	385	385	385	385	385	385	385	385	385	385	385	385	4,620
Utilities	460	440	265	265	460	460	460	485	285	285	290	440	4,400
Other	1,155	1,270	1,220	1,205	1,325	1,255	1,175	1,170	1,195	1,230	1,350	1,850	15,400
Debt Service	1,250	1,250	1,250	1,250	1,250	1,250	1,250	1,250	1,250	1,250	1,250	1,250	15,000
Total Outflow*	33,515	19,000	13,380	17,750	17,055	17,565	13,485	13,010	14,305	18,495	11,560	26,206	215,320
NET CASH FLOW	($23,195)	($2,940)	$745	($3,870)	$1,645	($1,375)	($1,230)	$1,270	($1,565)	($3,955)	$10,310	$28,840	$4,680
ENDING CASH BALANCE	$4,805	$1,865	$2,610	($1,260)	$385	($990)	($2,220)	($950)	($2,515)	($6,470)	$3,840	$32,680**	

* For simplification purposes no allowance or plans have been made for provisions of income taxes.

** To verify accuracy of calculations: Add the Beginning Cash Balance for January ($28,000) to the Total Net Cash Flow for the year ($4,680), and compare to the Ending Cash Balance for December ($32,680). If not equal, a mathematical error has been made in the calculations.

Figure 14-2. Monthly cash flow forecast.

```
           DAILY CASH FLOW PLANNER

       Beginning balance    $2350

       May 1   Friday       2350
               deposit       650
               utilities    (475)

       May 2   Saturday     2525
               deposit       850

       May 4   Monday       3375
               deposit      1125
               rent        (1275)

       May 5   Tuesday      3225
               deposit       450
               vendors     (2350)

       May 6   Wednesday    1325
               deposit       450
               misc.        (200)

       May 7   Thursday     1575
               deposit       675
               payroll     (1200)
```

Figure 14-3. Daily cash flow planner.

upon second presentation. It will not be the first time they have received an NSF check.

In the event there looms a large deficit ahead, you will need to visit the bank and request a short-term loan to get you over the hump. It is quite helpful to have a prearranged line of credit with the bank. They should be favorable to setting up an agreed-upon amount of monies available for you, as a regular depositor, to borrow for short-term emergencies. If this is arranged you will only have to call the bank and request that they deposit x number of dollars into your account immediately from your credit line. This saves you the time and inconvenience of application forms and committee approval meetings. The only requirement will be to share financial statements with the bank on a regular basis and to make sure the loans are paid back at the agreed-upon time.

MONTHLY CASH FLOW FORECAST
3 F 178A REV 12 84

CASH FLOW ITEMS	January	February	March	April	May	June
BEGINNING CASH BALANCE						
CASH INFLOW						
SALES						
LOAN PROCEEDS						
TOTAL INFLOW						
CASH OUTFLOW						
PURCHASES						
RENT						
PAYROLL						
UTILITIES						
SUPPLIES						
ADVERTISING						
INSURANCE						
MAINTENANCE						
TAXES						
MISCELLANEOUS						
DEBT SERVICE (PRINCIPAL & INTEREST)						
INCOME TAXES						
TOTAL OUTFLOW						
NET CASH FLOW						
CUMULATIVE CASH FLOW						

Figure 14-4. Cash flow planning form.

Understanding credit

Successful cash flow planning requires the entrepreneur to understand credit properly. In addition to understanding the bank obligations, you must know all the terms and conditions that apply toward purchasing on credit. There are numerous types of trade credit arrangements, most of them offering discounts for prompt payment. This incentive works well for both buyer and seller. The buyer saves money and the seller receives the money early in order to put it to use for other purposes. Discounts will be stated in various ways and in various amounts, depending on the industry. The invoice may carry terms of 2/10/30, which translates into a 2 percent discount if paid by the tenth of the following month, or pay the net amount by the thirtieth. Another example may read 8/10 which means an 8 percent discount is available if the invoice is paid within 10 days of the invoice date. Discount taking equals a sizable savings to the business.

The longer you can hold onto your money and take advantage of discounts, the easier your cash flow. Look at the terms before deciding on suppliers. An extra 30, 60, or 90 days in which to pay a bill and still receive a discount is added cash available that can turn into more profits. The ideal arrangement is buying the inventory and not paying for it until after it has been resold and the monies received. This can take the form of dated invoicing. In retailing it is often possible to buy Christmas merchandise in August or September and not have to pay for it until after Christmas. These types of terms will be helpful in that all of this merchandise sold during the pre-Christmas season will add to extra cash flow. Therefore, shop around for terms. Ask your suppliers for special terms—it can't hurt to try.

There will likely be times when all the bills are not paid on time. It is not the end of the world, but must be handled properly. The initial response of the creditor will be a past due notice, followed by a second notice, and if still not paid, the telephone will start ringing. They will likely add late charges of 1½ percent monthly on the unpaid balance and eventually turn your account over to a collection agency or their legal department. Needless to say, this will end your credit relationship with that supplier and can lead to a poor credit standing throughout the industry. This can be avoided by working closely with the creditor. Understand that they need to collect from their customers just as you do from yours. If you foresee a problem, let them know in advance and they will work out a payment plan to enable you to fulfill your obligation. In these days of overnight bankruptcy, most creditors will work with you, as opposed to helping to cause a bankruptcy and not receiving their monies at all.

Many manufacturers prefer to use industry factors to handle their accounts receivable. Factors are organizations whose sole purpose is to collect receivables for manufacturers for a specified percent of the amount invoiced. They are not collection agencies who handle only delinquent accounts. They are large financial organizations who act as agents for the manufacturer. They relieve the manufacturer from the cumbersome clerical work of an accounts receivable department.

One other item to consider in your cash flow analysis is how the small business receives its revenues. The bank card systems, mainly MasterCard and Visa, have been a great help in relieving the small business of carrying charge accounts. The merchant is charged a percent of the sale for this service. Depending on the amount of charge business done on an annual basis, the rates will range from 1 to 5 percent of the transaction. This is normally a savings as opposed to the cost of operating an accounts receivable system which requires bill preparation, mailing, and handling delinquent accounts. It also saves you losing customers due to delinquent bills. Normally, charge deposits are paid to your account the same day that you deposit them at your bank.

Accounts receivable are monies that you do not have the use of. If the average collection time on the bills is 37 days, that means that 37/365, or approximately 10 percent of your annual revenues, are always outstanding. This money will always be outstanding until the business is closed or sold. If not properly managed, the accounts receivable will be disastrous to the business's cash flow.

The entrepreneur spirit project—step 14

- Fill out a cash flow chart as shown in Fig. 14-4, using your monthly sales projections. Target the times of excess or too little cash and form a plan of action.

- Discuss with your bank ways to have a short-term line of credit established for your business.

- Find out the payment terms you will be asked to adhere to from your suppliers.

- Decide if you will need the use of bank cards or an accounts receivable system.

15

Inventory Control: Having the Right Goods, at the Right Place, at the Right Time

The ultimate frustration of owning a business is when a customer wants to buy something that you have sold out. Proper inventory management prevents out-of-stock conditions in retailing and downtime in manufacturing. Both are very expensive experiences. Imagine having to shut down an assembly line because you are missing a production piece, or owning a flower shop that has no flowers to sell on Valentine's Day. A proper buying plan and well-planned scheduling of shipments will prevent this from occurring.

Mindful that there is not unlimited capital available for inventory purchase, it is the small businessperson's goal to secure maximum sales on a minimum investment. In other words, how many units of x are needed to reach a sales objective that produces the maximum profit possible for the least amount of dollars invested. How to find that point is the challenge, because it constantly changes with market and industry fluctuations.

Inventory is the number of units, and the amount of value attached to these units, that is available for sale or manufacture in the normal course of business. All businesses are required to keep track of their inventory. It is necessary for proper record keeping, reporting to the Internal Revenue Service, and reporting to local and state taxing authorities for tangible property tax purposes. All businesses take a physical inventory at least once a year. This requires an actual and complete physical count of all items needed in the revenue-producing activities of the enterprise. For some businesses (like a hardware store), it is a very tedious chore. Once the inventory is established it should be constantly re-evaluated. This can be done by a monthly or a regular physical count of the inventory or by keeping a perpetual inventory count through purchase and sales records. The perpetual inventory method requires keeping a daily tracking of any products received and subtracting out all units sold or deleted. The accuracy of this method is determined at the time the physical inventory is taken. Any discrepancy in the two totals will have to be explained by shrinkage, spoilage, theft, accident, or poor record keeping. The value placed on the inventory is expressed using the cost value or market value, whichever is lower.

This is important to note because there can be quite a difference between what you paid and what it is worth. If a women's fashion store has out-of-style merchandise, the market value may be considerably below the original cost. Since the owner pays taxes based on the value declared, he will want to make sure the value assigned is fair to him.

Buying

Finding the best sources available to supply the business is a searching exercise. There will be some suppliers and vendors that the business will rely on its entire life, while many others will be used once and discarded. Finding reliable, good service, good product companies will reduce many of the entrepreneur's problems.

The entrepreneur should attend industry trade or merchandise shows. These are expositions of wholesalers and manufacturers which are intended to introduce sellers to buyers. In almost all industries there are annual, semiannual, or quarterly trade shows held in major cities in each region of the country. They generally last from four to seven days and are held in convention centers, large hotels, or merchandise marts. The new entrepreneur should plan on attending one of these shows. To register, you will have to show proof of operating a business, usually a state sales tax certificate. During the show, the customer is exposed to just about everything available and new in the industry. It is a carnival type of atmosphere with hundreds of separate booths set up for the different sellers. The potential customer walks the aisles looking at all that is available for her business. When an idea catches her attention she can stop and chat with the salesperson and possibly place an order. It is a fascinating and enjoyable experience, often complete with evening entertainment offered by the industry.

How good a buying plan the business owner comes up with is dependent on the accuracy of his sales projections. For the new business it is certainly much more difficult as he must rely on a sales projection estimate made without the advantage of historical data. The more history you have, the more accurate the buying plan.

A buying plan is designed to encompass a particular period of time, or in retailing, a particular season. It is necessary to have a beginning inventory figure, a sales forecast, and an end-of-period inventory objective.

Let's look at an example of a women's clothing store purchasing for the fall and holiday selling period that runs from July 1 to December 31. First, list the anticipated beginning and ending inventory levels that hope to be realized. In this case, using strictly retail value figures, the July 1 inventory is $50,000, with the goal of increasing inventory to $55,000 December 31.

If available, the business uses historical information to arrive at monthly sales projections, or, if not available, a percent of gross sales projection taken from industry sources. If the store has projected a $250,000 annual sales volume, the industry standards may show it is broken down as follows for the months being planned.

Month	Percent		Amount
July	6		$ 15,000.00
August	7		17,500.00
September	8		20,000.00
October	8		20,000.00
November	11		27,500.00
December	16		40,000.00
		Total sales	$140,000.00

In addition, the store will have to take into consideration the amounts of markdowns anticipated, in this case 10 percent of retail sales, in order to successfully achieve its planned ending inventory objective, illustrated by the following:

Beginning inventory	$ 50,000
plus purchases	+159,000
minus sales	−140,000
minus markdowns	−14,000
Ending inventory	$ 55,000

The total purchase to be planned, therefore, is $159,000. This will allow for $140,000 to be sold at full retail, $14,000 to be sold at a cost price, and an inventory growth of $5000. The total purchase plan will look like Fig. 15-1.

By planning the beginning and ending inventory for each month in anticipation of the month ahead, the buyer is assuring that the inventory will stay at a level high enough to withstand demand. It doesn't always work out as planned. Some merchandise will arrive earlier than desired, some later, and markdowns might be greater or less. To accommodate for these fluctuations, you utilize cash flow charts and short-term borrowing reserves. Unless something drastic happens to the business or the economy, the business activity should equate well to the total plan.

The purchase budget, often referred to as the open-to-buy budget, needs to have flexibility. There must be monies available to take advantage of special

	JULY	AUG.	SEPT.	OCT.	NOV.	DEC.	TOTAL
BEG INVENTORY	$50,000	$52,500	$55,000	$55,000	$62,500	$75,000	
+ PURCHASES	$19,000	21,750	22,000	29,500	42,750	24,000	$159,000
(−) SALES	$15,000	17,500	20,000	20,000	27,500	40,000	$140,000
(−) MARKDOWNS	$ 1,500	1,750	2,000	2,000	2,750	4,000	14,000
= END INVENTORY	$52,500	55,000	55,000	62,500	75,000	55,000	

Figure 15-1. Purchase plan.

purchase opportunities that will arise with very short notice. Good buyers do not commit all of their monies too far in advance. They leave an allowance available for unplanned purchases or a safety valve to use, if it is necessary, to drop inventory levels in the event there are cash flow problems. They also tend to be on the bold side in regards to planning, as there is always the factor of unshipped goods due to factory shortages or delays. You do not want to take the risk of being short on goods, which will mean lost sales. In the event of inventory surplus, the business must rely on taking markdowns or cutting planned orders the next season to get inventory back in line.

Just-in-time inventory

Small businesses should try as much as possible to perfect a just-in-time inventory control system. The idea behind this system is to have suppliers deliver goods just in time to go on the retail shelf or assembly line. By doing this a minimum amount of money is invested in inventory. In order to do this, it requires a tremendous amount of confidence and cooperation with suppliers. There is a downside to this control system in that unplanned interruptions, such as weather, can hamper delivery. Also there is the added cost of more frequent, smaller deliveries. However, if successful, the entrepreneur is able to free up money which can be used to better promote the business.

Successful just-in-time inventory systems require detailed planning in conjunction with the supplier. Deliveries should be monitored closely from a supplier before implementing the system. The supplier must be one who is able to ship quickly and also have access to a substantial inventory base to prevent sellouts. Most businesses will implement a just-in-time system with only those suppliers who they are assured can respond, while maintaining a more standardized system with their other suppliers.

Season ordering

Season purchasing for a particular holiday carries the risk that what is not sold will be in inventory for at least another year until that season comes around again. Many businesses have gotten into serious trouble because they have listened too optimistically to a sales pitch on how "hot" a particular item will be this coming Christmas season. Carrying over too much of a product for a season will significantly reduce the profit projection of a season. If a retail store sells 80 percent of its strictly Christmas merchandise and carries over 20 percent, its profit margin is reduced by 40 percent. For instance, $5000 cost or $10,000 retail of Christmas home decorations are purchased. The store is hoping to sell $10,000, making a gross profit of $5000; instead it sells $8000 or 80 percent, meaning it made $3000 on an investment of $5000, 60 percent instead of the 100 percent it had hoped for. The other option is to have a half-price sale after the season to clear out the inventory. However, this still does not assure you of selling everything and you have consequently put the notice out to your customers that if they wait until after the season they can buy for half-price. Buying holiday merchandise must be done conservatively. It is often advisable to buy only enough season-tailored products to present the necessary look to better sell your usual product assortment during the season. It is imperative accurate records be kept of season item buying for the purpose of planning the next year's purchase. Keep track of the items ordered and when they sold. By knowing a holiday item sold out early in the season, it will help you to remember to order more for the following season. If an item did not sell out until the last day of the season or was carried over until next year, you will know to use caution.

The same conservative outlook should be employed in buying fad-type products. They are usually short-lived and timing is of the essence. Many never experienced the consumer acceptance expected. The ET dolls of a few years ago are a good example. With the tremendous success of the movie, retailers could not wait to get their hands on the ET doll. They ordered in reckless numbers and got stuck. What no one realized was that the vinyl material used in making the doll was not the soft plush feel that children wanted to take to bed with them. The retailers lucky enough to get into the Cabbage Patch doll craze experienced the opposite. Demand exceeded production. Because of the lack of merchandise available, very few merchants made substantial profits.

The point is that the risk often outweighs the benefits. You might get stuck or, in the case that it proves successful, you may not be able to secure enough merchandise to really make the risk worthwhile.

Case study: Stevens-Kern Company

The following scenario shows a typical buying decision. The deal being offered by the manufacturer's sales representative was impressive. John R. Kern, owner and manager of Stevens-Kern Company, could not resist serious consideration of the proposal, despite his resolution to keep stereo inventory to a minimum.

The price reduction was substantial—35 to 50 percent off the customary wholesale price. There was no question that the manufacturer intended to move some merchandise. Sale of stereos nationally had been slow for some months—a fact that may have prompted the offer.

If stereos were purchased at the sharply reduced price, they could be sold at a correspondingly low price to retail customers. By also reducing the store's margin slightly, Stevens-Kern Company could offer its customers a "real buy." The normal and special prices on one of the popular models would compare as follows:

	Normal price	Special offer
Retail price	$289	$174
less wholesale cost	−204	−128
Gross profit	85	46
Gross profit %	29.4	26.4

By paying the normal wholesale price for appliances, he could do no more than break even. "If a salesperson wants me to listen now," he said, "he'd better have some kind of a deal to offer me." The present offer could be a very good deal. Kern had operated on the principle that it was better to be a little long on inventory than a little short on sales. His inventory position in stereos at the time was thin, but only six to eight stereos were needed to bring it up to a normal level.

The store's inventory investment (for all types of appliances) exceeded $150,000; the decision to expand inventory was not to be made lightly. Warehouse space was at a premium, with some inventory being kept in a public warehouse. Insurance and taxes added further to building inventory. Kern recalled that the cost of maintaining an inventory for just six months might be as high as 15 percent of its value.

Kern knew all too well that his leading competitor, in the same city, was getting the same offer. If the competitor bought, Stevens-Kern should also buy to remain competitive. If the competitor passed up the opportunity, purchasing could give Stevens-Kern a chance for a competitive advantage.

Unfortunately, the offer came during the off season for stereos. The big question was whether a stereo priced at $174 (below its normal wholesale price) would be a "hot" enough item to bring in customers during the off season.

One condition of the offer was that any purchase must be made in lots of 30. The most conservative course of action was to buy none. This would minimize inventory cost. The larger purchases would involve correspondingly greater risk but would maximize profit in the event the sale proved to be extremely popular. During the preceding year the store had sold 160 console stereos, about 60 percent of the sales occurring in the fourth quarter.

In a situation like this the success of the decision will depend on the planning steps made at the time of the purchase. First, consider the financial decision. If the store is six to eight stereos short at this time, it would indicate that there probably is a plan to buy, approximately $1200 to $1500 for stereos (6 or 8 times $204, the normal wholesale cost).

The purchase of 30 will not offer a great profit incentive since selling all the units would gain Stevens-Kern a gross profit of only $1380. If the owner subtracts the advertising costs and other additional costs involved, he will realize that buying 30 units will not be worth anything except staying competitive. If making a profit is his goal, he will do better buying 60 or 90, which represent profit potentials of $2760 and $4140. The decision should be based on the amount of confidence he puts into his selling plan, and the profit potential that becomes available to him if his competitor does not buy. In that event, he may not want to give such a large retail price discount, or he might decide to hold them back, and offer the special at Christmas as a vehicle for attracting customers. A good plan of attack, with various contingency strategies, is needed in any purchase decision like this.

The entrepreneur spirit project—step 15

- Plan your first buying season to arrive for the period following your initial opening.

- Design a strategy to be used in the case of too little or too much inventory.

- Design your selling strategy for all product groups that you are considering purchasing.

- Plan a trip to an industry trade show.

16

Managing Your Business: Keeping on Top of Things

Once opened, the entrepreneur turns her attention to the most efficient method of managing the operation. She will find that the same management principles and functions that hold true for the large business apply to the small business.

Getting organized

Start with an organization chart. It is used in the same way as the large corporate chart. Its purpose is to indicate the flow of communications and the delegation of responsibilities. It may appear similar to the one for the card and gift shop illustrated in Fig. 16-1.

Very seldom will there be staff positions, since everyone will be occupied directly with producing and selling the product, at least in getting started. The communication flow always leads to the top, which is occupied by the owner. There is no passing the buck. Everything goes through her and there is much less information compressing than in the large organization. In other words, the top position in the small business will be involved with all decisions regardless of their importance, whether it's a refinancing decision or if there is a need for more toilet paper in the restroom.

By assigning a position to each employee, it allows for the use of job descriptions. By writing out and reviewing each employee's job and the duties assigned,

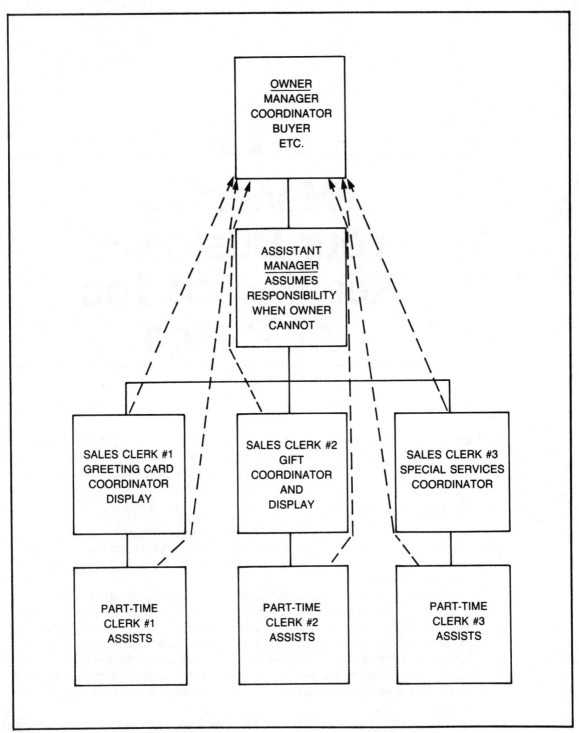

Figure 16-1. Small business organization chart.

everyone should know exactly what he or she is responsible for. By doing this it is possible for the organization to have a performance evaluation system tailored to its needs. The entrepreneur runs a complete management system of delegation, job description, and periodic evaluations to use as a control tool on performance.

The most difficult part of setting up this system is that just as the entrepreneur's duties overlap into so many areas, so do the employee's duties. Since there is not the capital available to hire specialists, employees will wear many different hats. This must be recognized in the implementation of job descriptions and performance evaluations.

The best management philosophy to use for motivating employees is management by objectives. This requires that, whenever possible, a quantitative objective be set in each area of performance to monitor results. By setting goals, whether they be to sell x units, or produce x units for shipment by a specific date, the employer and the employee will have a reference point by which to evaluate performance. The owner should set realistic goals, after discussing objectives with the employee, to ensure fairness and goal completion.

The small businessperson often has trouble delegating authority. This is particularly true after the business starts to mature and its growth demands more employee participation. In the beginning the owner does make all the decisions. However, with growth and development, this is not always possible. Since the entrepreneur has been used to handling all aspects of the organization, it may be difficult for him to trust other people with a direct responsibility. Often the business will grow to the point where it will become impractical and inefficient for the owner to make all the decisions and he will be forced to delegate. It is possible to delegate without losing control.

Design the organization so that it is comfortable to you and fits the needs of the customer. The reason you decided to start a business was your desire to do things your way. The organization structure should complement the way you like to manage. If you are one who does not care for committee meetings, design the communication flow so that everything arrives on your desk in whole. If, on the other hand, you believe that more heads are better than one, design your organization to take advantage of group study and decision. Management textbooks often center around three recognized organization theories: classical, human relations, and systems.

Organizational theories

Classical refers to the old school. All communications flow directly to the top through a very regimented chain of command. Strict policies, rules, and regulations control the behavior of the members of the organization. Employees are primarily considered to be motivated by money and will increase performance commensurate with the amount of pay. It is a no-nonsense philosophy that has been employed for years by many large organizations such as the military. Its biggest downfall is that it tends to build a bureaucracy within middle management.

In the past few decades there has been a trend toward the human relations theory. Management bends over backward to appease employees, believing that a good working environment equals improved performance. Many programs are implemented with the intent of gaining employee involvement and participation. The organizational structure is a far less formal chain of command, which allows more freedom to assume additional responsibilities.

The systems theory has evolved from contemporary theorists and is based on the efficient handling of information. With the advent of the computer age, businesses are able to handle much more information. Believing that the more information gathered, the less risk involved, the emphasis is to design the best organization structure to process information. Depending on the technological status of the industry, information gathering may be the key to success. Therefore, design the organization to gather information efficiently, translate the information effectively, and get the information quickly into the hands of the decision makers. The organization relies heavily on a team approach of gathering and dispersing information.

The successful entrepreneur designs his organization to incorporate the parts of each theory that best fit his organization. He recognizes the importance of strong policies and firm control; however, at the same time the entrepreneur knows that a small business must be participatory and alert to the needs of its employees. As the head of the enterprise, it will not take long to find out the importance of proper gathering and disseminating of information. Therefore, your organization must have an information-collection system built into it. You represent the leadership and how successfully the organization responds to market demands and conditions will be a reflection on your management style.

Five functions of management

The five functions of management—planning, organizing, controlling, staffing, and directing—are all present in the small business, but may take a slightly different form.

Planning requires looking ahead and being optimistic. Pessimism cannot survive in the small business world. The good manager finds some time in each working day to think about the future. Plans should be in mind for tomorrow, next week, next year, and five years from now. Some of this will happen automatically. All business activity of ordering inventory, creating advertising programs, and making financial requests must be made well in advance of the date needed. The retailer orders a large percentage of Christmas merchandise in March in order for the wholesaler to inform the manufacturer how much to plan for production. Advertising copy must be created in advance if it is to reserve the necessary space. The bank will need time to consider financial requests before approving. All of these functions require planning.

Organizing the work responsibilities in the small business is difficult due to the overlapping of many responsibilities among a small group of workers. Assign the primary responsibility of a task to one individual with backup support from other members of the staff. This will designate one person as ultimately responsible, while at the same time sharing the work.

Your own personal organization abilities will be tested as well. Since the entrepreneur is a generalist, handling many duties, a sound organizational plan is required. Because no one is looking over your shoulder with a stick, it takes self-discipline to accomplish the less enjoyable tasks.

The controlling function of a small business is handled on a very personal basis. There are usually no formal reports sent to the home office for review. You are the home office, and since it is a small business you can stay on top of things on a daily basis. Sales quotas may be checked on a daily basis by one-on-one visits with staff members or by phone calls to salespeople. This is another advantage the small business has over the larger ones. By knowing what is happening on a daily basis, corrective measures can be taken quickly to improve performance. It is not necessary to wait for a committee review to instill a new directive.

Employee evaluations are also handled on a more personal basis. There may not be the necessity of a formal evaluation form that is the same for everyone. Many effective evaluations have been conducted over a cup of coffee, lunch, or at the local tavern. The object of a performance evaluation is an honest analysis of performance and a review of future goals, designed to motivate the employee. As a small businessperson you have hired and know personally all the employees; therefore, you are in an excellent position to evaluate and motivate. Needs cause motivation, and since you know the needs, you should be able to motivate. The key ingredient is not the type of system utilized, but in the ability of the owner to be honest and tactful in his approach. Build on the employee's strengths, do not concentrate on their weaknesses.

The objective of proper staffing is to offset weaknesses with strengths. The baseball team with a future Hall-of-Fame center fielder does not trade for another center fielder, it tries to acquire players in positions that it is weak in. Start with yourself. If you are a technical person you may need to hire someone with marketing expertise to offset your weakness in that area. When it is necessary to hire someone, take inventory of the strengths of your organization and its weaknesses.

Directing requires that the entrepreneur practice the art of managing and its functions on a daily basis. Letting down in a particular area will cause a snowball effect of problems getting away from you in all areas.

Marketing management

The administrative and financial management functions of a business require attention to detail and discipline, the marketing management function requires creativity and insight. Marketing management is complex and demands flair. Doing it differently and with excitement pays dividends.

Many believe the key to successful marketing management is outspending the competition. This is not true; the key is outthinking the competition. First, understand where your product stands in regard to your competition and plan your strategy accordingly. Figure 16-2 shows the product life cycle and the suggested marketing strategies to be utilized at the various stages.

In addition to knowing the product position on the life cycle, it is important to understand your objectives in gaining market share. Businesses that handle multiple product lines strive to put together a proper product balance. Not all products

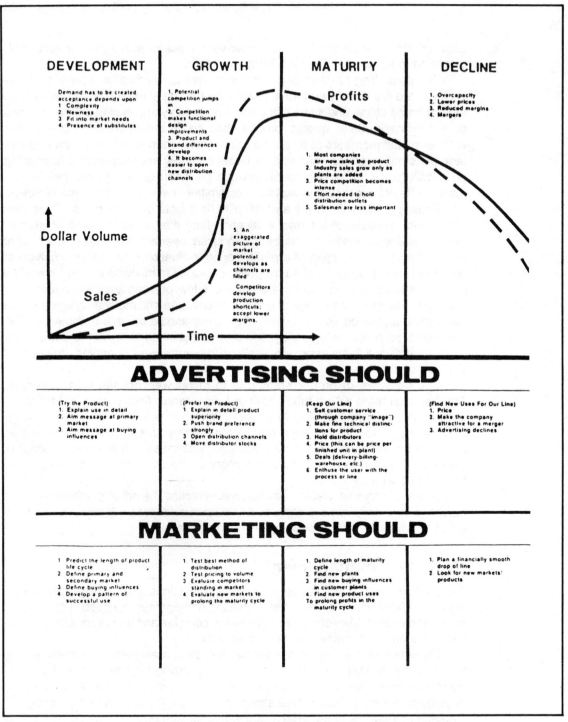

Figure 16-2. Product life cycle with suggested advertising and marketing strategies.

will perform at the same rate at the same time. Due to seasonal fluctuations, stage of life cycle, and market changes, some product groups will carry the others at various times. There will be some products that will generate more cash than is needed to maintain their growth rate and market share. The extra cash from these can be used to feed other products that are growing fast but need additional marketing help to gain market share. Other products that are faring poorly will have to be eliminated or used for traffic-generating purposes, such as loss leaders in sales promotions. Proper marketing management will recognize the life-cycle and market-share status of its various products and integrate them in order to secure maximum profits using limited cash and managerial resources.

Often objectives become confused. Andy, a department store manager, was looking forward to a visit from his district manager. He was coming off the highest sales volume quarter in the store's history and was looking forward to receiving his due recognition. Quite the opposite happened. Andy almost lost his job when the district manager pointed out that although sales were recordbreaking, the store's profit figure was the worst ever due to the misuse of marketing expenditures.

Increasing sales is not the sole objective. By overspending marketing resources and increasing inventory levels, anyone can increase sales. Sales gains must be achieved through the proper use of the marketing mix without ever losing sight of the bottom line—the net profit.

Marketing management must properly define what markets should be served, what form the product should take to appeal to its market, and what the product should do for the user. It must be able to anticipate changes in the market and respond to them.

When you enter a new market, you will cause a disruption in the marketplace. Competition will react to your entry. Be prepared for attempts to sidetrack your ambitions. Your competition has one big advantage—experience. They will use it against you. It may come in the form of lower prices or a change in marketing strategy. It may not come immediately, but sooner or later, the competition will raise its head. One warning, do not decide your future based on the success or failure of your initial opening. Many businesses take time to grow while implementing their marketing strategies. Other businesses will start off with a bang, only to face a letdown after the competition reacts or the customer curiosity subsides.

New restaurants always cause quite a stir because everyone wants to try them. After a few weeks many of the new customers will return to the restaurants where they have traditionally dined. Customer habits are difficult to change and it takes time. Proper marketing management should take a long-term outlook of the environment.

Keep your priorities straight and you will keep your sanity. You are an entrepreneur because you are a risk-taker. Risk takers lose sometimes. It will not always run according to plan. There will be pressures and disappointments. Since there are long hours, expect some burnout times. Remember you also had problems in your previous position. Maybe they were different, but they were just as real. Owning a business is not utopia. Design some escape mechanisms for your personal use. One major objective of becoming self-employed was to control your own destiny. Too often, when entrepreneurs get so caught up in their work, they forget their original goals. Don't forget hobbies, family, friends, and leisure time. If you are a golfer, play golf—an angler should fish—these are important escape valves. Play that weekly game, even if it means going back to work afterwards to catch up. As an entrepreneur, you can only blame yourself if you lose your freedom to the organization.

By keeping your morale high, you will keep the morale up of the people who work for you. It all starts at the top. A relaxed and confident leader transfers the feeling down the line. Your good morale will help motivate. Any sudden change in behavior in a member of a group will affect the entire group. This is particularly true of the leader. Moody leadership will be detrimental. Do what is necessary to make sure the leadership remains confident, optimistic, relaxed, and involved.

The entrepreneur spirit project—step 16

- Draw an organization chart for your venture, showing communication flow and responsibilities.
- Write out the job descriptions for all positions.
- Decide the best manner to conduct performance evaluations.
- Make a list of possible strategies your competition might use to combat your market entry and how you might deal with them.

17

Bookkeeping: It Is Not as Bad as You Think

The accounting procedures of a small business are really not as difficult as the new entrepreneur usually envisions. Although sometimes rather tedious, it is quite simple to handle the everyday bookkeeping procedures required. The entrepreneur needs patience, but not the training of a CPA, to handle the books.

There are times to use an accountant, but accountants cost money and should be used for the more sophisticated problems and not for routine matters the owner can do. Starting from the beginning, let's discuss the forms and procedures the small business will ordinarily encounter.

Forms and procedures

In order to collect revenues, the business operation must register with the state to collect the necessary sales tax. This is a simple form, accompanied by a small one-time fee that is sent to the state department of revenue. In return, the business will receive a state registration certificate with an identification number, along with forms to include with sales tax collections. It will be necessary to complete a sales tax collection form each month and send it with a check to the state department of revenue.

The new business will need to register with the city and county in which it resides in order to receive an occupancy license. A small fee is involved with this, and it must be renewed each year. This registration also enables the county to include you on property tax roles. This is an annual tax and requires a form listing your assets to be filed each year.

The business will also need to apply for a federal tax identification number in order to comply with tax regulations involving FICA and federal income tax withholding procedures. Check with an accountant to make sure the business has complied with all the proper registration requirements. The complexity of the organization structure (sole proprietorship, partnership, or corporation) will be a factor in determining the amount of paperwork required.

The daily bookkeeping procedures of operating a business become pretty routine once the business is established. The basic tools used are the sales journal, the disbursement journal, and the master ledger. Keeping track of sales is normally a two-step process.

Keep a daily workbook if the business takes in revenues on a daily basis; this reconciles each day's activities to make sure all monies are accounted for. It lists reported sales, offset by any activity which affects that day's revenues. It is a very useful reference tool if completed in some detail. Not only will it reconcile the monies, but it can also be used to keep track of any unusual occurrences, such as bad weather or an unusual sale, that would cause a fluctuation in business activity. By keeping this record the businessperson has a storybook to refer to the following year to explain business activity for that particular day. Figure 17-1 is a sample daily worksheet from a retail business that records sales revenues from a cash register readout at the end of each day.

This information is condensed and recorded in the monthly sales journal. The monthly sales journal is used to report sales for tax purposes and financial statements. Figure 17-2 shows the posting in the sales journal.

The disbursement journal, as shown in Fig. 17-3 is the same as your personal check register, just more complete. Each check written is recorded as to the date, the amount, and the type of expenditure. The information recorded is taken from the checkbook stub. The accurate posting of this journal will save much effort and time when income tax reporting time comes around. By totalling all of the columns, it will give an accurate summary of all disbursement activity for each month.

All of this is daily activity and must be kept up on a daily basis. It is quite simple and can be completed by anyone who can read and write. The important thing is to keep up with it. Failure to do so will cause the frustration of accumulated work and not permit proper posting to the master ledger.

The master ledger is where the information comes together to show the overall condition of the business. It contains two sections, like a balance sheet—assets, as shown in Fig. 17-4, and liabilities, as shown in Fig. 17-5. Any information posted to the sales journal and the disbursement journal that affects the overall financial condition of the business is posted to the master ledger. The monthly difference between revenues and disbursements is posted to the cash account. Any purchases for equipment are posted to the capital asset sheet. A note reduction is taken out of the notes payable sheet, etc. The final result is an up-to-date picture of the business in book form.

```
DAILY CASH RECONCILIATION

May 12, Monday (rainy and overcast)

Gross sales    $1407.60

Register readings    #1 687.90
                     #2 325.30
                     #3 394.40


Cash         $897.00
Coin            4.67
Checks        345.90
Visa           67.80
Master ch      54.85
             ------
Total        1370.30

overrings    12.60
refunds      17.40
paid outs     6.50( postage)
             ------
Total        1406.80

Shortage       .80

Number of transactions   235
```

Figure 17-1. Daily sales record.

By keeping the master ledger, the sales journal, and the disbursement journal up to date, it is relatively simple to create informal financial statements.

Financial statements

An income statement is the record of revenues, minus the cost of goods sold, minus all operating expenses, equaling the net profit before taxes. These figures are taken from the monthly journals and master ledger and are arranged as shown in Fig. 17-6.

There is a difference between purchases and cost of goods. Purchases shows only what was paid for, not what was received. To receive a cost of goods figure, consult the following calculation.

FACSIMILE PAGE
ILLUSTRATING THE USE OF THIS
IDEAL SYSTEM FORM.

SALES AND CASH RECEIPTS

DISTRIBUTION OF SALES
IDEAL SYSTEM FORM 21
(REPLACES FORMS 41, 131, 141)

THE IDEAL SYSTEM, REG. U.S. PAT. OFFICE. MADE IN U.S.A.

	1	2	3	4	5	6	7	8	9	10	11	12	
DATE 19__	MEMORANDA	CASH SALES	CREDIT SALES	MERCHANDISE RETURNED OR ALLOWANCES	TOTAL SALES (1+2÷3)	CASH RECEIVED TO APPLY ON CREDIT SALES	OTHER CASH RECEIVED	TOTAL CASH RECEIVED (1+5+6)	Dept A	Dept B	Dept C		
1 Mar 1	Days Business	12200	1400		13700	1000		13300	8050	3850	1800		1
2	"	16120			16120	1650		17770	10350	3620	2150		2
3	"	11850			11850	925		12775	5480	4170	2210		3
4	"	13400	825	625	13600			13400	7620	3980	1800		4
5	"	11850	1600		14450			14450	7440	2700	2310		5
6	"	16060			16060	1650		18710	9110	4350	2600		6
7	"	12850			12850			12850	8050	3820	980		7
8	"	14200	2000	1000	15200	1250		15450	8010	4150	3040		8
9	"	13430			13420	810		14230	7520	3750	2150		9
10	"	11900	250		12150			11900	6110	3980	2060		10
11 12	Deposit Ideal Hdw Co. Days Cash Sales 1820 0				182.00		2500 2500	1820 0 11450		6750		WHEN MERCHANDISE THAT WAS PREVIOUSLY BEEN ENTERED IN THIS SECTION IS RETURNED TO YOU FOR CREDIT — ENTER AND CIRCLE THE AMOUNT (OR ENTER IN RED) — AND DEDUCT THE AMOUNT IN THE COLUMNS CONCERNED.	11 12
13	Cash Sales: R.Q. Smith	2100	2100		2100				8.00	2110			13
14	" Lou Works		8000		8000			8.00					14
15	Rec'd on acct R.A. Smith					1000		1000					15
16	Financial El Morgan			320	320						(320)		16
17	15-Days Cash Sales 1480 0	1480 0			148.00			14800	4400	3240	2150		17
18	Cash Sales: J. Brown	1650	1650		1650				1650				18
19	" Tom Jones	1810	1810		1810			1810					19
20	Rec'd on acct R. Riley					920	920	920					20
21 22 23	YOU MAY EITHER SUMMARIZE THE ENTIRE DAYS SALES AND CASH RECEIPTS ON ONE LINE EACH DAY - IN WHICH CASE YOUR ENTIRE MONTHS ENTRIES WILL BE ON ONE PAGE - OR YOU MAY USE AS MANY LINES DAILY AND AS MANY PAGES MONTHLY AS ARE NEEDED TO ITEMIZE EACH TRANSACTION EACH DAY.										COLUMNS WITH BLANK HEADINGS MAY BE USED TO KEEP TRACK OF ANY PARTICULAR CLASS OF SALES YOU WISH. FOR EXAMPLE: REPAIR DEPT.: APPLIANCE SALES; RETAIL SALES; WHOLESALE; LABOR; MATERIAL SALES; ETC; ETC.	21 22 23
24 Mar 25	Days Business	13000	2100		15100			13000	9490	5610			24
25	"	12026	1650		13676	2450		14476	10526	3150			25
26	"	14290			14290			14290	8070	6220			26
27	"	16574	810	600	16784			16574	9644	7140			27
28	"	14350			14350	900		15250	9750	1625	2975		28
29	"	12940	925		13865			12940	8365	2075	3425		29
30 31 32	TRANSFER ALL OF THE MONTHLY TOTALS TO FORM S-21 SUMMARY (LAST PAGE OF THIS SECTION). THIS GIVES YOU A MONTH BY MONTH COMPARISON OF YOUR SALES — IN EACH DEPARTMENT OF YOUR BUSINESS - SHOWING YOU EXACTLY HOW YOUR BUSINESS IS PROGRESSING.									THE MONTHLY TOTAL OF COLUMN 4 (TOTAL SALES) IS TO BE ENTERED ON LINE 1 UNDER THE PROPER MONTH ON THE SUMMARY FORM S-21 AND STATEMENT OF INCOME FORMS			30 31 32
33 TOTALS		251130	25130	25130	254502137 15	13515	2600	267 85 16445	779 56	298 20			33

Figure 17-2. Sales journal posting.

FACSIMILE PAGE
ILLUSTRATING THE USE OF THIS IDEAL SYSTEM FORM 23.

PAYMENTS — ALL CASH AND CHECKS PAID OUT

IDEAL SYSTEM . FORM 23

THE IDEAL SYSTEM, REG. U. S. PAT. OFFICE MADE IN U. S. A.

YOU MAY USE AS MANY LINES DAILY AND AS MANY PAGES MONTHLY AS ARE NEEDED TO ENTER ALL PAYMENTS

ACCOUNTS FOR ALL CHECKS AND FOR ALL CASH PAID OUT

USE TWO LINES WHEN NECESSARY.

ENTER THE DETAILS OF EACH EMPLOYEES EARNINGS AND DEDUCTIONS ON THE EMPLOYEES INDIVIDUAL COMPENSATION RECORD (FORM G-812) IN THE BACK OF THIS BOOK. THUS SIMPLIFYING THE PREPARATION OF YOUR VARIOUS PAYROLL TAX RETURNS.

AT THE END OF EACH MONTH — ENTER THE ENTIRE MONTHS TOTALS OF EACH COLUMN ON THE LAST LINE — AND ALSO ENTER UNDER THE PROPER MONTH ON FORMS 5-23 · 18 · 28 AT THE PAGES IN THIS SECTION) AND ON FORMS 1Y R B · C. SUMMARY OF BUSINESS AND STATEMENT OF INCOME.

Figure 17-3. Disbursement journal.

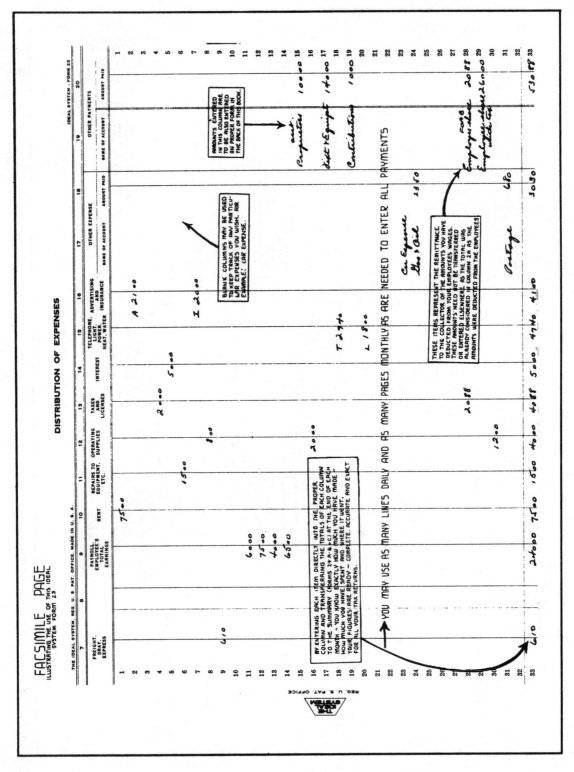

Figure 17-3. (Continued)

FURNITURE & FIXTURES. MACHINERY & EQUIPMENT. AND BUILDINGS

THE IDEAL SYSTEM, REG. U.S. PAT. OFFICE. MADE IN U.S.A.

IDEAL SYSTEM - FORM 9
(REPLACES FORM 18)

DATE 19	NO.	FROM WHOM BOUGHT	DESCRIPTION	COST OF FURNITURE & FIXTURES	PAYMENTS ON FURNITURE & FIXTURES	COST OF MACHINERY & EQUIPMENT	PAYMENTS ON MACHINERY & EQUIPMENT	COST OF BUILDINGS & IMPROVEMENTS	PAYMENTS ON BUILDINGS & IMPROVEMENTS	
JAN 15		ABC Supply	Lighted Jewelry Case	600 -	600 -					1
FEB 10		Norton's Office Supply	Used NCR Cash Register			475 -	475 -			2
FEB 15		Captain's Carpet	600 sq ft - Carpet					380 -	380 -	3
										4
										5
										6

BANK ACCOUNT   CASH RECORD

THE IDEAL SYSTEM, REG. U.S. PAT. OFFICE. MADE IN U.S.A.

IDEAL SYSTEM - FORM 0

DATE 19	NO.	MEMORANDA	DEPOSITS	CHECKS	BALANCE	CASH ON HAND	CASH RECEIVED	CASH PAID OUT	CASH DEPOSITED	BALANCE CASH ON HAND	
JAN		1st National Bank	6480 30	5970 50	1425 64						1
FEB		"	7963 14	8227 60	1161 ?						2
											3
											4
											5
											6
											7
											8
											9
											10
											11
											12
											13
											14
											15
											16
											17
											18
											19
											20
											21

THE IDEAL SYSTEM, REG. U.S. PAT. OFFICE

Figure 17-4. Asset ledger sheets.

LOAN AND NOTE RECORD

THE IDEAL SYSTEM. REG. U.S. PAT OFFICE MADE IN U.S.A. — IDEAL SYSTEM - FORM 90

DATE 19	NO.	TO WHOSE ACCOUNT AND WHERE PAYABLE	(TIME DAYS OR MONTHS)	DATE DUE	AMOUNT OF LOAN	PAYMENTS MADE ON PRINCIPAL	BALANCE OF PRINCIPAL	RATE OF INTEREST	INTEREST PAID	INTEREST PAID TO
Jan 15	1	1st National Bank (955.90)	60 mos.	June 98	15657 -	767 -	14890 -	11.5	188 90	1|15
Feb 15	2	1st National Bank (955.90)	60 mos.	June 84	14890	779 -	14111 -	11.5	176 90	2|15

ACCOUNTS PAYABLE

NAME Russell Stover Candies
ADDRESS 110 Baltimore   Kansas City, Mo. 64141

THE IDEAL SYSTEM, REG. U.S. PAT OFFICE MADE IN U.S.A.

DATE 19	NO.	MEMO	CHARGES	CREDITS	BALANCE
1 15	1	Inv # 64571	210 50		210 50
2 1	ct#2u0	Inv # 62571		210 50	

ACCOUNTS PAYABLE

NAME Fenton Glass Co.
ADDRESS Williamstown, W. Va. 52930
PAGE NO. _____

IDEAL SYSTEM - FORM 904

ACCOUNTS RECEIVABLE

DATE 19	NO.	MEMO	CHARGES	CREDITS	BALANCE
12 15		Inv #16-401	456 71	3 50	453 21
1 10	ct#170	Inv # 16-401		453 21	

Figure 17-5. Liability ledger sheets.

```
                    INCOME STATEMENT
           FOR THE YEAR ENDING DECEMBER 31, 19XX


SALES                               ACTUAL $      % of SALES
  Greeting cards                    $160,000        80.0%
  Gifts                              40,000         20.0
     Total Sales                    200,000        100.0
COST OF GOODS SOLD
  Cost of Sales                     100,000         50.0
  Freight                             4,000          2.0
  Discounts on merchandise          (1,000)         (1.0)
  Markdowns, empl. disc.             5,000          2.5
  Shrinkage                          6,000          3.0
     Total cost of goods sold       114,000         57.0

GROSS PROFIT                         86,000         43.0
OPERATING EXPENSES
  Payroll                            31,000         15.5
  Rent                               20,000         10.0
  Maintenance & Repairs              1,600          0.8
  Operating supplies                 4,200          2.1
  Taxes & Licenses                   2,000          1.0
  Utilities                          3,800          1.9
  Advertising                        3,000          1.5
  Insurance                          2,400          1.2
  Accounting & Legal                 2,000          1.0
  Miscellaneous                      3,000          1.5
    Total Cash Operating Expenses   73,000         36.5
  Depreciation                       5,000          2.5
  Interest                           6,000          3.0
Total Operating Expenses            84,000         42.0

PRE-TAX PROFIT                      $2,000          1.0%
```

Figure 17-6. Income statement.

Beginning inventory	$ 50,000
plus purchases	+140,000
minus ending inventory	−55,000
Cost of goods sold	$135,000

This is the true picture of your purchasing activity and is posted in the master ledger. By posting strictly purchases, you are showing cash flow as opposed to profit.

The balance sheet is a summary statement of the general ledger. Its purpose is to show the true capital value of the venture. By accurately posting to the general ledger, the owner can put together an informal balance sheet as shown in Fig. 17-7.

Following these procedures will provide sufficient information to allow the business owner to make financial decisions. They will also allow the entrepreneur to provide the bank with necessary updated information. It is possible to design the bookkeeping system yourself by purchasing the journal books and sheets at the local office supply store. There are also prepared bookkeeping systems for sale that can be tailored for your business. The best plan of action is to consult with an accountant on the most preferred system for your business, and then maintain it yourself.

```
                    BALANCE SHEET
                  DECEMBER 31, 19XX

                       ASSETS
CURRENT ASSETS
   Cash                                  $28,000
   Inventory                              47,500
   Other Current Assets                    1,000
      Total Current Assets                76,500

FIXED ASSETS                              30,000

TOTAL ASSETS                             106,500

        LIABILITIES AND OWNER'S EQUITY

CURRENT LIABILITIES

Accounts Payable                          27,000
Current Portion - long-term debt          10,000
      Total Current Liabilities           37,000

LONG-TERM DEBT                            40,000

TOTAL LIABILITIES                         77,000

OWNER'S EQUITY                            29,500

TOTAL LIABILITIES & OWNER'S EQUITY      $106,500
```

Figure 17-7. Balance sheet.

Of course you can hand the whole thing over to an accountant and he will do everything for you. However, he will charge you by the hour for work that you can do yourself. Also, if someone else does the work for you, you will not know the true financial status of the business on a daily basis.

Do as much as possible yourself and use an accountant for advice, and if necessary, at income tax time. There is also much help available now through the use of personal computers, which will be discussed in Chapter 19.

Tax forms

The accountant can also get you initiated to the many and various tax forms with numbers such as 941, 940, W-2, etc. Many of these forms you will become accustomed to, and will become very routine. A few of the more common forms are:

Sales tax reports—monthly. This is a simple report (Fig. 17-8) taken from the monthly sales journal.

Form 941—federal withholding and FICA report—quarterly. Information compiled from employee payroll sheets will be reported as in Fig. 17-9.

Depending on the amount of payroll, you may be required to make monthly deposits to a bank which handles federal deposits. These deposits are automatically deposited to your federal record.

Form 940—federal unemployment compensation-quarterly or annually, depending on size of payroll. This is the business's contribution to our welfare system. You will also contribute to the state's unemployment system as well. Although initially it is quite small, usually under 1 percent of payroll, it may rise if there are unemployment claims made against your firm.

When you are forced to lay off or fire someone, they have the right to collect unemployment. The payments that they receive are partially charged against your contributions, and your contribution rate will increase. It is very difficult to prevent an ex-employee from collecting unemployment unless the reason for termination is of a criminal nature. It is an example of the small business paying more than its share into our tax system.

There are a number of additional annual, quarterly, and monthly reports (property taxes, excise taxes, intangible taxes) that you may or may not have to comply with depending on the nature of your business.

The experience and expertise of the entrepreneur and the complexity of the business will determine how much income tax assistance is needed. Properly kept records will save time and money in tax preparation. Before attempting to complete the tax forms, it is essential to have a firm understanding of tax regulations, as well as tax loopholes. If the entrepreneur is not equipped with the necessary background, the use of a CPA at tax time will save money and headaches.

ST-3-ND (REV. 4/91)
DEALERS AND CONTRACTORS

SALES & USE TAX DIVISION
STATE OF GEORGIA
DEPT. OF REVENUE
P.O. BOX 105296
ATLANTA, GEORGIA 30348

IMPORTANT

This return must be filed and paid by the 20th of the month following the period for which the tax is due to avoid loss of vendor's compensation and the payment of penalty and interest. DEALERS AND CONTRACTORS MUST FILE TIMELY RETURN EVEN THOUGH NO TAX IS DUE.

DO NOT SEND CASH BY MAIL

SEE INSTRUCTION SHEET FOR PREPARING THIS REPORT. LOCAL TAX - BULLETIN UPDATE, SPECIAL COUNTY TAX UPDATE AND SALES TAX INFORMATION.

IF THERE IS ANY CHANGE IN TRADE NAME, ADDRESS OR OWNERSHIP, SO INDICATE IN SPACE PROVIDED BELOW AND CHECK BOX

SALES AND USE TAX REPORT
GEORGIA SALES AND USE TAX
MARTA/ SPECIAL, LOCAL OPTION
AND MOTOR FUEL

BULK RATE
U.S. POSTAGE
PAID
Atlanta, Ga.
Permit No. 144

SALES AND USE TAX FOR CALENDAR MONTH OR OTHER AUTHORIZED PERIOD OF _____ 19 ____

ATTACH REMITTANCE HERE

		COL. A 4% STATE	COL. B 1% MARTA (FULTON DEKALB) SPL / 2nd L/O	COL. C 1% LOCAL OPTION	COL. D 3% MOTOR FUEL
1.	SALES (Gross sales and/or rental proceeds) This amount should include all sales, retail and wholesale, with exempt sales indicated in proper area......				
2.	USE (See Instructions)				
3.	TOTAL SALES AND USE (Lines 1 & 2)				
4.	EXEMPT SALES (Must be itemized in Schedule below)				
5.	NET TAXABLE SALES (Lines 3 minus 4)				
6.	TAX DUE (4% Col. A & 3% Col. D)(1% Col. B & C)				
6a.	1% Sales and Use Tax due on sales of Motor Fuel from worksheet below See Instructions				
7.	EXCESS TAX (See Instructions)				
8.	GROSS TAX (Total of Line 6, 6a, & 7)				
9.	VENDOR'S COMPENSATION (A discount and deductable only on timely returns 3% of State, MARTA/Special, Local & Motor Fuel Tax)				
10.	SPECIFIC PENALTY (Applicable if paid after the 20th of the month following the period of the return. See Instructions)				
11.	INTEREST (1% per month or fraction thereof from date delinquent until paid. See Instructions)............				
12.	AMOUNT DUE (See Instructions)............				
13.	CREDIT MEMO				
14.	Estimated Tax paid last month—Amount from line 15 of previous month's return............				
15.	Estimated Tax due for current month (See instructions)				
16.	PAY THIS AMOUNT (See instructions) MAKE CHECK PAYABLE TO GEORGIA SALES AND USE TAX DIVISION.				

SCHEDULE OF EXEMPT SALES CLAIMED LINE 4 ABOVE (SEE INSTRUCTIONS BEFORE COMPLETING)		A STATE	B MARTA (FULTON DEKALB) SPL / 2nd L/O	C LOCAL OPTION	D MOTOR FUEL
Sales for resale and/or further processing	A				
Sales to State of Ga., counties & municipalities thereof or Federal Government (See Instructions since certain sales of motor fuels to State of Ga., counties and municipalities thereof, must not be entered in Column A or D)	B				
Sales in bona fide interstate commerce	C				
Sales exempt from MARTA/Special Tax, and/or Local Option Tax............	D				
Purchased, rented, furnished, fabricated or imported property on which tax was paid to supplier(s) or lessor(s) (See Instructions)	E				
Gasoline sold at retail for any purpose and/or other motor fuels for on-the-highway use only. (See Instructions)	F				
State Excise Tax on Motor Fuels (Effective 4/1/88 Federal Retailers Excise Tax is no longer exempt)(See Instructions)	G				
Other deductions authorized by law (specify)	H				
	I				
TOTAL OF ALLOWABLE EXEMPT SALES (LINES A THRU I) TOTAL(S) TO RESPECTIVE COLUMN ON LINE 4 OF REPORT ABOVE............					

SALES AND USE TAX ON MOTOR FUEL WORKSHEET (STMFW)

1. Sales of Motor Fuel (from Line 5, Column D)..
2. Exempt sales to State of Georgia, Counties, Cities and Municipalities thereof ....
3. Subtotal..
4. Add back 7½¢ per gallon only on sales to State of Georgia, counties, cities, and municipalities ....
5. Net taxable Motor Fuel Sales ....
6. Tax due (1% of Line 5, enter here and on Line 6a column A) ....

FOR ANY CHANGE OF TRADE NAME, ADDRESS, OWNERSHIP, OR TELEPHONE NUMBER, CHECK PROPER BOX(es) AND FURNISH APPLICABLE INFORMATION BELOW: (A change in location from one county to another requires new application except for contractor.)

( ) New business location: _____ ( ) New mailing address: _____

( ) New trade name: _____ ( ) Date business discontinued: _____

( ) Name and mailing address of owner(s): _____

( ) Telephone No.: _____

I certify that this return, including the accompanying schedules or statements, has been examined by me and is to the best of my knowledge and belief a true and complete return, made in good faith, for the period stated.

This ____ day of _____ , 19___ (Signature) _____

Return prepared by _____

(State whether individual, member of firm, or give title if officer of corporation)

WHEN WRITING THIS DIVISION ALWAYS STATE YOUR CERTIFICATE OF REGISTRATION. (SALES TAX NUMBER)

Figure 17-8. State sales tax form.

Form **941**
(Rev. January 1991)
Department of the Treasury
Internal Revenue Service

4141

Employer's Quarterly Federal Tax Return

▶ See Circular E for more information concerning employment tax returns.

Please type or print.

Your name, address, employer identification number, and calendar quarter of return. (If not correct, please change.)

Name (as distinguished from trade name)   Date quarter ended

Trade name, if any   Employer identification number

Address and ZIP code

OMB No. 1545-0029
Expires: 5-31-93

T
FF
FD
FP
I
T

If address is different from prior return, check here ▶ ☐

IRS Use

1 1 1 1 1 1 1 1 1 1   2   3 3 3 3 3   4 4 4

5 5 5   6   7   8 8 8 8 8   9 9 9   10 10 10 10 10 10 10 10 10 10

If you do not have to file returns in the future, check here . . . ▶ ☐   Date final wages paid . . . ▶

If you are a seasonal employer, see **Seasonal employers** on page 2 and check here . . ▶ ☐

1a Number of employees (except household) employed in the pay period that includes March 12th . ▶	**1a**	
b If you are a subsidiary corporation AND your parent corporation files a consolidated Form 1120, enter parent corporation employer identification number (EIN) . . ▶ **1b** −		
2 Total wages and tips subject to withholding, plus other compensation . . . . ▶	**2**	
3 Total income tax withheld from wages, tips, pensions, annuities, sick pay, gambling, etc. . . ▶	**3**	
4 Adjustment of withheld income tax for preceding quarters of calendar year (see instructions) . ▶	**4**	
5 Adjusted total of income tax withheld (line 3 as adjusted by line 4—see instructions) . . . ▶	**5**	
6a Taxable social security wages **(Complete** $ × 12.4% (.124) =	**6a**	
b Taxable social security tips **line 7)** $ × 12.4% (.124) =	**6b**	
7 Taxable Medicare wages and tips . . . . . $ × 2.9% (.029) =	**7**	
8 Total social security and Medicare taxes (add lines 6a, 6b, and 7)	**8**	
9 Adjustment of social security and Medicare taxes (see instructions for required explanation) . .	**9**	
10 Adjusted total of social security and Medicare taxes (line 8 as adjusted by line 9—see instructions) ▶	**10**	
11 Backup withholding (see instructions) . . . . ▶	**11**	
12 Adjustment of backup withholding tax for preceding quarters of calendar year. . . . . . ▶	**12**	
13 Adjusted total of backup withholding (line 11 as adjusted by line 12)	**13**	
14 **Total taxes** (add lines 5, 10, and 13)	**14**	
15 Advance earned income credit (EIC) payments made to employees, if any . . . . . . ▶	**15**	
16 Net taxes (subtract line 15 from line 14). **This should equal line IV below** (plus line IV of Schedule A (Form 941) if you have treated backup withholding as a separate liability)	**16**	
17 **Total deposits for quarter,** including overpayment applied from a prior quarter, from your records. ▶	**17**	
18 **Balance due** (subtract line 17 from line 16). This should be less than $500. Pay to IRS. . . . ▶	**18**	

19 **Overpayment,** if line 17 is more than line 16, enter here ▶ $ _____ and check if to be:

☐ Applied to next return   **OR**   ☐ Refunded.

Record of Federal Tax Liability (You must complete if line 16 is $500 or more and Schedule B is not attached.) See instructions before checking these boxes.

Check only if you made deposits using the 95% rule ▶ ☐   Check only if you are a first time 3-banking-day depositor. . . ▶ ☐

Show tax liability here, **not deposits.** IRS gets deposit data from FTD coupons.

Date wages paid	First month of quarter		Second month of quarter		Third month of quarter	
1st through 3rd	A		I		Q	
4th through 7th	B		J		R	
8th through 11th	C		K		S	
12th through 15th	D		L		T	
16th through 19th	E		M		U	
20th through 22nd	F		N		V	
23rd through 25th	G		O		W	
26th through the last	H		P		X	
Total liability for month	I		II		III	

Do NOT Show Federal Tax Deposits Here

▶ **IV** Total for quarter (add lines **I, II,** and **III**). **This should equal line 16 above** . . . . ▶

Sign Here

Under penalties of perjury, I declare that I have examined this return, including accompanying schedules and statements, and to the best of my knowledge and belief, it is true, correct, and complete.

Signature ▶   Print Your Name and Title ▶   Date ▶

For Paperwork Reduction Act Notice, see page 2.

Figure 17-9. Form 941 tax return for reporting payroll withholding.

The entrepreneur spirit project—step 17

- Meet with an accountant to receive assistance in setting up the bookkeeping system for the business.
- List all registrations, forms, and procedures to be filled out before opening the business.
- Budget an affordable amount for the use of an accountant.
- Visit the office supply store to become familiar with the availability of supplies to assist you with bookkeeping.

18

Taxes:
The Never-Ending
Headache

As they say, two things are certain, death and taxes. There is no way around income taxes, so you might as well do the smart thing and learn about them. Let's look first at the reporting differences between the proprietorship, partnership, and corporation.

Proprietorship income taxes

As we discussed in Chapter 7, one of the advantages of the proprietorship is its simplicity of form and control. This becomes very apparent when it comes time to do your income tax. Income tax reporting for a proprietorship is simply declaring the profits or losses made in the course of business activity on a Schedule C (Fig. 18-1) and posting that amount to the front of your personal 1040 tax return.

For most small business owners filling out the Schedule C is simply a matter of totaling up their monthly sales journal sheets, totaling the monthly columns from the disbursement journal, and taking a physical inventory. By doing this you will be able to calculate the gross receipts, the cost of goods, and the deductions to subtract out from the gross income.

A couple of explanations might help. Cost of goods is not just the amount of goods or materials purchased. It must account for any change of inventory to be accurate. On the back of the Schedule C there is a formula that states ending inventory plus sales minus purchases minus beginning inventory equals cost of goods. Using this formula raises the cost of goods when inventory has increased

Profit or Loss From Business
(Sole Proprietorship)
Partnerships, Joint Ventures, Etc., Must File Form 1065.

▶ **Attach to Form 1040 or Form 1041.**   ▶ **See Instructions for Schedule C (Form 1040).**

OMB No. 1545-0074

19 90

Attachment
Sequence No. **09**

Name of proprietor	Social security number (SSN)

A Principal business or profession, including product or service (see Instructions)

B Enter principal business code
(from page 2) ▶

C Business name and address ▶ ....
(include suite or room no.)

D Employer ID number (Not SSN)

E Accounting method: **(1)** ☐ Cash   **(2)** ☐ Accrual   **(3)** ☐ Other (specify) ▶ ....

F Method(s) used to
value closing inventory: **(1)** ☐ Cost   **(2)** ☐ Lower of cost or market   **(3)** ☐ Other (attach explanation)   **(4)** ☐ Does not apply (if checked, go to line H)

	Yes	No
G Was there any change in determining quantities, costs, or valuations between opening and closing inventory? (If "Yes," attach explanation.)		
H Are you deducting expenses for business use of your home? (If "Yes," see Instructions for limitations.)		
I Did you "materially participate" in the operation of this business during 1990? (If "No," see Instructions for limitations on losses.)		

J If this is the first Schedule C filed for this business, check here . . . . ▶ ☐

Part I Income

1 Gross receipts or sales. **Caution:** If this income was reported to you on Form W-2 and the "Statutory employee" box on that form was checked, see the Instructions and check here . . . . ▶ ☐	**1**	
2 Returns and allowances	**2**	
3 Subtract line 2 from line 1. Enter the result here	**3**	
4 Cost of goods sold (from line 38 on page 2)	**4**	
5 Subtract line 4 from line 3 and enter the **gross profit** here	**5**	
6 Other income, including Federal and state gasoline or fuel tax credit or refund (see Instructions)	**6**	
7 Add lines 5 and 6. This is your **gross income** . . . . ▶	**7**	

Part II Expenses

8 Advertising	**8**		**21** Repairs and maintenance . . .	**21**	
9 Bad debts from sales or services (see Instructions)	**9**		**22** Supplies (not included in Part III) .	**22**	
			23 Taxes and licenses	**23**	
10 Car and truck expenses (attach **Form 4562**) .	**10**		**24** Travel, meals, and entertainment:		
11 Commissions and fees	**11**		**a** Travel	**24a**	
12 Depletion	**12**		**b** Meals and entertainment .		
13 Depreciation and section 179 expense deduction (not included in Part III) (see Instructions). . .	**13**		**c** Enter 20% of line 24b subject to limitations (see Instructions) . .		
14 Employee benefit programs (other than on line 19)	**14**		**d** Subtract line 24c from line 24b .	**24d**	
15 Insurance (other than health) . .	**15**		**25** Utilities	**25**	
16 Interest:			**26** Wages (less jobs credit)	**26**	
a Mortgage (paid to banks, etc.).	**16a**		**27a** Other expenses (**list type and amount**):		
b Other	**16b**		....		
17 Legal and professional services .	**17**		....		
18 Office expense.	**18**		....		
19 Pension and profit-sharing plans .	**19**		....		
20 Rent or lease (see Instructions):			....		
a Vehicles, machinery, and equip. .	**20a**				
b Other business property. . .	**20b**		**27b** Total other expenses . . .	**27b**	

28 Add amounts in columns for lines 8 through 27b. These are your **total expenses** . . . . ▶	**28**	
29 Net profit or (loss). Subtract line 28 from line 7. If a profit, enter here and on Form 1040, line 12. Also enter the net profit on Schedule SE, line 2 (statutory employees, see Instructions). If a loss, you MUST go on to line 30 (fiduciaries, see Instructions)	**29**	

30 If you have a loss, you MUST check the box that describes your investment in this activity (see Instructions). . .

If you checked 30a, enter the loss on Form 1040, line 12, and Schedule SE, line 2 (statutory employees, see Instructions). If you checked 30b, you MUST attach **Form 6198.**

30a ☐ All investment is at risk.
30b ☐ Some investment is not at risk.

For Paperwork Reduction Act Notice, see Form 1040 Instructions.

Schedule C (Form 1040) 1990

Figure 18-1. Form 1040 tax return for reporting profit or loss of a sole proprietorship.

to account for the added assets, and lowers the cost of goods if the inventory has decreased to account for lost assets.

Depreciation is calculated to show the wear and use of equipment, furniture, fixtures, and leasehold improvements. The government allows this as a reserve expense in order to replace the fixed assets of a business. In other words, if the business owner invests $50,000 in fixed assets to operate a business, he or she is allowed to deduct from profits a percentage of this cost each year. The owner has the option of deciding over what period of time the property can be depreciated. If in the case of the $50,000 investment it was decided to write the use of the equipment off over five years, the owner could deduct $10,000 for depreciation expense. Often a new business owner is relieved to find that a sizable depreciation expense can be deducted from net profit. You should check with an accountant to determine the best depreciation schedule to follow for your type of business.

It is important to understand that interest paid on a business loan is a fully deductible expense. Loan principal reduction is not deductible and will not show on the Schedule C.

When completed, the net profit is posted as business gain (loss) on the individual's 1040 and Schedule C is attached as support. Net profit is not the same as what you have paid yourself. In a proprietorship or partnership, money taken out as compensation for the owner is not salary, it is strictly considered a draw against the assets of the business. It is quite possible, particularly for a new business, that although you paid yourself $24,000 during the year, the net profit was only $20,000. The minus or plus of net profit to owner's draw might show up as part of depreciation or travel allowances.

Partnership income taxes

As a partnership you will be required to file a form 1065 (Fig. 18-2). Page 1, as shown, looks similar to the Schedule C in reporting revenues and expenses. However, you are also required to attach supporting schedules which show the partnership's balance sheet, division of profits, and a reconciliation of partner's capital accounts. Each partner must declare their percentage of profit or loss on their respective 1040 form, and the 1065 is sent separately. Since it involves more than one party, the government wants to keep up on who is receiving what share of profits or property disposition. The reconciliation is often complex and might require the use of an accountant.

Corporation income taxes

There is a different form to use depending on whether the business is a Subchapter S corporation or a regular corporation.

The S corporation uses form 1120S (Fig. 18-3), which requires the normal revenue, expense, and net profit calculation and a balance sheet for the corporation. The balance sheet is more complex than the partnership because there must be a declaration of capital stock and undistributed retained earnings. Subchapter

Form **1065**

Department of the Treasury
Internal Revenue Service

U.S. Partnership Return of Income

For calendar year 1990, or tax year beginning _____, 1990, and ending _____, 19 ___ .

▶ **See separate instructions.**

1990

A Principal business activity	**Use IRS label. Otherwise, please print or type.**
B Principal product or service	
C Business code number	

Name

Number, street, and room or suite no. (If a P.O. box, see page 9 of the instructions.)

City or town, state, and ZIP code

D Employer identification number

E Date business started

F Total assets (see Specific Instructions)
$

G Check applicable boxes: **(1)** ☐ Initial return **(2)** ☐ Final return
(3) ☐ Change in address **(4)** ☐ Amended return

H Check accounting method: **(1)** ☐ Cash **(2)** ☐ Accrual
(3) ☐ Other (specify) ▶ _____

I Number of partners in this partnership ▶ _____

	Yes	No
J Is this partnership a limited partnership?		
K Are any partners in this partnership also partnerships? . .		
L Is this partnership a partner in another partnership? . .		
M Is this partnership subject to the consolidated audit procedures of sections 6221 through 6233? If "Yes," see "Designation of Tax Matters Partner" on page 2		
N Does this partnership meet **all** the requirements shown in the instructions for **Question N**?		
O Does this partnership have any foreign partners? . . .		
P Is this partnership a publicly traded partnership as defined in section 469(k)(2)?		

	Yes	No
Q Has this partnership filed, or is it required to file, Form 8264, Application for Registration of a Tax Shelter? . . .		
R Was there a distribution of property or a transfer (for example, by sale or death) of a partnership interest during the tax year? If "Yes," see the instructions concerning an election to adjust the basis of the partnership's assets under section 754		
S At any time during the tax year, did the partnership have an interest in or a signature or other authority over a financial account in a foreign country (such as a bank account, securities account, or other financial account)? (See the instructions for exceptions and filing requirements for form TD F 90-22.1.) If "Yes," enter the name of the foreign country. ▶ _____		
T Was the partnership the grantor of, or transferor to, a foreign trust which existed during the current tax year, whether or not the partnership or any partner has any beneficial interest in it? If "Yes," you may have to file Forms 3520, 3520-A, or 926		

Caution: *Include **only** trade or business income and expenses on lines 1a through 21 below. See the instructions for more information.*

Income

1a Gross receipts or sales	1a		
b Less returns and allowances	1b		1c
2 Cost of goods sold (Schedule A, line 7)			2
3 Gross profit—Subtract line 2 from line 1c			3
4 Ordinary income (loss) from other partnerships and fiduciaries *(attach schedule)* . . .			4
5 Net farm profit (loss) *(attach Schedule F (Form 1040))*			5
6 Net gain (loss) from Form 4797, Part II, line 18			6
7 Other income (loss) (see instructions) *(attach schedule)*			7
8 **Total** income (loss)—Combine lines 3 through 7			8

Deductions (see instructions for limitations)

9a Salaries and wages (other than to partners)	9a		
b Less jobs credit	9b		9c
10 Guaranteed payments to partners			10
11 Rent			11
12 Interest			12
13 Taxes			13
14 Bad debts			14
15 Repairs			15
16a Depreciation (see instructions)	16a		
b Less depreciation reported on Schedule A and elsewhere on return	16b		16c
17 Depletion **(Do not deduct oil and gas depletion.)**			17
18a Retirement plans, etc.			18a
b Employee benefit programs			18b
19 Other deductions *(attach schedule)*			19
20 **Total** deductions—Add lines 9c through 19			20
21 Ordinary income (loss) from trade or business activities—Subtract line 20 from line 8			21

Please Sign Here

Under penalties of perjury, I declare that I have examined this return, including accompanying schedules and statements, and to the best of my knowledge and belief, it is true, correct, and complete. Declaration of preparer (other than general partner) is based on all information of which preparer has any knowledge.

▶ _____
Signature of general partner

_____
Date

Paid Preparer's Use Only

Preparer's signature ▶	Date	Check if self-employed ▶ ☐
Firm's name (or yours if self-employed) and address ▶		E.I. No. ▶
		ZIP code ▶

Preparer's social security no.

For Paperwork Reduction Act Notice, see page 1 of separate instructions.

Form **1065** (1990)

Figure 18-2. Form 1065 (page 1) tax return for reporting revenues and expenses for a partnership.

Form **1120S**

Department of the Treasury
Internal Revenue Service

U.S. Income Tax Return for an S Corporation

For calendar year 1990, or tax year beginning _____, 1990, and ending _____, 19___

▶ **See separate instructions.**

1990

A Date of election as an S corporation

B Business code no. (see Specific Instructions)

Use IRS label. Otherwise, please print or type.

Name

Number, street, and room or suite no. (If a P.O. box, see page 7 of the instructions.)

City or town, state, and ZIP code

C Employer Identification number

D Date incorporated

E Total assets (see Specific Instructions)

$

F Check applicable boxes: (1) ☐ Initial return (2) ☐ Final return (3) ☐ Change in address (4) ☐ Amended return

G Check this box if this is an S corporation subject to the consolidated audit procedures of sections 6241 through 6245 (see instructions before checking this box) . . ▶ ☐

H Enter number of shareholders in the corporation at end of the tax year . . . . ▶

Caution: Include **only** trade or business income and expenses on lines 1a through 21. See the instructions for more information.

Income

1a Gross receipts or sales |_____| **b** Less returns and allowances|_____| **c** Bal ▶		**1c**	
2 Cost of goods sold (Schedule A, line 7)		**2**	
3 Gross profit (subtract line 2 from line 1c)		**3**	
4 Net gain (loss) from Form 4797, Part II, line 18		**4**	
5 Other income (see instructions) *(attach schedule)*		**5**	
6 **Total** income (loss)—Combine lines 3 through 5 . . . . ▶		**6**	

Deductions (See instructions for limitations.)

7 Compensation of officers		**7**	
8a Salaries and wages |_____| **b** Less jobs credit |_____| **c** Bal ▶		**8c**	
9 Repairs		**9**	
10 Bad debts		**10**	
11 Rents		**11**	
12 Taxes		**12**	
13 Interest		**13**	
14a Depreciation (see instructions) **14a**			
b Depreciation reported on Schedule A and elsewhere on return . . **14b**			
c Subtract line 14b from line 14a		**14c**	
15 Depletion (**Do not deduct oil and gas depletion. See instructions.**) . .		**15**	
16 Advertising		**16**	
17 Pension, profit-sharing, etc., plans		**17**	
18 Employee benefit programs		**18**	
19 Other deductions *(attach schedule)*		**19**	
20 **Total** deductions—Add lines 7 through 19 . . . . ▶		**20**	
21 Ordinary income (loss) from trade or business activities—Subtract line 20 from line 6 . . .		**21**	

Tax and Payments

22 Tax:			
a Excess net passive income tax *(attach schedule)* **22a**			
b Tax from Schedule D (Form 1120S) **22b**			
c Add lines 22a and 22b (see instructions for additional taxes)		**22c**	
23 Payments:			
a 1990 estimated tax payments **23a**			
b Tax deposited with Form 7004 . . . . **23b**			
c Credit for Federal tax on fuels *(attach Form 4136)* **23c**			
d Add lines 23a through 23c		**23d**	
24 Enter any **penalty** for underpayment of estimated tax—Check ▶ ☐ if Form 2220 is attached .		**24**	
25 **Tax due**—If the total of lines 22c and 24 is larger than line 23d, enter amount owed. See instructions for depositary method of payment		**25**	
26 **Overpayment**—If line 23d is larger than the total of lines 22c and 24, enter amount overpaid ▶		**26**	
27 Enter amount of line 26 you want: **Credited to 1991 estimated tax** ▶ |_____| **Refunded** ▶		**27**	

Please Sign Here

Under penalties of perjury, I declare that I have examined this return, including accompanying schedules and statements, and to the best of my knowledge and belief, it is true, correct, and complete. Declaration of preparer (other than taxpayer) is based on all information of which preparer has any knowledge.

▶ _____
Signature of officer

Date _____

▶ _____
Title

Paid Preparer's Use Only

Preparer's signature ▶	Date	Check if self-employed ▶ ☐	Preparer's social security number
Firm's name (or yours if self-employed) and address ▶		E.I. No. ▶	
		ZIP code ▶	

For Paperwork Reduction Act Notice, see page 1 of separate instructions.

Form **1120S** (1990)

Figure 18-3. Form 1120S tax return for reporting revenues and expenses of an S corporation.

S corporations are required to claim all profits or losses in the calendar year in which they occur. Since you are a corporation, the money you are paid is declared as salary, not a draw against assets; therefore the corporation must issue you a W-2 statement to include with your 1040. Money left in the corporation as a result of profits will be taxed to the corporation.

A regular corporation will file form 1120. In addition to the net profit calculation, schedules must be attached for the balance sheet, dividend deductions, compensation for officers, tax computation, and reconciliation of income with books, with income stated on the return. Filing taxes for a corporation normally takes the training of an accountant due to the degree of complexity.

Where to go for help

If this all sounds very confusing, don't despair; there is help available. Using an accountant when necessary is appropriate; however, it will help if you have an understanding of what the accountant does. Many small business owners save a lot of money by taking training that helps reduce their dependency on accountants.

The best place to go for assistance is the Internal Revenue Service. They have a training program available to small business advisers called STEP, The Small Business Taxpayers Education Program. The goal is to equip advisers, often associated with small business development centers in local communities, to conduct workshops on preparing small business tax returns. Check with your local assistance center to learn where and when the program will be available in your area.

The STEP program comprises eight 2-hour modules of instruction covering the following small business tax topics:

1. *Business assets: depreciation and selling depreciated property.* Discusses depreciation and amortization methods and reporting, equipment record keeping, and sale of business property.

2. *Business use of the home.* Discusses what qualifies as business use in the home, how to calculate business use percentage, and deduction limitations.

3. *Employment taxes.* Discusses how to get an employer identification number, how to use federal income tax reporting tables, filing quarterly employment tax reports, and filling out employee W-2 forms.

4. *Excise taxes.* Discusses who must pay federal excise taxes and how they are to be reported.

5. *Starting a business—record keeping.* Reviews decisions about formation of sole proprietorships, partnerships, and corporations, how to make basic financial statements, accounting, and record keeping methods.

6. *Schedule C and SE, and form 1040.* Gives instruction as to completing a Schedule C for proprietorship, how to calculate and report self-employment (social security) tax, and how to enter on the individual's 1040 tax return.

Form 1120

Department of the Treasury
Internal Revenue Service

U.S. Corporation Income Tax Return

For calendar year 1990 or tax year beginning _____, 1990, ending _____, 19 ____

▶ Instructions are separate. See page 1 for Paperwork Reduction Act Notice.

OMB No. 1545-0123

1990

Check if a—

A Consolidated return ☐
B Personal holding co. ☐
C Personal service corp.(as defined in Temp. Regs. sec. 1.441-4T—see Instructions) ☐

Use IRS label. Other-wise, please print or type.

Name

Number, street, and room or suite no. (If a P.O. box, see page 2 of Instructions.)

City or town, state, and ZIP code

D Employer identification number

E Date incorporated

F Total assets (see Specific Instructions)

$

G Check applicable boxes: (1) ☐ Initial return (2) ☐ Final return (3) ☐ Change in address

Income

1a	Gross receipts or sales	**b** Less returns and allowances	**c** Bal ▶	1c	
2	Cost of goods sold (Schedule A, line 7).	2	
3	Gross profit (line 1c less line 2)	3	
4	Dividends (Schedule C, line 19)	4	
5	Interest	5	
6	Gross rents	6	
7	Gross royalties	7	
8	Capital gain net income (attach Schedule D (Form 1120))	8	
9	Net gain or (loss) from Form 4797, Part II, line 18 (attach Form 4797)	9	
10	Other income (see Instructions—attach schedule)	10	
11	**Total income**—Add lines 3 through 10 ▶	11	

Deductions (See Instructions for limitations on deductions.)

12	Compensation of officers (Schedule E, line 4)	12	
13a	Salaries and wages	**b** Less jobs credit	**c** Balance ▶	13c	
14	Repairs	14	
15	Bad debts	15	
16	Rents	16	
17	Taxes	17	
18	Interest	18	
19	Contributions (**see Instructions for 10% limitation**)	19	
20	Depreciation (attach Form 4562)	20	
21	Less depreciation claimed on Schedule A and elsewhere on return	21a	21b	
22	Depletion	22	
23	Advertising	23	
24	Pension, profit-sharing, etc., plans	24	
25	Employee benefit programs	25	
26	Other deductions (attach schedule)	26	
27	**Total deductions**—Add lines 12 through 26. ▶	27	
28	Taxable income before net operating loss deduction and special deductions (line 11 less line 27)	28	
29	**Less: a** Net operating loss deduction (see Instructions)	29a	
	b Special deductions (Schedule C, line 20)	29b	29c	

Tax and Payments

30	**Taxable income**—Line 28 less line 29c	30	
31	**Total tax** (Schedule J, line 10)	31	
32	Payments: **a** 1989 overpayment credited to 1990	32a	
	b 1990 estimated tax payments	32b	
	c Less 1990 refund applied for on Form 4466	32c ( )	**d** Bal ▶	32d	
	e Tax deposited with Form 7004	32e	
	f Credit from regulated investment companies (attach Form 2439)	32f	
	g Credit for Federal tax on fuels (attach Form 4136). See Instructions	32g	32h	
33	Enter any **penalty** for underpayment of estimated tax—Check ▶ ☐ if Form 2220 is attached	33	
34	**Tax due**—If the total of lines 31 and 33 is larger than line 32h, enter amount owed	34	
35	**Overpayment**—If line 32h is larger than the total of lines 31 and 33, enter amount overpaid	35	
36	Enter amount of line 35 you want: **Credited to 1991 estimated tax ▶**	Refunded ▶	36	

Please Sign Here

Under penalties of perjury, I declare that I have examined this return, including accompanying schedules and statements, and to the best of my knowledge and belief, it is true, correct, and complete. Declaration of preparer (other than taxpayer) is based on all information of which preparer has any knowledge.

▶ Signature of officer   Date   ▶ Title

Paid Preparer's Use Only

Preparer's signature ▶	Date	Check if self-employed ☐	Preparer's social security number
Firm's name (or yours if self-employed) and address ▶		E.I. No. ▶	
		ZIP code ▶	

Figure 18-4. Form 1120 tax return for reporting revenues and expenses of a regular corporation.

7. *Self-employed retirement plans.* Discusses what and who qualifies for a self-employment retirement plan, the merits of a Keogh plan, simplified employee pensions (SEPs), IRAs, and how these plans are reported.

8. *The small business as a partnership.* Reviews reporting procedures for a partnership, how to form a partnership, and the different types of partnership formations.

9. *Tip reporting and allocation rules.* Discusses tax laws related to paying employees who receive compensation through tips, minimum wage for tip recipients, and how tips are to be reported.

Workshop participants are provided workbooks and are led through the learning exercises with case studies and other hands-on learning exercises.

In addition, the IRS offers toll-free telephone tax assistance at 1-800-424-1040.

When is an employee an independent contractor?

There has been a lot of confusion over the issue of when a worker qualifies as an independent contractor versus an employee. It is a very important consideration for many small employers because if a person is classified as an independent contractor, as opposed to an employee, the employer does not have to deduct withholding taxes or pay the employer contribution toward social security. It also alleviates paying worker's compensation. If your workers fit the description of an independent contractor, it will save you money. To be an independent contractor, a worker:

Should not have to follow instructions about where, when, and how the work is to be done.

Should not have to receive training from the employer in order to do a job in a particular manner.

Cannot have paid employees of the business acting as assistants.

Should not be required to devote his or her full-time occupational endeavor to one particular business.

Should not be required to submit regular reports to the business.

Should be paid for the job, or a commission, and not on a regular hourly, weekly, or monthly schedule.

Should be subject for dismissal only for nonperformance of contract specifications.

Should furnish his or her own tools.

Should not be reimbursed for business expenses except as provided by a performance contract.

In deciding if you are able to classify a worker as an independent contractor, discuss the particulars with a qualified accountant or IRS adviser to see if the worker meets these and other criteria set forth by the IRS.

The entrepreneur spirit project—step 18

- Inquire of the closest IRS office the availability of tax assistance training in your area.
- Attend appropriate workshops.
- Discuss income tax regulations with an accountant.

19

Computers in Small Business: The Brains Behind the Organization?

It wasn't too long ago that the small businessperson was delighted that she could purchase an electronic pocket calculator for $125; now she can purchase that same tool for $7.95. The pocket calculator was followed closely by the electronic cash register, available initially to retailers for approximately $3500. A comparable electronic cash register now sells for under $1000.

Then came the small computers. The small businessperson relished the thought of owning one, but at a price of over $5000 it could not be justified. Now with the continued decline in cost for computers, it could prove very justifiable. It may not be a necessity item for the initial opening of the business, but, once established, the small business should seriously consider making the investment in consideration of the number of time saving functions it can handle.

What the computer can do

The computer can be a tremendous help with bookkeeping and inventory management. The proper system will save you time and money, whether it is in the form of accounting and bookkeeping costs, or in the better use of your own time. It will not manage for you, but it will enable you to manage better. Here are a few examples of areas that will be better served through the use of a computer.

Payroll.   Payroll procedures are the most time-consuming of the bookkeeping procedures you will encounter; computing salaries, computing deductions or additions (federal withholding taxes and FICA payments, overtime, bonuses, etc.), entering the information on each individual's payroll sheet, and writing the checks and payroll vouchers. In addition, there are quarterly 941s, 940s, monthly federal deposits, annual W-2s, W-3s, and a number of other minor reports and forms to fill out. Once installed, the computer can handle all of these functions in a fraction of the time required to do it manually. Figure 19-1 is an example of a computerized payroll summary. Depending on the size of the operation, the computer can even write the checks. If the business carries more than five employees, a payroll program can be of benefit to the owner.

Sales reports and financial statements.   It is not difficult to keep your own financial records by posting information from the general ledger to an income statement and a running balance sheet. It is made easier, more complete,

Pay period ending 01-10-XX

	Hours	Base Salary	Comm'n	Makeup	Total Salary		Bonus	Total Pay	FICA	W/H	Store Charge	Insur	Total Deduc	Net
	Kitchen Hours	Kitchen Salary	Waitrs Hours	Waitrs Salary	Total Salary	Tips	Bonus	Total Pay	FICA	W/H	Store Charge	Insur	Total Deduc	Net
Women's	152.75	639.63	0.00	0.00	639.63	0.00	0.00	639.63	45.09	49.13	63.00	0.00	157.22	482.41
Restaurant	230.50	833.83	69.50	145.10	978.93	87.73	0.00	1066.66	75.20	73.47	20.00	16.43	185.10	793.83
Cards & Gifts	185.25	711.12	0.00	0.00	711.12	0.00	0.00	711.12	50.13	41.78	0.00	0.00	91.91	619.21
Management	0.00	0.00	0.00	0.00	923.07	0.00	0.00	923.07	65.08	133.96	0.00	0.00	199.04	724.03
Clerical	44.25	199.13	0.00	0.00	199.13	0.00	0.00	199.13	14.04	18.23	0.00	0.00	32.27	166.86
Totals	612.75	2383.71	69.50	145.10	3451.88	87.73	0.00	3539.61	249.54	316.57	83.00	16.43	665.54	2786.34

Figure 19-1. Computerized payroll summary sheet.

and more accurate with the use of a computer. Having such information as the percentage of each expense item to total revenue, year-to-date totals, etc., stored in a computer can quickly produce a neat, nicely organized presentation. When the bank requests a review of your financial information, it is as easy as pushing a button.

Accounts payable and accounts receivable. If you need to know when a bill is due or the last time a supplier was paid, ask the computer for a printout of all accounts payable activity. Information that normally requires a manual recording on separate records for each supplier can easily be entered into the computer whenever the payment obligation is received. An accounts receivable program will immediately tell you the status of everyone who owes you. This printout will show you how much and how old the debt is.

Inventory management. Most businesses will operate on a minimum/maximum reorder system for most of their basic products. When the inventory level of a specific item falls to a predetermined minimum inventory level, it is time to reorder. The maximum level is the quantity amount that you do not want to exceed for a given item. By entering into the computer the number of units received of an item and then continuously posting the number sold, the computer will be able to tell the buyer when it is time to reorder an item, or when an item becomes too excessive. Using such a system the owner is able to make a regular review of all inventory on hand and on order.

These are examples of basic functions the computer can perform. How elaborate will be determined by the size and type of system installed and the needs of the business. Many businesses will do away with the manual aspects of a disbursement journal by entering checkbook activity directly into the computer. By using a code to indicate type of payment, the computer will automatically post that information to the proper expense account. It can replace the sales journal and general ledger just as easily. The computer can store and sort all financial activity of the business and make it available to the owner, whenever needed. The only precaution needed is to make backup copies in the event of damaged diskettes or memory failure. It is also necessary to check for accuracy when entering information, since the computer is only capable of digesting the information given to it.

How much to spend and what to buy

Deciding on the type of computer hardware and software is difficult due to the tremendous selection available. If terminology such as floppy disk, database, and daisy wheel are not in your vocabulary, you will need a friend well versed in computer technology to assist you.

Popular software

More important than deciding on what type of computer to buy, is what computer software best fits your needs. The ideal way to buy a computer system is to find the software that is best tailored to your business and then buy the hardware that will run it. Many business programs are written to fit many types of general business applications, while others are written for particular types of business activity. For example, an auto parts retail store has many inventory items and would do well with programs that allow computerized counter sales and inventory control for purchases. Once you decide on the best software programs, the computer hardware decision becomes easier.

Word processing software can be used by small businesses to keep tab of all supplier correspondence, assist in making professional-looking announcements, and keep a written history of the activities of the business. The three most commonly used programs are Multimate, Wordstar, and WordPerfect. All three are quite adequate, although WordPerfect is probably the easiest to use and the most flexible.

If you plan on keeping customer lists or doing your own direct mailings, you will need a database program. The most comprehensive program is DBase III, but it requires a fair amount of training time to get up to speed. If you don't have the time (or inclination), several ready-to-go packages are available: Alpha, Q&A, or File Express. All three will allow you to create forms and/or letters and to merge documents with a mailing list.

There are numerous accounting software packages available. Many are quite extensive and will offer more application than you will actually need. It is a good idea to check with your accountant before you purchase, since software that is compatible with the accountant's software might save time, which will save you money.

Businesses that are involved with any type of financial analysis will need a financial spreadsheet program. You will need some training and practice with this type of program, but once mastered the program will perform wonders. The most common is Lotus 1-2-3. Excel is another that might be easier to learn, but is not as universally used.

Popular hardware

Any one of the well-known machines can handle basic business needs. One general rule with computers is that you pay for speed. An inexpensive computer can do the job just as well as a more expensive one, but with a sacrifice in speed. Speed may not impress you as a necessary need with machines that are already fast, but it can make a big difference. Don't forget to budget in a printer and the other accessories that you will need. (See Fig. 19-2 for a computer setup.) Buy the most computer that you can afford and you probably won't be sorry in the long run.

In your search for the right equipment, you may wish to consider some of the following units which are considered practical and capable for small business needs:

IBM and its clones and compatibles.   This would include NCR, Corona, Leading Edge, PC's Limited—to mention just a few. This would be the safest

Figure 19-2. Example of a typical computer setup.

group to be in, with the most application software available and the best potential for the future.

Apple family computers, including the Macintosh. Apple has made considerable penetration into the education market and has software available for business.

Tandy. Radio Shack has a full line of computers from inexpensive game computers to a line of IBM compatibles.

Commodore and Atari. Both have new computers which have the potential to be good business computers if the software comes along for them. Their older computers do have some business software and are quite economical, but are overshadowed by IBM and its compatible computers.

It is a very competitive market and you must take the time to shop around. Make sure that wherever you buy, that the company will back up the equipment with knowledge as well as guarantees.

Buying a system too advanced or one that cannot handle your needs is a waste of money. Often this purchase is better put off until the business is established and the entrepreneur is confident of the direction he wishes to pursue. With the decreased costs of computer ownership, it is normally more economical to buy than to lease. Leasing might be preferable if you are uncertain of your present and future needs.

The entrepreneur spirit project—step 19

- Make a thorough study of the computer market and how it can assist you. Involve a friend if this is not your interest.

- Budget this purchase for now, or for a future time, if it is decided there is a need.

- Investigate computer leasing if available.

20

Insurance

Just as the small businessperson views his customer as representing total value to the business over its lifetime, so does the insurance industry view its clients. The insurance company is betting at pretty good odds that the risk it is covering will not happen.

The insured person is putting up money against these long odds to make sure that he is covered in the event the long shot occurs. The odds are squarely in favor of the insurance company. The risk of not playing is too great for the business owner. Insurance, in its proper perspective, is a necessity to the small business.

Guidelines to follow

- Determine the true needs for protection, those that are legally required, and those that can be identified as common business risks. By law, if you have employees, you will have to carry worker's compensation insurance; this provides medical insurance for all employees while they are on the job. If an employee is injured while on the job, all medical costs will be covered by the employer's worker's compensation insurance.

The cost of the policy is determined by the type of work and is charged on a per hundred dollars of payroll basis. It may be as low as $.41 per hundred dollars of clerical payroll, or higher than $5 per hundred for more hazardous work. The rates are regulated by the state; therefore, all insurance companies charge the same.

The same company that insures your property will write your worker's compensation policy. It is billed using projected payroll and will be adjusted, upward or downward, depending on an annual payroll audit performed by the insurance company. You may also have a legal requirement to carry a specified amount of insurance, if requested in your lease agreement. The landlord will demand that you carry liability insurance in order that she would be held harmless in the event of an accident on the leased property.

Common business risks are those that can legitimately occur in the normal conduct of business. Fire would certainly be a risk common to all business establishments. However, inventory theft may not be a common risk for service-oriented businesses such as a small catering service. You must be familiar with the risks that are considered legitimate to your industry.

- Insurance coverage should only be acquired for those losses that the business cannot afford to pay for. Since the odds are against the occurrence happening, do not pay money to cover those incidents that even if they do happen you could afford to pay for. Paying a $20 annual premium for five years to insure the loss or damage to a $75 strip of outdoor carpeting by your front door is not good use of capital. Utilize that $100 in a manner to make additional profits for the business.

- There must be a reasonable correlation of the cost of insurance to the probability of loss. If the probability of sustaining the loss is exceptionally low, the premium for insuring it should be exceptionally low. If it isn't, don't insure it. You cannot afford to insure yourself against every possible incident that can occur. If you feel comfortable that something could not occur to your business, take the chance that it won't.

Insurance premiums are skyrocketing throughout the industry due to ludicrous claims, and it is becoming more practical for the businessperson to assume more risks. Do not be so insurance rich that you cannot afford to meet your other obligations.

- Investigate all possible ways of reducing your insurance premiums. There are some things that you can do to help control risks. All insurance premiums are calculated as to the likelihood of occurrence and the extent of loss that could be sustained. Ideas such as firewalls, sprinkler systems, and security alarm systems all reduce risks and decrease exposure to loss; therefore, insurance companies can reduce premiums.

Insurance companies use actuarial tables to assign risks. These tables are designed to calculate the risk difference by situation, such as the difference of loss risk in being one block away from a fire station or one mile away. Or the crime exposure risk of being located in one section of the city versus another. It is a gambler's game.

- Find an agent who knows the business. A good insurance agent will save a small business money by knowing the best way to write a policy. He will know the ins and outs of proper protection at reasonable costs. For instance, if the business operates out of two locations, the good agent will write a blanket policy to cover both, as opposed to writing separate policies for each. He may designate the owner as clerical work, if he is not directly involved with physical operations, thereby reducing the rate of worker's compensation coverage. Good insurance agents, like good accountants, will work to save their clients' money.

In order for a risk to be insurable it must meet certain requirements. It must have a tangible or monetary value, not sentimental. The insured must have little or no control over the risk. The risk must exist in large numbers and must be calculable in order that the insurance company has developed an actuarial table showing the probability of loss. Insurance companies offer protection in areas they are familiar with, and insure only clients who have an insurable interest in the property. They will not allow Sam to buy insurance to cover insurable risks at Joe's.

Types of insurance

The comprehensive insurance policy is called a multiperil policy. This policy will contain two parts, property and liability. The property coverage will explain all conditions and stipulations in effect in the event of physical damage to the business. The carrier will agree to indemnify (compensate) the insured to the agreed-upon limit of the policy. The limit of the policy will be for the replacement value of the damaged property. The dollar amount will have to be verified by the insured if requested.

The liability coverage will insure against three conditions: criminal behavior against the insured (not including customer and employee theft); legal responsibility by a contract, which harms the insured; and tort liability, which covers harm done due to negligence, which produces bodily or intangible injury.

Included within the property and liability coverage will be a multitude of additional coverage options the small businessperson may or may not decide to include. Some of these optional coverages are:

Vandalism or malicious mischief

Comprehensive crime (burglary, employee theft)

Sign damage

Loss of earnings

Sprinkler leakage

Glass

General liability (additional coverages)

Any of these coverages can be added with additional premiums. The insured should apply the five principles just discussed in deciding which is necessary. Get yourself a good insurance agent and study insurance options. Shop around for rates. You may want to consider co-insurance, in which you are insured only to a certain stipulated percentage of the loss, usually set at 80 percent.

Making a claim

It is quite possible that you may encounter a less-than-helpful hand when you have to make a claim. The most common practice of the insurance companies is to offer a quick settlement after an initial inspection of the damage. Their objective is to have the matter resolved quickly and have the insured sign the settlement agreement. However, hidden damages may appear later, and if the case is closed there will be no recourse.

In the event you have a claim, be patient and study the settlement. You have paid the premiums and you deserve complete compensation for any damages. No matter how good your agent is, remember that he is paid by the insurance company. It is the insured's responsibility to make sure she is adequately compensated.

A major claim may require the assistance of an attorney. This will slow down the procedure; it also tells the insurance company that you expect proper compensation. In the case of a liability claim against you, it is quite advisable to secure legal counsel, particularly in the current era of exaggerated claim compensation.

Another source of claim assistance available is the public insurance adjuster. The public insurance adjuster works for you, the insured. In states which require licensing, the adjuster is a professional insurance contract analyzer. He studies the insured's contract and then puts together the most complete package of information he can generate, to present to the insurance company.

His knowledge of the industry should assure the insured of receiving full compensation for damages. Normally, the public adjuster works for a percentage of the total reimbursement (usually 10 percent). Depending on the circumstances it may be well worth it. This is particularly true in an incident involving two insurance companies. Look at the plight of Tim.

"Oh my God, how could this happen?" was the first thing out of Tim's mouth when he witnessed the damage. The entire inside ceiling above the ladies' clothing and bridal department had collapsed under a deluge of water.

The roofing company that had been replacing the roof had evidently quit working the day before and had not covered up their work. The tremendous rain during the night had come through the exterior roof and had forced the entire acoustical tile ceiling to cave in. The result was devastating. Every piece of clothing, the wooden fixtures, and the carpet in the 2000-square-foot department was ruined. "What a mess," thought Tim. "What do I do now?"

The roofing contractor was already there and was ready to clean up. The man in charge told Tim that they would clean it up and their insurance agent was on his way. Tim acted quickly. "Hold everything, I think I'll need some pictures before anything is moved." He found his camera and started clicking away. Next, he placed a call to his insurance agent, Bill. "I am really sorry to hear of this happening to you Tim, but don't worry. I am sure the roofing company's insurance company will cover your loss. If you have any problems, give me a call, and if I can help I will."

Later in the day Tim talked to the insurance adjuster representing the roofing company. "My company will certainly cover your loss, Tim. What did you pay for this carpet and how old is it? We will depreciate it for its usage and write you a check for the net amount. As soon as you can get us the invoices together on all merchandise and fixtures destroyed we will get to work on a settlement for their value as well."

"Wait a minute," cried Tim. "The depreciated value and the cost to replace that carpet are two different things. I expect replacement at least, and what about the damage to the wallpaper, the lost business and the employees' wages while we are shut down?" "Tim, my company's policy will cover strictly the loss value of the damage. Anything else would have to come through your insurance company. Has your agent been by yet to see the damage?" "No, he hasn't," sighed an exasperated Tim. "I am getting the feeling I've got some problems."

Tim realized he was confronted with the problem of two insurance companies arguing over who pays what. He knew that he had a good policy, which included loss of earnings, and felt agitated that there was no one overly eager to help him. In discussing the problem with a friend, the suggestion was made to contact a public insurance adjuster. Although he was unfamiliar with how they operated, he called the one listed in the yellow pages and met with her the following morning.

After inspecting the damages, the adjuster was eager to help for a 10 percent commission of the total reimbursement. She would take over for Tim in collecting all information and presenting it to Tim's insurance company for the claim. She explained to Tim that she would go directly to Tim's insurance company, as they were the ones responsible to him. It was their problem to negotiate a settlement with the roofing company's insurance agency, not Tim's. She felt confident that she would be able to collect full replacement value, plus any loss of earnings and expenses incurred, due to the department being closed for at least three months for repairs and restocking.

Tim had roughly calculated that he would have a potential $40,000 total claim, but was afraid the insurance company representative he had spoken to from the roofing company was thinking more in terms of $20,000 on a depreciated value. That $20,000 difference could involve legal action, expenses, and time. The public insurance adjuster seemed preferable to a lawyer; therefore he signed the agreement. The public adjuster went immediately to work, taking pictures, meeting with the store's bookkeeper, securing estimates, and making contact with the insurance company. Tim was not involved, except to answer questions.

Six weeks later, a finished report of some fifty pages was ready to present to the insurance company. This report cited the past personal history of the business, past financial information, listed all damages with their replacement value, and projected all losses using graphic presentations to show the impact of the closed department on the overall business for as long as a year later. It was complete, elaborate, and successful. The final reimbursement was for $50,000. After paying the 10 percent commission, Tim ended up with $45,000, $5000 more than he had originally planned.

The final result was fair. Tim was fully compensated and avoided the pitfalls of the inexperienced in dealing with insurance companies. His decision to utilize an experienced, licensed, and ethical public insurance adjuster had proven to be a good one.

Security

One area the small businessperson does not usually receive insurance protection with is internal security. Unfortunately, the reports that are published showing the tremendous amount of employee pilferage are not exaggerated. It can be a staggering problem. Employee trust is a wonderful thing; however, it does have a limit. Any employees involved with the handling of monies or items of value should be routinely evaluated for honesty. Circumstances in personal lives change, which in some cases can make a trusted employee a questionable one.

The number one safeguard is in the hiring process. Do a thorough check on an applicant's background. Ask pertinent questions, check with previous employers, and call the police department to make sure there is no history of dishonesty. Many businesses, including small ones, are using lie detector tests. The fee for lie detector tests, although not exorbitant, can add up if used for each applicant. You may have to consider their use for certain positions. If there is any doubt whatsoever, do not hire that person.

Always keep an eye and an ear out for any strange behavior or comments. If the small businessperson has built an environment of trust and loyalty throughout his organization, the dishonesty of one employee will often be reported by another. Instill precautions, such as bag checks or locker checks for everyone at periodic, but random times. Any businessperson who has been victimized by employee theft knows the shock and dismay of discovering the truth. Once discovered, act decisively. You will be setting an example to all other employees by your actions. This is no time for sympathy or else you will be taken advantage of at a later date by a different employee. The guilty party must be removed from the organization, and, if possible, legal action taken.

The best course of action for all security matters is firmness. Whether it is employee theft or shoplifting, the owner's action speaks the loudest. Shoplifting, which continues to grow at an astounding rate throughout the retail industry, is best prevented by having a tough reputation. Arresting all shoplifters, regardless of age or circumstances, will give a retailer the reputation of a store that prosecutes. Once a teenager is apprehended and arrested at the store, the word flows quickly through colleagues and fellow students that the business where he or she was caught does not fool around. With no exceptions, arrest anyone over ten years old. The young child will not be severely punished by the law and will learn a valuable lesson for the remainder of his or her life.

Shoplifting legislation has been revamped in most states to be more favorable to the merchant. It is no longer necessary to wait until a suspect leaves the store carrying stolen merchandise to make an arrest. The merchant has the right to request inspection of parcels, bags, or clothing at any time without fear of legal proceedings. She may apprehend the suspect in the store and detain him until the law enforcement authorities arrive. Convictions are possible even without seizure of the stolen merchandise as illustrated by the following story.

During an unusually slow Sunday afternoon at the Clothes Tree, the salesclerk Alice noticed a suspicious-looking shopper browsing through the fine dress department. Alice's observations were interrupted by an inquiry from another customer, who happened to be a personal friend, in another area of the store. When she returned to her previous position she noticed the suspicious-looking customer had left and she continued on with her normal duties. She had no other customers the remainder of the day.

The next morning, Laura, the owner of the store, immediately noticed four dresses missing, valued at $800 retail. She immediately called in Alice for a report on the Sunday afternoon. Alice gave a full description of the suspicious shopper; she also recalled that the friend that she had waited on had mentioned she knew the name of the woman. Laura called Alice's friend to get the name and then called the police department to report the theft. The police went to the suspect's house and arrested the woman on suspicion of shoplifting.

The trial convened approximately one month later. Based on the testimony of Alice and her friend that the suspect was the only person in the store at the time the merchandise was stolen and by the prosecuting attorney introducing the suspect's previous criminal record of shoplifting, the jury returned a verdict of guilty even though the stolen merchandise was never found. She received a six-month prison sentence and was forced to reimburse the store $800 as a condition for her release.

This was a case of enough incriminating circumstantial evidence to find the defendant guilty. A conviction was made without an eyewitness to the actual theft. It serves as an example that our legal system is becoming more intent on protecting the rights of the small business.

There are many preventative methods available to use for shoplifting. Two-way mirrors, electronic checkout machines which will go off if a tag passes them, fake and real cameras, are ideas to consider. The retailer is better off spending time and effort trying to prevent shoplifting as opposed to trying to catch the thieves. Employees must be well versed in procedures to follow in preventing and apprehending shoplifters. There are always bound to be some losses, but the astute business will find ways to keep this problem to a minimum.

There also are the problems of bad checks, counterfeit money, counterfeit credit cards, and fast-change artists. Use your local police department for assistance. A good idea is for you and your employees to attend security seminars which are given by the police department in every community. These seminars will teach you how to recognize counterfeit monies, how to make sure the bearer of a check or credit card is legitimate, and the proper way of handling cash transactions. They will also give precautionary ideas on the best way of making cash deposits at the bank and other security measures to follow.

The entrepreneur spirit project—step 20

- Interview three insurance agents to learn about policies. Remember a good insurance agent will save you money.

- Put all suggested coverages to the guidelines mentioned in this chapter.

- Discuss your in-house security program with a law enforcement agency.

PART FOUR

Looking Toward the Future

21

Expansion: Expansionitis Can Be a Fun Disease

When you plan your venture, you should do it with long-term goals. If expansion is a goal of the future, start to plan immediately. Design a timetable of goals to achieve in chronological order. Pinpoint that time when expansion would be wise and work toward it. Your projected plan may change quite a bit; however, the goal should not.

When to expand

The most reliable barometer is the business's sales and profits report. At what point will it be necessary and advisable to increase the size of the business in order to continue increasing profits? There may come a time when profits and sales will decrease if an expansion move is not made. There is usually an ideal time to expand or enter a new market. Often referred to as the *strategic window,* it is that limited period of time when all key indicators are favorable to react to the market. The finances are available, the market demand is increasing, competition has been weakened, there has been a change in the marketplace—these are all key indicators. The business that you started at the introductory level of the life cycle has entered the rapid-growth period and is contemplating an expansion move before entering the maturity stage (Fig. 21-1).

Successful businesses will reach a period of substantial profits. They will need a large amount of cash to finance their rate of growth. To protect the market share, it is necessary to reinvest the earnings into product improvements, new

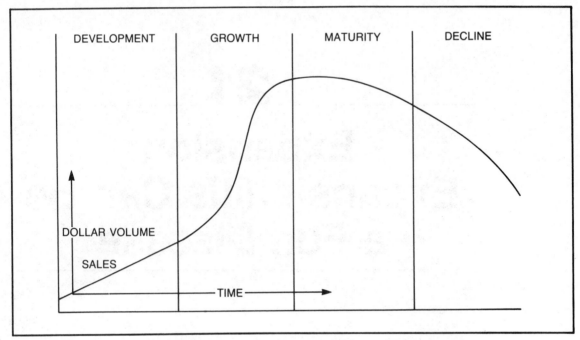

Figure 21-1. Business life cycle.

products, or more space. The eventual goal is to generate more profits than are required to maintain and increase market share.

The decision to expand requires answering many of the same questions confronted initially. Does the market have a high enough growth potential? What is competition doing? Is the value added to the business going to produce the necessary additional capital needed to pay back the owner over a reasonable period of time? Are there new markets to be served? Has anything happened to change the marketplace?

Expansion has to be founded on more than just a whim to grow. Expanding is too often thought of as a way to show success to friends and relatives. There is a tremendous temptation to expand in order to achieve recognition. Also, the ambitious have trouble sitting still. Opening a new business is like a new romance—exciting, vibrant, and challenging. Just as in a romance, a bit of the initial luster will subside as time passes and the entrepreneur will become anxious to try something bigger. Just as a good romance needs time to mature into a lifelong relationship, so does the business need to mature to the point where it can sustain expansion. The decision to expand must be made based on facts, figures, and solid projections, not just on wishes.

The entrepreneur needs to go back to step number one. Study the demographics for any changes. Talk to suppliers, bankers, and all interested parties. Conduct surveys among your present clientele. Examine your present physical facilities to see if there is expansion space available before going through the expense of moving. It is often possible, through redesigning a business layout, to expand an operation appreciably.

A 2000-square-foot gift shop can conceivably expand 25 percent by adding a fifth display shelf to all four-shelf wall and aisle fixtures. This requires no additional leasable floor space, no redecorating expenses, and no moving costs. It may be an excellent method of testing out expansion ideas.

When a business outgrows its space, either physically or environmentally, it is time to expand. Physically, you must be able to house the operation in an efficient manner. Environmentally, you must be able to please your customers if they are to continue buying. A retailer selling quality goods at suggested retail prices cannot overclutter his store without taking on the appearance of a discount environment. Needless to say, if this occurs the customer will shop at the discounter. Adding space will increase sales if it accommodates more product. The extra rent may be easily covered by additional sales.

Mary Lawrence and Jane Fitzgerald, two long-time friends, each invested $5000 into a small women's ready-to-wear boutique in Titusville, Florida. Both young women were quite fashion-minded and although neither had any retail background, they felt confident they could buy successfully for the 18- to 40-year-old, well-dressed women of the area.

After carefully surveying the area they decided upon a 500-square-foot store located on the outside of the major mall of the community. The rent of $7 per square foot was more attractive to their tight budget than an indoor mall location at a much higher price. They opened with $8000 retail inventory and used the rest of their monies to attractively lay out their store in an early 1900s decor, and to set up an operating account.

The store, The Fashion Attic, opened with very little fanfare on a 10 a.m. to 6 p.m., six-day-per-week operation. Business started very slowly, with many days not doing enough to pay for basic operating costs. Within a three-month period it showed enough improvement to hire a part-time sales clerk, and proceed with the next season's buying plans. At the end of the first year sales were $38,436 with a net profit of $2264. Neither partner took any draw against profits. Business continued to grow and at the end of the second year the store showed the profit and loss shown below:

Sales	$48,701
less cost of goods	−25,900
Gross profit	$22,801
Operating expenses	
Rent	$ 3,500
Operating supplies	655
Salaries	3,073
Advertising	433
Insurance	186
Taxes	2,076 (4% sales tax)
Utilities	2,117
Depreciation	775
Travel	967
Miscellaneous	767
Accounting	295
Total operating expenses	$14,844
Net profit	$ 7,957

Inventory had grown to $11,000 retail. The partners had withdrawn some net profit for compensation. Mary proposed to Jane that they consider moving to an inside-the-mall location with more space, based on their somewhat encouraging improvement. At the time there were two available spaces.

One store was 800 square feet (20′ × 40′) which leased for $8 per square foot or 6 percent of gross sales, whichever was highest. It was available on a three-year lease with a three-year option to renew, with a cost-of-living increase built into the base rent. It would require a total redecoration at $20 per square foot of sales area and $10 per square foot of stockroom space.

Mary figured inventory would have to approximately be doubled to accommodate the extra space and increased sales volume. She also figured she would have to sell a minimum of $72,000 to cover additional overhead. There would be additional salaries, of at least 80 percent, and additional utilities of at least 50 percent, due to the longer mall hours (10 a.m. to 9 p.m. daily) and paying their share of air conditioning in the mall. All other operating expenses, and cost of goods sold, should maintain approximately the same percentage level to sales as before.

The other space was 1750 square feet (25′ × 70′) for $6.50 per square foot or 6 percent of gross sales. It was also available on a three-year lease. It would also have to be redecorated using the same cost basis. A store this size would require increasing inventory approximately 400 percent over the current operation. Sales would need to be a minimum of $110,000 to cover additional overhead. In relation to their present operation, salaries would increase 300 percent, utilities 100 percent, and a more consistent advertising program of 3 percent of gross sales would be needed. As in the other location under consideration, Mary figured all other operating expenses and cost of goods could be maintained at the same percentage level of sales.

Jane was not sure she wanted to take such a gamble and told Mary, "If you want me to get interested you'll have to show me three things. Estimated profit and loss statements for both locations, a general store layout indicating basic decor, cash register area, dressing rooms, and stockroom space. Also, I would like to see some kind of general buying plan for the upcoming fall season. Right now I don't believe I am interested, and if you want to give me back my $5000, you can have the whole thing."

Mary went to work on Jane's request, including the fall buying plans. She knew from past history that her sales were 7 percent of gross for September; 8 percent, October; 8 percent, November; and 16 percent, December. Using these percentages as guidelines, and maintaining at least minimum inventory as calculated for each location, she could come up with a basic dollar buying plan. She also made a note to remember to figure in her markdowns, which at that time of the year were 5 percent of gross sales per month.

In order to decide, Mary worked out both proposals and studied each carefully.

- To stay in her present location with her partner until she achieved a longer history?

- To expand to the 800- or the 1750-square-foot store?

- Whether to end her partnership with Jane?

There are numerous arguments to be put forth, both pro and con, on the decision to be made. The first factors to consider are experience and goals. Although two years in some businesses may be too limited, in this instance, it may be sufficient coupled with the proper goals and ambition. Mary does have the ambition, and the proper objectives needed to pursue expansion. Jane does not. This indicates incompatible goals and is enough to dissolve the partnership. Although the past is not a glorious success, it does indicate potential growth.

This potential needs to be tested in the manner of least risk. If you worked through the figures given, you would have projected that both new locations have a greater potential than the current operation for more profits or greater losses. The 800-square-foot store appears to be the logical stepping stone for Mary. She can presume that there will be other 1700-square-foot opportunities available in the future, if she is successful. She might be able to reserve the adjacent space when it becomes available in negotiating her new lease. In consideration of her somewhat limited experience, and operating without Jane's help, the 800-square-foot store will be ample to challenge her ambition and creativity.

Selling a business

Once established and proven successful, there will be opportunities to sell the business. Your decision to sell or not will largely be a personal one, but should be intelligently thought out.

The first question to ask yourself is what are you going to do to make a living? It may take a while to re-enter the job market and you might have to enter at an entry-level position. This might mean a big drop in pay. Often, an offer to buy your business appears very tempting, as it may mean a substantial return on your investment.

Don't leap without looking. Many small businesspeople who have sold for a great profit have regretted their decision. While looking to replace her livelihood, by the time taxes are paid on the profits and the family has lived off the income, there may be little left and the one-time entrepreneur may be punching a clock. Do not sell a business unless your next step has been fully laid out.

Selling a business may be great if you are using the monies to buy a better opportunity. Selling a business for retirement years may be great, if there is enough money left to enjoy a long retirement. Instead of selling, you may want to consider other options. If a lump sum of monies is not necessary, consider changing the status of your business, from being a livelihood to being an investment. Hire and train management. There may be enough money available to pay the management, and still give you a healthy dividend each year, for many years. This gives you the option of being as involved as you wish to be. The idea of being able to tinker with a business interest, as opposed to total retirement, appeals to many. In your own business there is no mandatory retirement age. Businesses can also be passed down through the family. It may be a great inheritance to pass on.

Setting a price

There are many approaches employed in arriving at a selling price for a business. Some say a business can be sold for its annual sales volume, others say five times its net profit, some arbitrarily assign the value they would like to receive. However, the real selling price depends on what a buyer is willing to pay and what rational sales presentation can be made to influence that decision. The bottom line is that if you have made the decision to sell, put a fair price tag on it that will allow a mutually beneficial sales agreement. To do this, put yourself in the place of the potential buyer.

An astute buyer wants a solid investment that will pay him or her a salary and also pay a dividend on the investment. Remember that if an investor puts money into a relatively conservative mutual fund, he can usually count on a 10 percent dividend, or return on investment, a year. In order to entice that person to buy a business with a significantly higher degree of risk, you will have to prove a return of investment significantly higher than the mutual fund. A 20 percent return, or double the conservative investment, should be fair. At 20 percent, you are telling the buyer that if the business is managed correctly and the market stays intact, the new owner should receive the initial investment back in five years, generally the time period most mentioned to develop a business.

As an example, presume your business made a pretax profit of $30,000 the past year, after the owner's salary or draw. If you are able to substantiate that the business should continue that trend or better for the next five years, the selling price can be realistically set at $150,000.

Some factors can increase or decrease that price to a certain extent. If there has been a dramatic recent change in the marketplace, that will either cause a substantial increase or decrease to the projected profit, the price can be adjusted either way to show the anticipated change. If there has been a recent fluctuation in the amount of assets being sold, the price should be adjusted either way to indicate the change of value.

Selling price = pretax profits × 5, plus or minus anticipated changes
in market or asset conditions

The proper sales presentation should take the shape of a business plan for the future. If the seller takes the time to carefully lay out a realistic sales and profit scenario for the next five years, which shows anticipated growth and changes in the market, he or she will be confident of the selling price and will not have to sell at a drastically lower price through poor negotiating.

One word of caution: Be prepared for buyers to request assistance in financing the purchase. The buyer would rather have the seller do the financing as opposed to borrowing from the bank. In this situation the seller must stay involved with the business to be assured payments will be made or else run the risk of being forced to take back the business. If this is the case the seller should be paid a fair interest on the portion financed to pay for the risk incurred. The seller should run a careful credit check on the buyer and request as much security and collateral as possible on the loan.

The best selling situation is when the buyer approaches the seller. Always be open to offers. Unless the timing is critical, do not be overly aggressive in soliciting potential buyers.

The entrepreneur spirit project—step 21

- Design a timetable that indicates possible expansion periods.
- Review your designed floorplan to find expansion possibilities in the present operation.
- From industry sources, investigate selling opportunities for your type of business.

22

The Global Entrepreneur

The business world has changed. Advanced communication and transportation technologies have made doing business with the other side of the world almost as easy as doing business with the other side of the country. We are hearing about the global market of the nineties. The exciting part is that it is not just for the large businesses anymore. More and more entrepreneurs are learning that they can engage in global marketing and that the opportunities are exciting.

Although only a small percentage of the 300,000 manufacturers in the United States export their products, the number is growing, particularly among small businesses. Thirty-seven percent of companies with less than 500 employees are exporting. One-quarter of exporting companies employ less than 100 employees. The majority of exporters experienced a significant increase in sales from 1989 to 1990. Exporting will continue to grow through this decade because of the slow-down of U.S. population growth and the increasing internationalization of our economy.

Exploring opportunities

The U.S. government encourages small businesses to export goods. For too long there has been a balance-of-trade deficit—more imports than exports—which is hurting our economy. There are numerous avenues open to export goods successfully to overseas markets, as more companies make the effort. In the past only the large businesses dared to enter the export market, but now more and more small businesses are pursuing opportunities. If you are considering a manufacturing or wholesaling business, take time to explore the foreign markets. The starting place for seeking information is the International Trade Administration (ITA) of the United States Department of Commerce.

The ITA receives information about export opportunities from U.S. Foreign Commercial Service offices located in 125 foreign countries. The ITA gathers and shares information regarding:

Which markets are growing and changing.

Which foreign markets are buying, or want to buy, products and what those products are.

Tariff and nontariff trade barriers, import regulations, policies, and product standards.

Domestic and foreign competition.

Distribution practices.

Foreign media that effectively promote products throughout their market.

The ITA will provide you with information about your specific product in specific countries, including sales potential in the market, comparable products, distribution channels, going prices, competitive factors, and qualified purchasers. Other assistance available includes export mailing list, credit checks on foreign countries, and opinions as to reliability as a trade contact.

The ITA will also help put you in contact with foreign visitors looking for trade contacts. They set up seminars, plant visits, trade shows, and other arrangements for these visitors to attend while in our country.

For more information regarding the ITA, contact one of their 47 district offices or 21 branch offices throughout the United States. Another source for answers is to call the Export Opportunity Hotline of the Small Business Foundation of America, toll free 1-800-243-7232 (inside Massachusetts 1-800-244-7232).

There are a number of publications put out by the Department of Commerce to keep you informed of international business developments and help you investigate markets.

Business America magazine reports every two weeks on international markets and economic conditions.

Commerce Business Daily summarizes U.S. government procurement activity.

Overseas Business Reports addresses trade regulations, marketing profiles of foreign countries, and basic economic data.

Foreign Economic Trends and Their Implications for the United States contains reports on business conditions in individual countries.

Market Share Reports contains statistical data on over 1000 commodities by 88 countries.

The Export-Import Bank of the United States (Eximbank)

Eximbank is the government agency responsible for assisting the export of U.S. goods and services by providing loan guarantees to banks that extend loans to U.S. exporters. Although the program is not available to offer start-up assistance, it provides valuable help to small businesses in obtaining inventory, carrying accounts receivable, and meeting payroll. Its eligibility requirements are determined primarily by the creditworthiness of the borrower and how the money is to be utilized. It gives preference to loans needed to complete a specific export order. The funds cannot be used to repay existing debt or to purchase fixed assets.

Other financing sources for the small exporter besides local banks and government agencies are certain foreign banks, such as Europe's National Westminster Bank USA and Japan's Daiwa Bank Ltd.

Getting started as an exporter

To start your export business follow these steps:

1. Assess your export potential. Look at industry trends, your financial capabilities, the effects it might have on your domestic operations.

2. Get expert counseling. Check with the Department of Commerce, state development agencies, and any other public or private assistance firms.

3. Select the one or two best markets. Conduct market research utilizing the available network of assistance centers.

4. Formulate your export strategy. Set your objectives, choose the tactics you will use, schedule marketing and networking activities, and allocate your financial resources. This will require contacting trade consultants, scheduling trips to trade fairs, and making contacts with potential agents or distributors.

5. Decide on a selling technique. You will have to decide between selling direct or indirect. If you sell direct you will sell through sales representatives, distributors, foreign retailers, or in some countries state-controlled trading companies. If you sell indirect you might use commission agents, country-controlled buying agents, export management companies, or export trading companies.

6. Obtain financing through regional or international banks, or Eximbank.

7. Contact bankers and government specialists to learn how to arrange for payments from foreign buyers.

Trends in international trade

There will continue to be growth in U.S. exports to the European Community. The European Community is the biggest market in the world for United States' products. In 1992 there will be further elimination of restrictions on the free movement of goods and services in these countries.

The new environment in Eastern European countries and the USSR should create a boom in sales to these countries, particularly regarding computers, tele-communications, and other high-technology equipment. There should continue a lessening of trade barriers to these countries.

The uniting of Germany has meant a common, freely convertible currency—the deutsche mark. This opens an untapped market in East German trade, par-ticularly in the areas of medical equipment, energy-related equipment, computers, and chemicals.

Growth of export opportunities to Finland and Sweden should continue to be strong.

Opportunities have been created from the Iraqi war, particularly export of construction materials to Kuwait.

Competition from the Japanese will continue to be stiff; U.S. exports to Japan have been under scrutiny for poor quality.

Foreign market entry requires diligence and planning. The marketer must stay abreast of current happenings at all times. Using an ambitious distributor who knows both the product and the chosen market well is cited by many as the key to success.

The entrepreneur spirit project—step 22

- Evaluate the potential of your business to export.
- If there is potential, contact the nearest ITA office for assistance.

23

Your Business at One Year Old

When a baby reaches his or her first birthday, remarkable things are happening. The personality is taking on its own unique characteristics, features are becoming better defined, and the child is learning to respond to its environment. The same is true for a one-year-old business. It is a thrilling and rewarding time.

When the first birthday is a happy one

The year-old business is no longer new. The owner has learned a lot and for the first time is feeling comfortable as an operator. He or she has climbed the learning curve at an astonishing pace. The anniversary allows for the first sigh of relief for a number of reasons.

1. It will start to become easier and more manageable the second year. The experience gained should translate into more profits.

2. There is now a history to measure results by and to use as a reference. Sales trends will now appear, allowing for the first time a guide for exact planning. Inventory can be ordered with the knowledge of what sold well previously and in what quantities.

3. The customers know you. No longer are you spending money simply to tell people that you exist. It is time to enter that second stage of the advertising cycle—competitive. The confidence gained will be used to take on the competition head-on by announcing why you are better than anyone else.

4. If the plan has been successfully followed, new avenues of credit will be opened. Suppliers now know you and credit arrangements can be more

easily entered into. The banks who were afraid of taking a risk on a new business will now listen to your requests for financing.

5. You have learned from observation what your customers expect. The initial setup and design of the business have probably changed to reflect what you have learned. The business is now better tailored for its particular customer.

6. The customer profile can be refined and adjusted to reflect the true target market. You know the unsatisfied needs and the lifestyles of those the business serves.

7. The business has a sound pricing strategy. The customers have spoken as to what price they are willing to pay and the owner has adjusted appropriately.

8. The group of strangers who started working at the new business are now a coordinated, cohesive team. They know their responsibilities and they have learned their roles. The misfits have been weeded out. The owner has molded a team to fit the image of the business.

9. The cash flow surprises of the first year will not be quite the shock the second year. Plans will be implemented that will make the cash shortage times more manageable.

10. Initial goals will have been revised to focus on realistic targets for the future.

When the first birthday is not a happy one

Unfortunately for many the picture won't be as clear. If the initial plan was poor, it will be evident by the end of the first year. A number of problems will show their nasty selves.

1. Poor initial capitalization will be strangling the fledgling business. The gamble that instant profits would cure cash shortages failed, causing inventory shortages or not enough equipment or people to serve the customer.

2. The choice of a bad location will now be clear. Plans to move to another location are hampered by lease restrictions and the added cost of making a move.

3. The pricing strategy of getting rich quick or trying to compete with the discounters has backfired in the form of either driving customers off or not making the necessary profit needed to keep growing.

4. The inconsistent management practices of the owner have created chaos and turnover among the employees, which has caused payroll cost to soar past the initial projection.

5. Purchasing in ill-advised quantities to get a discount or buying "fad" products too heavily has created inventory surpluses of unwanted items.

6. Missing the target market has wasted the money spent on advertising and promotion. The business is still looking for its market niche.

7. The hastily put together bookkeeping system has not been kept up to date and the accountant is having a field day charging you for the hours it is taking to decipher the business's finances.

8. All of the above have made it impossible to put together a sound plan for the upcoming year. The purchase plan for inventory or materials will have no justification.

9. Creditors are clamping down on terms. COD is the norm allowing no time to sell before paying causing catastrophic cash flow problems. The hoped-for good bank relationship is a distant dream.

10. The owner has no reason for a sigh of relief. The problems have extended into his or her personal life and there seems to be no hope.

Sizing up the situation

As the preceding indicates, the start of the second year can be rewarding beyond your wildest dreams or might take on the resemblance of a nightmare. Most one-year-old businesses will find themselves with a combination of rewards and concerns. Seldom is it clear sailing; however, if the entrepreneur has stayed on top of the situation and learned, he or she will be much more prepared to take on the problems encountered than during the first year. Using the experience gained, the business owner should enter the second year with a plan for growth. It will be a very important year, since it tells the results of the efforts expended.

In terms of the business life cycle (see Chapter 14), the business should be coming out of the development stage and into a strong growth period. The marketing strategy should reflect this. In most businesses growth should be at least twice the industry growth rate. If the industry is showing sales growth of 7.5 percent, the one-year-old business should be moving along at a clip of 15 percent or more, since it has established a customer base it did not have in the first year. Repeat sales should be evident in most businesses at this point. A business that is not generating strong growth at this juncture is most likely headed for an early demise. Figure 23-1 illustrates the market position of the one-year-old business.

Dusting off the business plan

It is helpful at this point to pull out the initial business plan and see how you have done. A business plan is not only used for getting a business started; it is a guide that should be constantly updated as the business passes through its various cycles. The first year anniversary is certainly a time to review and update the business plan.

The review should be done just as it has been stressed before, in writing. The owner should find the time, and a quiet working environment, to address the ac-

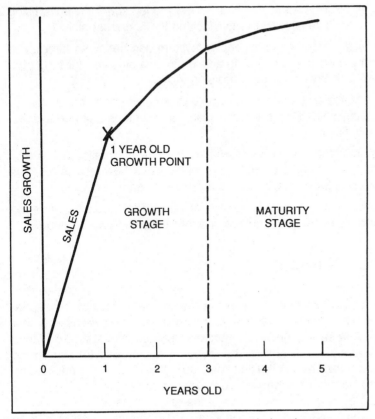

Figure 23-1. Typical business growth trend showing one year growth point.

complishments and problem areas of the first year. Make a list of the key areas and proceed as follows:

1. Look at the personal objectives that were set. Have you achieved the minimum financial needs for your personal living expenses? Are the personal satisfiers present? In other words are you happy with what you are doing and meeting your personal financial obligations. If things are not in sync, this might be your last chance to change them.

2. Analyze the financial statements indicating what areas the objectives were achieved and what ones were missed. A typical review will look similar to the one in Table 23-1. The written review should comment on all areas as to why it was a plus or minus and what plans are in process to improve a particular expense, revenue, asset, or liability classification.

3. The target customer should be redescribed. Redo the target center and its outer rings, as shown in Fig. 23-2. Note what changes you have learned about the customer. Are you ready to expand your marketing ef-

Table 23-1
Typical One Year Review

	Projected	Actual	Variance (%)
Sales	$200,000	$188,000	– 6
Cost of goods	108,000	102,000	– 5
Gross profit	92,000	86,000	– 7
Operating expenses			
Rent	14,600	14,600	—
Employee payroll	18,000	16,450	– 8
Owner's pay	20,000	16,200	– 17
Utilities	6,200	6,450	+ 2
Maintenance	1,200	780	– 30
Insurance	1,500	1,520	—
Legal, accounting fees	700	700	—
Advertising	6,000	5,200	– 11
Taxes, payroll	2,800	2,150	– 24
Interest	4,800	4,800	—
Miscellaneous	5,200	7,460	+ 40
Total operating expense	81,200	76,310	– 6
Net operating profit	10,800	9,690	– 10
Debt reduction	6,000	6,000	—
Retained earnings	4,800	3,690	– 20
Assets			
Inventory	24,000	22,100	– 10
Furniture, fixtures	31,000	31,800	+ 1
Equipment	7,800	7,800	—
Leasehold improvements	15,500	16,600	+ 6
Total assets	78,300	78,300	—
Liabilities			
Accounts payable	8,500	8,150	– 1
Bank note	44,000	44,000	—
Total liabilities	52,500	52,150	—

forts to an outer circle or do you need more time to build the core customer base?

4. Make a new cash flow projection for the next year. Refer to the initial year and plug in realistic growth figures. Write a description for each month defending your estimates. For instance if your estimate for the second July is for a 20 percent increase, explain how and why it will happen. Perhaps it is because you are planning a special promotion or, if retail, perhaps there is an extra weekend as opposed to the last July calendar. The same holds true for any change in an expense classification. If you show an expense reduction for payroll in a month, explain the reasoning behind the decision to cut payroll. If you do this it will serve as a disciplinary tool. Stick to it unless something happens in the marketplace that forces a change.

5. Review your inventory purchase plan in recognition of the recent history. This year will be a great improvement in your ability to plan purchases;

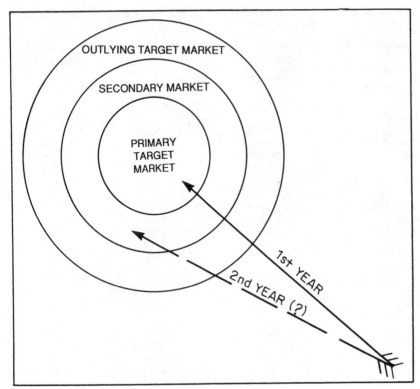

Figure 23-2. Changes in the target market.

however, it is still limited history, therefore your purchase plan will have to be flexible.

6. Redesign your advertising direction. Since the business is now considered in the competitive advertising stage, take the time to study the competition's advertising thrust. Look for their weaknesses and capitalize on them. Figure 23-3 illustrates the difference.

7. Compare the personnel organizational chart you are currently operating under to the initial plan. Do all employees fully understand their responsibilities? Are communication lines open? Is there money available to reward good work? Have you discussed individual performance with each employee? Consider implementing a bonus program as opposed to permanent raises. The business is still too young to make long-term financial commitments to employees. Check for skills and talent voids that should be addressed.

8. How are the relationships with creditors? Spot any problem suppliers and make a plan to contact them directly to improve relationships. Request a meeting with your banker to review your progress. This does not have to

```
┌─────────────────────────────────────┐
│                                     │
│           INTRODUCING...            │
│                                     │
│        VINCENT'S ITALIAN            │
│                                     │
│             CUISINE                 │
│                                     │
└─────────────────────────────────────┘
```

```
┌─────────────────────────────────────┐
│                                     │
│          FOR THE BEST IN            │
│                                     │
│        ITALIAN CUISINE...           │
│                                     │
│          IT'S VINCENT'S             │
│                                     │
└─────────────────────────────────────┘
```

Figure 23-3. Contrasting advertisement head-lines—one year later.

be a loan request meeting. The banker will be impressed that you arranged a meeting strictly for the benefit of keeping him abreast.

9. It is time to analyze insurance needs. Since the business has gone through changes, very possibly it requires a change in insurance coverage.

10. Run a recheck on the demographics of the market. Has the market grown or weakened? What are the present economic indicators saying nationally and locally? It is also a good time to get out and take a close look at your competition. Since you have entered the market they had to make adjustments. What are they doing differently to combat you? What creative edge can you come up with to let them know you are here to stay?

Once you have written out an analysis of your study, you will be pretty close to having a business plan for the second year. Eliminate reference to the first year's statistics and announce the objectives for the coming year in a separate report. Analyze it with people who can give you valuable input, particularly employees. When you are satisfied with the plan, formalize it and file it as a guide to follow. Keep it handy and remember it is a guide not a law. It can be changed, and should be when circumstances change around you.

A better look at the future

Just as you have used the first year's results to plan for the second, you can use them to re-evaluate the long-term goals. Since you are now able to sense a trend and you have a history, it is the ideal time to look at the five-year objective that you had originally set. It might not be realistic based on the first year. If it is out of line, make the necessary changes, but don't change the objective date. Defend your argument in writing as to why you are making the changes. Once again review it with family, investors, and key employees so that they are aware of the direction you are taking.

This is the first time that the word expansion might creep into your mind. There might be some minor changes you can implement. A new product line that complements what you are selling is an idea. Adding some shelves or additional fixtures, machinery, or equipment might be timely. It is probably too soon to make a major move or investment; however, it is not too early to start making some preliminary plans.

Planning is the most important management function of the business owner. It is your defense against the unexpected. The successful small business must be able to react to changes and be flexible to serve the needs of its market. Without a plan you will not be organized enough to cope with the demands placed upon you. Planning never stops. It is an ongoing activity.

The entrepreneur spirit project—step 23

- Presume that you came within 10 percent of achieving your first year's projections. What specific programs might you look at to improve the business? List a new plan of action for the second year. How would this change your long-term objective?

24
Retirement Planning

If you have worked for a large organization, more than likely you have belonged to a retirement or pension plan program. When you become self-employed, it is imperative that you give thought to your retirement. You will not work forever.

Many aspiring entrepreneurs do not take this into account when forming a business plan. They mistakenly presume that the business will flourish and that eventually it will be sold for large profits that will serve as retirement income. To some that happens; however, it is not a definite, but retirement is and it must be planned for with a regular investment program. There are numerous alternatives to choose from and, with a little discipline, the entrepreneur can build a solid retirement foundation.

Whole life insurance

Whole life insurance differs from term life insurance in that it builds a cash value over time, in addition to protecting your business and family in the event of an untimely death. A certain portion of the premiums paid are invested by the insurance company in various funds or ventures that in time pay dividends to the policyholder. Eventually the cash or investment value will become higher than the amount of premiums put in. The other attractive bonus of a whole life policy is that you will be able to borrow against the cash value of the policy from the insurance company at an interest rate considerably below the prevailing bank rates. Therefore the whole life policy serves three purposes:

1. Life insurance protection against the unplanned death of the business owner.
2. A growing investment that can serve as retirement income.
3. A means of borrowing money at a low interest rate.

Since it is necessary to carry life insurance anyhow, the small business owner is wise to buy whole life insurance versus term.

IRAs

In addition to a sound insurance program, the entrepreneur should be setting aside money in investments for the future. Individual Retirement Accounts (IRAs) offer a method of investing, in some instances tax-free, until it is time to withdraw the investment at the age of 55 or older. Recent tax changes have stipulated certain requirements for the tax-free IRAs and have curtailed the amount of money that can go into such a fund; however, they are still a program designed for the small business owner. Even though not all the money you might wish to put into your IRA will be tax-free, all interest and dividends that accrue will be. Check with a financial planner on the most advantageous method of setting up an IRA for your future.

Many small business owners will create a simplified employee pension (SEP). An SEP allows an employer to make contributions toward his or her own retirement and his or her employees' as well. The limit is 15 percent of the owner's net earnings and 15 percent of an employee's annual pay, not to exceed $30,000. For example, if you are a sole proprietor with net earnings of $50,000 and you have one employee who has been paid $20,000, you would be able to deduct $7500 (15 percent of $50,000) from your taxable personal income and the employee would not have to declare $3000 (15 percent of $20,000) for the year the contributions were made. The $3000 would also be a deductible business expense to the business. An SEP allows an employer to offer a simple-to-understand pension plan to employees.

Keogh plans

Keogh plans are another pension plan method for self-employed individuals. As a sole proprietor you are permitted to invest up to 30 percent of the business's net profit into a Keogh plan. Taxes are not paid on this amount until the Keogh plan is drawn against. The maximum amount you can deduct is $30,000 per year. A Keogh plan differs from an IRA in that it is required that employees meeting certain criteria be included in the business's Keogh plan. It can serve as a good motivator and benefit for those employees that have served long and well for the employer. Since the monies are invested tax-free going into the fund, and if the plan is able to generate a 9.5 percent interest growth per year, the business owner that is in the 28 percent tax bracket would, in actuality, be earning a 37.5 percent interest return the first year.

A Keogh plan for a corporation is known as a 401K plan. A corporation retirement plan allows a maximum tax deductible contribution of 15 percent of an employee's salary, which applies to your salary as the owner. The corporation also is permitted to contribute up to 15 percent of its net profits to the plan as well. For example, as a small corporation owner-employee with a salary of $30,000, the corporation can contribute $4500 (15 percent of $30,000) to a retirement plan to draw on later. In addition, if the corporation has a net profit of $20,000 it can contribute an additional $3000 (15 percent of $20,000) to the pension plan.

How investments grow

If the business owner starts by consistently putting money aside for investment, he or she will find it will grow quite quickly even in a rather conservative investment fund. Let's look at a typical example.

The new business owner deletes his or her savings or retirement fund by $50,000 in order to start a business. If the business is a viable one, he or she should be able to recapture $10,000 or 20 percent of that investment back each year. By investing that $10,000 in a fund paying 9.5% interest, the fund will grow to $66,188 at the end of the five-year period. If all goes well the business owner will have received all invested money back and have a handsome start to a generous retirement income. (See Table 24-1.)

On a smaller scale, let's look at what happens if the business owner is able to invest $5000 each year into a 9.5 percent fund for twenty years. (See Table 24-2.)

Not bad for starters. Add to this the profits received from the possible sale of the business and it makes a very nice retirement income.

Other considerations

For many, selling the business is not the goal. They might wish to hand the business down to the next generation of family members. The idea of establishing a profitable concern to be shared by many for years to come is a very exciting motivation. It can be very gratifying, if planned correctly. If not it can be a nightmare. One particular problem is designating the heir to the leadership of the business if a number of family members are involved. Many family units have been destroyed over the politics, greed, and jealousies associated with determining who will inherit what when the founder decides to step down. The use of proper management tools of performance evaluations, job descriptions, and a clear communication system will help to alleviate these problems. The business must be viewed as a separate entity from the family relationships and operated as a business. Un-

Table 24-1
Five-Year Investment at 9.5 Percent Interest Rate, $10,000 per Year

Year	End-of-year value
1	$10,950
2	22,940
3	36,069
4	50,446
5	66,188

_____ **Table 24-2** _____
Twenty-Year Investment at 9.5 Percent Interest Rate, $5000 per Year

Year	End-of-year value
1	$ 5,475
2	11,470
3	18,034
4	25,223
5	33,094
6	41,713
7	51,151
8	61,485
9	72,801
10	85,192
11	98,760
12	113,618
13	129,886
14	147,701
15	167,207
16	188,567
17	211,956
18	237,567
19	265,611
20	296,319

fortunately, this is much easier to say than do. Once again, the skills of the leader will be put to the test.

There are many who really do not want to retire. The business gives them such satisfaction that they wish to stay associated with it until death. In this event they might opt for an absentee management operation which allows them to stay involved as an investor and adviser. This form of semiretirement works out well if the operation can be turned over to capable hands. In order to do this the plans must be put into motion long before the semiretirement is in place. Proper management must be schooled and trained in the operation of the business. This might take years of coaching and working alongside the new operations manager. The succeeding manager might be an employee or a family member. The founder still continues receiving compensation without undergoing the daily headaches of managing the concern. Often this is best accomplished by giving up partial ownership to another to assure their long-term interest. An agreement should be written as to the eventual disposition of the business upon the death of the founder.

All of these plans have one thing in common—a successful business operation. Without success there is no investment plan, nor is there concern about the eventual disposition of the business. Good plans = good management = successful business operations.

The entrepreneur spirit project—step 24

As part of the business plan, a retirement program should be devised from the very beginning. Consult with a financial planner and determine the following:

- The amount of money to be budgeted for a retirement plan.
- Plans to consider. The total program should include insurance plus a tax-free annuity investment plan.
- A projection as to the value of the program at the time of anticipated retirement.
- A stated objective as to the eventual disposition of the business. Whether the ultimate plan is to sell, pass on to family, absentee management, or a gradual buyout from a dedicated associate, the goal should be written out, even if changed in later years.

25

The Problems
of Small Businesses

A chart like the one shown in Fig. 25-1 would scare most people away from pursuing their small business goal.

A closer look would indicate it is not quite as bad as it first appears. The tremendous mortality rate is slightly exaggerated. It is actually an accounting of business closings, not necessarily business failures.

There are many reasons businesses close besides failure. A great many would-be entrepreneurs find it is not their cup of tea and liquidate their assets instead of continuing. Many businesses are sold to larger businesses, which is a transfer of assets, not a business failure. If these adjustments are taken into account, the picture would appear a little more hopeful. However, these statistics still show a magnitude of problems.

Reasons for failure

If you were to survey owners of failed businesses, you would hear a lot of stories about unfair competition, economic depression, bad debt losses, and other reasons beyond their control. It all translates into one broad category of inefficient management.

Inefficient management can be due to poor initial capital planning, ineffectual sales effort, poor choice of location, or improper organizational structure. All of these problems are due to the owner not being prepared to handle the operation, most likely due to inexperience. As the chart demonstrates, the longer the business survives, the mortality rate declines proportionately. After five years, the prognosis is more favorable. This points out that with experience comes success. Gaining success means persevering. The impatient fail. Hang on to the philoso-

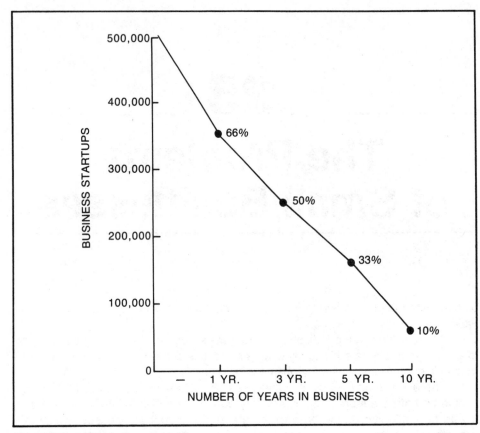

Figure 25-1. Business closings.

phy that your business will not fail, because you will not allow it. Reach that five-year plateau, and then decide if you wish to continue. Put up with the hard times to get to the good times. Do not fall victim to first-year mistakes as George did in his attempt to join Bob in his retail operation.

"Okay George, here's your opportunity to become an entrepreneur." Bob was speaking to his old fraternity brother George on the telephone, concerning George's long-held ambition to own a men's clothing store in Florida. "I am opening a small specialty department store and I have approximately 1500 square feet available for men's wear. I will either sublease you that space, or, if you would rather, I will sell you stock in my corporation and we will use that capital to buy your inventory and fixtures."

George responded enthusiastically, "You could not have called at a better time. The company I am with is having all sorts of problems and I may get laid off. Anyhow, I am sick of cold New England weather. Let me see what I can put together and I will call you back in a few days." George was in sales for a company that manufactured golfing and resort sportswear. He had been involved with the wholesale selling of apparel for five years and had always wanted to try the retail end.

Three days later he called Bob. "I can come up with $25,000. If you think that will cover us I will buy your stock and we will try it. I would rather do that than sublease, this way I can use your retail experience to help me out." Although Bob, who had owned successful card and gift shops, had no experience in men's clothing, he calculated that $25,000 might be enough to get started with for initial merchandise and fixtures and he consented to give it a try. He recommended that George give his notice, and be prepared to travel to the Atlanta Men's and Boy's Apparel show in four weeks, to place orders for their fall opening. The store was scheduled to open on October 1.

Bob went to work on the store layout as shown in Fig. 25-2. He had five departments to lay out in approximately 10,000 square feet of sales floor: cards and gifts, women's fashions, men's wear, bridal shop, and a restaurant. The store was located in a 55-store enclosed mall, and would have a mall entrance and an outdoor entrance. Since it had previously been occupied by a restaurant, the only preset space was the kitchen area. Therefore, he located the 1000-square-foot

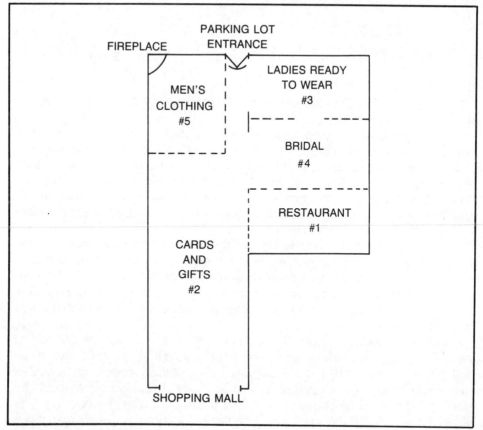

Figure 25-2. Store layout.

restaurant (department 1) adjacent to the kitchen. Knowing that the cards and gifts were impulsive merchandise requiring high traffic, that department (department 2), was placed at the mall entrance. With window exposure from the outside, it was thought women's ready-to-wear (department 3) would show off well in that area. Bridal and tuxedo (department 4) were placed beside the women's fashions. That left the back corner, 1500 square feet, for men's wear (department 5). That area also included a brick fireplace and would decorate well for men. Bob, along with the women's fashions manager, went to work designing, decorating, and remodeling the restaurant and other departments, into an attractive department store.

With 80 percent of the store finished, George arrived one week before opening.

The first thing Bob and George did was review the merchandise orders placed in Atlanta for the men's shop. Approximately $20,000 cost merchandise was ordered for the initial base inventory. It was broken down as follows:

Original monies	$25,000
Fixtures and equipment	6,300
Casual slacks, shirts	2,400
Dress slacks, shirts	1,900
Sweaters	700
Belts, accessories	1,225
Sport coats	3,900
Suits	5,600
Ties, billfolds	2,850
Total (paid in advance)	$25,075

In addition, $15,600 of fall and holiday merchandise was ordered for October and November delivery.

Bob and George were both somewhat concerned about the suit order. With over 25 percent of the original order in expensive suits it cut into the selection presented for more casual wear. In addition, that same percentage was ordered for fall, and holiday orders. They agreed that if they were to have a "complete look" the suit selection was necessary. It was also necessary to think about spring, since the orders had to be placed at the mid-October apparel show, before any sales history would be realized.

They went to work immediately unpacking and pricing the merchandise, which had been arriving the past two weeks. It was noticeable that George's taste in colors and designs were very oriented toward the golf and resort look. This concerned Bob, because he knew the community was composed mainly of engineers from the nearby aerospace industry. George was confident, however, that it was the right way to go.

The final week before opening was spent setting up merchandise and adding the finishing touches. Bob became somewhat annoyed at George's meticulous work habits, as everything had to be done by plan. With so much to do, in such a busy week, it didn't seem appropriate that so much of George's time should be spent in doing a lot of detailed charts and plans, until after the opening. The women's manager felt the same way. Bob thought it should prove advantageous in the long run to have at least one well-organized person in the firm.

Grand opening was set for 7 p.m. on a Thursday. It was a big affair. Ribbon cutting, champagne, entertainment, and a lot of advertising was used to make it a successful evening. George's first customer bought two suits, $450, and everything looked great.

Unfortunately, the first night was the highlight of the men's department. While the rest of the store performed pretty much up to expectations, the men's wear floundered. At the end of the fall and Christmas quarter, the total men's department sales were a disappointing $14,560. Since the first year's projections for the department were $150,000, the store had a major problem. The actual figures are given below:

Sales	$ 14,560
less purchases	−34,375
less payroll (George)	−11,200
less share of overhead	−6,450
plus end inventory	+27,500
Net loss	$−9,965

Of immediate concern was the $18,000 worth of merchandise on order for the spring. They tried to cancel as much as possible, particularly in the category of suits, but since most of it had already been cut and was ready to ship they took in over $16,000 of cost merchandise.

The January through March quarter was a disappointing $11,700 sales period, followed by an equally disappointing April through June sales period of $13,400. During this period, an additional $4500 of summer merchandise arrived. Bob looked at the end-of-June figures for the department and knew something had to be done.

They had already borrowed short-term monies to cover the loss and were now confronted with buying decisions for the upcoming fall. In addition to the financial problems, George continued to show no flexibility in changing plans in midstream. He worked everything out based on prescribed formulas he had learned while working for a large corporation. In addition to annoying Bob and the women's manager, two employees had quit over the frustration of working within George's guidelines. A meeting was held to confront the problem.

"George, I suggest we liquidate the department. The rest of the store cannot continue to support it, and I am not willing to borrow more money to purchase the fall season. If we liquidate, we can raise enough capital to purchase your stock at the same price you paid for it. We can either expand one of our other departments into that area, or carry a limited line of men's wear and accessories, which will be self-service and require one-half the investment. I am afraid you will have to go as I cannot afford your salary."

George was confused and disappointed. There seemed to be no other alternatives.

The problems created here were very burdensome. However, if George was determined to succeed it was still possible. There would have to be some changes of attitude and relationships, among all parties concerned. There would have to be new capital generated and a better business plan incorporated. A business that had been born was not given sufficient time to mature.

An attempt could have been made to concentrate efforts in the areas that showed promise, while discontinuing the most disappointing activities, until they were prepared to handle them. George may have to moonlight another job while waiting for business growth. Did they explore the possibilities of moving the department to another area? The most important point to be made is, that anyone expecting quick success is very likely a candidate for failure. Success is achieved through realistic goal setting, careful planning, sufficient training, and listening to proper advice.

Where to go for help

Although the small business owner often feels isolated since he or she is the single leader of a business, there are places to turn for assistance. The Small Business Administration (SBA) is a federal agency created by Congress in 1953 to assist in the development of the small business sector of our economy. The SBA helps small business owners meet their financial needs as discussed in Chapter 7 with their loan programs and also offers counseling assistance at no charge through SCORE, Service Corps of Retired Executives, who are volunteers. There are over 100 SBA offices located in the United States.

There are over 600 Small Business Development Centers (SBDC) throughout the United States. Often located on university campuses, these assistance centers are funded by a combination of state and federal SBA money. They offer no-charge counseling through trained small business consultants and low-cost seminar training. Small business owners and potential owners should contact the closest SBDC office and take advantage of this service. SBDC offices specialize in assisting with the development of business plans and are backed by the university system resources for information. Appendix D is a complete directory of SBDC offices.

There is also help available through your local Chamber of Commerce. The mission of the Chamber of Commerce is to promote commercial growth within its community and it will be glad to help guide you to appropriate resources in your local business community.

As mentioned, a major part of this education process is to learn not to be afraid to ask for help. You cannot possibly know all the answers, so seek the experience of others while your experience grows.

The entrepreneur spirit project—step 25

- Research through the library, and find all sources of help that are available to you. Make a running bibliography of publications to read.
- Check the area for any seminars or educational forums that you would be able to attend.
- Stop by the office of a small business development center, if there is one in your area, and discuss your needs to discover if there is any assistance available.

APPENDIX A

Case Study: Homeless Entrepreneurs

St. Luke's Economic Development Company (SLEDCO) is an Atlanta inner-city nonprofit organization whose mission is to provide opportunities for the homeless to gain employment and stability in their lives. The idea was introduced at a board of directors' meeting to attempt to create jobs for their clients through enterprise development. In searching for an idea requiring minimum investment and work for low-skill employees, it was decided to explore the possibility of manufacturing and assembling novelty buttons. A group of college students working with a local Small Business Development Center was asked to do a feasibility study and present its findings to the board.

The group of four students laid out a four-step approach to a business plan. The first assignment was to gather information regarding the competition and the market in the local industry. They then proceeded to analyze the cost to produce and distribute the buttons. This was followed by preparing pro forma financial statements. Finally, a conclusion was reached as to the feasibility of the project.

The competition and market analysis was completed mainly through in-depth interviews with the four largest button producers in the area. The interviewees were quite cooperative, because for each the manufacture and sale of novelty buttons was but one small part of their total operation. The students were able to identify the strongest potential customers as schools, athletic organizations, political candidates, shopping malls and stores, and all promotion-minded companies including radio stations. The pricing of the buttons fell in a range of 26 cents to 75 cents for the standard 2¼-inch button, depending on quantity ordered.

In conducting the cost analysis, a company called Badge-A-Minit was found to offer a simple-to-operate machine that would cut and assemble buttons. The company could also supply pin backs and plastic covers. The students costed out the production using three employees and two machines (Table A-1).

After a careful survey of potential customers ranging from political candidates to restaurants, the students were able to make the financial projections shown in Tables A-2 to A-4.

Based on the collected and analyzed information, the students recommended to the board of directors that SLEDCO proceed to develop an enterprise that would initially employ three full-time people in the manufacturing and marketing of 2¼-inch novelty buttons. The board of directors agreed to appropriate $3000 seed money for equipment, starting inventory, and a small operating account.

Start-up

Once the initial equipment of two machines and inventory for 5000 buttons was received, three of the most able of the homeless clients were chosen to begin production to fill orders received from a local church, a college business department, and three political candidates. It was quickly recognized that for this to be an ongoing enterprise, a major contract would have to be secured. The attention of the workers turned to getting the contract for one of Atlanta's professional

Table A-1
Numerical Cost Analysis

Equipment

2 Badge-a-Matic Plus	$667.90
1 Cut-a-Circle II	69.95
1 Cut-a-Circle	18.95
Capital equipment cost	$756.80

Cost per Button

	One-Color Type No Logo	One-Color Type and a Logo	Three-Color Type and a Logo
Pin-back button	$0.11	$0.11	$0.11
Paper	0.04	0.04	0.04
Artwork	0.05	0.06	0.33
Cost	$0.20	$0.21	$0.48

Cost per Button Including Labor

$0.43	$.044	$0.71

Annual Cost of 3 employees at $4.50 per hour equals $28,080.

Table A-2
Capitalization and Net Worth

Requested Capitalization	
Initial inventory	
(35,000 button sets)	$ 5,250
Capital purchases	
(2 button machines, 2 cutters, 1 computer)	2,500
Utility deposits	300
Promotional costs	800
Miscellaneous	150
Cash on hand	2,500
Inventory reserve account	13,500
Total initial capitalization	$25,000
Pro Forma Statement of Worth, July 1991	
Cash	$ 2,500
Reserve account	13,500
Inventory	5,250
Capital equipment	2,500
Deposits	300
Total assets/net worth	$24,050

Table A-3
Pro Forma Income Statement

	Year 1		Year 2	
Sales	$52,380		$96,500	
Cash injection	13,500		———	
Total revenues		$ 65,880		$ 96,500
Purchases		(13,500)		(35,500)
Gross profit		$ 52,380		$ 61,500
Operating expenses:				
Gross wages	31,680		44,240	
Payroll taxes	2,400		3,080	
Graphic services	5,900		2,400	
Supplies	1,200		1,200	
Advertising	1,200		1,200	
Delivery	1,200		1,200	
Telephone	1,200		1,200	
Utilities	1,200		1,200	
Insurance	600		700	
Miscellaneous	3,000		3,000	
Total operating expenses		49,580		59,420
Net operating profit		$ 2,800		$ 2,080

Table A-4

SLEDCO: Monthly Cash Flow Projections for the First Eighteen Months

	JULY 91	AUG 91	SEP 91	OCT 91	NOV 91	DEC 91	JAN 92	FEB 92	MAR 92
Projected Number of Buttons Sold	5,000	7,000	10,000	10,000	10,000	10,000	10,000	10,000	10,000
Cash on hand	$2,500	$ 860	$ 20	$ 380	$ 740	$1,100	$1,460	$ 1,820	$2,180
Cash receipts									
Cash sales	2,250	3,150	4,500	4,500	4,500	4,500	4,500	4,500	4,500
Loan or other cash injection				4,500				4,500	
Total cash available	$4,750	$4,010	$4,520	$9,380	$5,240	$5,600	$5,960	$10,820	$6,680
Cash paid out									
Purchases (merchandise)				$4,500				$ 4,500	
Gross wages	$2,640	$2,640	$2,640	2,640	$2,640	$2,640	$2,640	2,640	$2,640
Payroll expenses (taxes, etc.)	200	200	200	200	200	200	200	200	200
Outside services (graphics)	250	350	500	500	500	500	500	500	500
Supplies (office and operating)	100	100	100	100	100	100	100	100	100
Advertising	100	100	100	100	100	100	100	100	100
Car, delivery, and travel	100	100	100	100	100	100	100	100	100
Telephone	100	100	100	100	100	100	100	100	100
Utilities	100	100	100	100	100	100	100	100	100
Insurance	50	50	50	50	50	50	50	50	50
Miscellaneous	250	250	250	250	250	250	250	250	250
Total cash paid out	$3,890	$3,990	$4,140	$8,640	$4,140	$4,140	$4,140	$ 8,640	$4,140
Cash position	$ 860	$ 20	$ 380	$ 740	$1,100	$1,460	$1,820	$ 2,180	$2,540

sports teams. Another dream would be to do promotional buttons for the newly organized Atlanta Olympic Committee. The question was how to get their attention. The answer turned out to be through the political candidates.

Since it was the political season, the idea occurred to have publicity generated concerning the homeless making buttons for some of the high-profile congressional and state office candidates. The *Atlanta Constitution* ran a feature story on the workers. There was a follow-up plan of action scheduled to get the attention of the Atlanta Olympic Committee, but it was not necessary. The day following the newspaper story, the Atlanta Olympic Committee called SLEDCO to inquire if they had the capability to produce buttons for the first stage of Olympic promotion in Atlanta.

Meetings were held to review the licensing requirements and production specifics. Working with a local printer the SLEDCO button prototype was approved. SLEDCO was given permission to manufacture and distribute the AOC official button (Fig. A-1) through Atlanta retail stores for a three-month period. At the end of this period the Atlanta Olympic Committee would be replaced by the International Olympic Committee in preparation for the 1996 Olympic Games, and all future licensing agreements would have to be approved by the new committee.

The homeless entrepreneurs went to work, spreading out through the city and suburbs soliciting orders from leading retail outlets. Additional equipment was

APR 92	MAY 92	JUN 92	Annual Totals	JUL 92	AUG 92	SEP 92	OCT 92	NOV 92	DEC 92	6-Month Totals
12,000	12,000	12,000	118,000	12,000	12,000	12,000	15,000	15,000	15,000	81,000
$2,540	$3,460	$ 4,380		$ 5,300	$ 6,220	$ 7,140	$ 8,060	$ 5,170	$ 6,780	
5,160	5,160	5,160	$ 52,380	5,160	5,160	5,160	6,000	6,000	6,000	$33,480
			4,500	13,500						
$7,700	$8,620	$14,040	$ 87,320	$10,460	$11,380	$12,300	$14,060	$11,170	$12,780	$72,150
		$ 4,500	$ 13,500				$ 4,500			$ 4,500
$2,640	$2,640	2,640	31,680	$ 2,640	$ 2,640	$ 2,640	2,640	$ 2,640	$ 2,640	15,840
200	200	200	2,400	200	200	200	200	200	200	1,200
600	600	600	5,900	600	600	600	750	750	750	4,050
100	100	100	1,200	100	100	100	100	100	100	600
100	100	100	1,200	100	100	100	100	100	100	600
100	100	100	1,200	100	100	100	100	100	100	600
100	100	100	1,200	100	100	100	100	100	100	600
100	100	100	1,200	100	100	100	100	100	100	600
50	50	50	600	50	50	50	50	50	50	300
250	250	250	3,000	250	250	250	250	250	250	1,500
$4,240	$4,240	$ 8,740	$ 63,080	$ 4,240	$ 4,240	$ 4,240	$ 8,890	$ 4,390	$ 4,390	$30,390
$3,460	$4,380	$ 5,300	$ 24,240	$ 6,220	$ 7,140	$ 8,060	$ 5,170	$ 6,780	$ 8,390	$41,760

Figure A-1. Sample of the Atlanta Olympic Committee licensed button.

added and four more employees. Over the three-month period 30,000 buttons were sold at a wholesale cost of $0.625. The income statement for the contract is shown below.

Sales	$19,353
Cost of goods	−6,219
Gross profit	$13,134
Operating expenses	
Payroll	$ 8,559
Supplies	355
Royalties	3,838
Miscellaneous	272
Total operating expense	$13,024
Net profit	$ 110

It was an overwhelming success for a nonprofit organization. Seven formerly homeless, unemployed people had work and SLEDCO's mission was brought to the attention of the Atlanta citizens. With the contract concluded, the SLEDCO entrepreneurs are waiting for approval to produce the official button for the 1996 Olympic games. If received, it is anticipated production for worldwide distribution of buttons and related items could be in the millions and employment guaranteed for many homeless for at least four years.

APPENDIX B
Case Study: Bodywear, Etc.

The "health boom" of the seventies ushered in an era of leg warmers, running shoes, and sweatshirts. Twenty or more years later, the "boom" is still as loud as ever. Health spas are springing up everywhere; aerobic classes are held in schools, county buildings, and hospitals. Spas are included in the construction of large hotel and motel chains. Large corporations now have wellness centers and aerobic classes. For these reasons, we believe that there is a great demand for retail outlets that specialize in exercise clothing, shoes, and light equipment for the jogger, aerobic dancer, and free weight enthusiasts.

Our company name, Bodywear, Etc., was selected because it best describes the type of products we will sell and indicates that other similar items are also available there.

We also investigated the attributes of an existing business compared to a new business and concluded that our specialized needs would necessitate major changes to any currently existing business. We believe that Bodywear, Etc., will supply all products required by our target customer so he or she needs to make only one stop.

Organization, management structure, personnel

Organization

Bodywear, Etc., will be formed as a Subchapter S corporation. Articles of incorporation are included as an attachment to this section.

Management structure

Company objectives are

- To earn a profit.
- To provide a service to the community.
- To achieve continued growth.

Functions of employees

- Directors-owners will meet once a month with the store manager to discuss profits, plans, policies, and future growth. Directors-downers will hire/fire.
- General manager, appointed by the directors, will oversee the entire management of the store and work closely with the store manager to assure the objectives of the company are met. (Initially the directors will share this responsibility.)
- The store manager is responsible for the day-to-day operations of the store and makes recommendations to the directors on new merchandise, changes in policies, and hiring and firing of store salespeople.
- Clerks will be responsible for selling merchandise and ensuring fair and equal treatment to all customers.

Functions of the directors-owners

- Accounting and legal
- Audit
- Budget and forecasting
- Consulting
- Financial statements
- Taxes
- Marketing
- Production and operations
- Personnel
- Risk management
- Advertising and selling

Personnel

Store hours will be 10 a.m. to 9 p.m. Monday through Saturday. Two salespeople will be hired at $3.35 per hour each. One will work 10 a.m. to 3 p.m., Monday through Saturday, and the other will work 3 p.m. to 9 p.m., Monday through Saturday.

One salesperson will be hired at $5 per hour and will serve as the store manager. This employee will work Monday through Friday, 8 hours per day, and will be responsible for store opening.

The directors will work one Saturday each month in addition to serving in the position of general manager. There will be a schedule developed to ensure that at least one director is on hand for store closing every night.

This schedule will also be developed so that at least two salespeople and/or directors are in the store at all times.

Market demographics and psychographics

A demographic study was conducted by contacting the Chamber of Commerce and the Brevard County Development Commission and visiting the public library. Information acquired through these sources included:

- Family income characteristics by geographic areas.
- Median family income by geographic areas.
- Educational levels by planning area.
- Age composition by planning area.
- General population characteristics.

Our studies indicated a larger population in the south mainland and the south beaches. The median family income was higher in the south beaches. Educational levels were higher in the south beaches and the south mainland. The south mainland was more densely populated with the age group we had selected (20 to 50 years old).

Additionally, we conducted a separate survey of all major health spas in north, central, and south Brevard, requesting the total number of memberships and median age in each spa. The number of spas and total memberships were greater in the south mainland. The median age ranges from 28 to 34 years. We believe that with the great emphasis on health, America is getting younger. Our target customer is the modern male and female between 20 and 50 years of age, with an income of $20,000 to $40,000 per year. Our target customer thinks young with an emphasis on lean, clean lines.

Location

The demographic study and the spa survey played a major role in our decision to locate in south Brevard. Subsequently, we surveyed various realtors and leasing corporations to obtain leasing information.

We agreed to locate in a community mall, adjacent to the Melbourne Square Mall. The Melbourne Square Mall Promenade is a prime location, is newly constructed, and has adjoining shops including a health spa and a tanning salon. The mall construction is a modern design with a totally "today" look, which projects the theme and mood we wish to portray at Bodywear, Etc. Base rent is $13 per square foot for 1365 total square feet.

$17,745	base rent/year
4,778	triple net/year
$22,523	total yearly rent
$ 1,877	total monthly rent

The triple net lease includes the following items with charges of $3.50 per square foot.

- Common area maintenance
- Real estate tax
- Insurance

We acquired a three-year lease with a three-year option.
The lessor provides:

- Interior (unfinished) walls
- Bathroom (one)
- Drop-in grid ceiling
- Heat and air-conditioning unit
- Lighting
- Electrical 120/208, 3-phase
- Water connection

We must provide:

- Finished interior walls (dry wall)
- Carpeting
- Painting and wall covering

Building improvements

The directors agreed on the layout and type of materials to be used based strictly on aesthetic considerations without regard to cost. This information was given to a general contractor and we received an estimate for labor and materials. The cost was greater than we had anticipated. In order to reduce cost, we elected to change some of the materials and do some of the work ourselves.

Some of the changes include using a vinyl walkway rather than oak. We agreed to paint the walls ourselves and to change the circular glass wall to Plexiglas. Subsequently we intend to reduce the costs to $12,000.

Environmental merchandising

The store's interior will be bright and modern, designed to set the mood of the "lean, clean" look. The furniture and raised dressing room area are made of oak, which promotes the exterior design. The center walkway will be covered in an oak-look vinyl. The oak will create a warm, accommodating, gracious environment. We selected beige carpeting and off-white walls to (1) blend with the warm, friendly atmosphere and (2) to provide a quiet background for the bold, bright, arrows and designs to be painted on the walls that will direct the customer to specific merchandise. The accent colors for spring include bold yellow, electric blue, lush orchid, savage red, tropical green, and humid pink. Bright posters with "beautiful bodies" will be displayed on the wall in the weight and leotard areas. Mirrors are located in two areas to accommodate the customer.

Merchandise will be located in the store as follows:

- Right front section—jogging suits for men and women.
- Right center section—leotards, tights, and leg warmers.
- Right rear section—weights, fleecewear (sweatsuits). These items are unisex and will be sold as separates.
- Left rear section—shoes (running and aerobic). This area will include minishelves which will display the shoes, oak chairs, and a three-way mirror for customer convenience.
- Left center section—socks and T-shirts (unisex).
- Left front section—check out and impulse-buying display area.

Our office will be located in the left rear of the store. It is designed with a curved glass wall which promotes our modern look. The furniture is oak and the walls will display a poster of a "muscular male body" and a "curvaceous female body." The glass wall design creates an open friendly atmosphere.

The display window will exhibit new merchandise every two weeks. Posters and clothing will be displayed with the use of nylon line suspended from the ceiling and attached to the floor. This display will complement and complete our "lean, clean" look of today.

Advertising

Promotional advertising

Our grand opening will be held during a long weekend. It will start on May 23, 19XX (Friday) and continue through May 26, 19XX (Monday). Our grand opening will include:

1. Mailouts

2. Free T-shirts

3. Door prize

We plan to mail out or otherwise distribute 1000 flyers to our friends, coworkers, neighbors, and to the Atlantic Nautilus spas. A portion of the flyers will be distributed to local colleges and universities.

The door prize of a full one-year membership at the Atlantic Nautilus health spa will be awarded by a drawing on Monday, the last day of our grand opening. Free T-shirts with our business name on the back will be given to the first 100 customers who purchase $25 worth of merchandise.

Flyers	$ 146.85
Spa membership	150.00
T-shirts—100	447.00
Newspaper ads	
Sunday, ¼ page, *Today*	894.30
Daily, 1 column inch, *Today,* the *Times,* and *The Tribune*	160.20
Miscellaneous	300.00
Total	$2098.35

Long-range advertising program and plan (nine-month projection)

For the first nine months of operation, Bodywear, Etc., plans to place one advertisement per month (1 column inch) as "reminder ads," and one appreciation sale ad (¼ page). The one appreciation ad would be run approximately 60 days after the start of operation. We will also look into the neighborhood shopper for advertising possibilities.

Both the Donnelly Yellow Pages and the Southern Bell Yellow Pages were considered for ad placement and we decided to go with the better known—Southern Bell—even though it is more expensive. (Donnelly is $68 per month.) Donnelly assured us that they delivered a book to every business and residence in Brevard County. However, after conducting a survey of friends and relatives, we discovered that most had never heard of the Donnelly Yellow Pages.

Effectiveness of advertising and success of business will be analyzed at nine months to decide the course of future advertising.

Southern Bell ($96.00 per month)	$ 864.00
¼ page Sunday newspaper ad	894.30
Daily newspaper ad ($26.70)	240.30
Business cards (500 per director)	96.00
Total 9 month	$2094.60

Inventory

Our inventory selection was based on purchasing more items in the midrange sizes and fewer items in the smaller and larger sizes.

Color selections were mixed with the exception of pastels. More pastels were ordered in the smaller sizes. These items include fleecewear and T-shirts. Socks were mixed with brights and pastels for women and whites with stripes for men.

Jogging suits were ordered in primarily the same colors for men and women, with the exception of pastels for women. Nylon jogging suits were ordered in lighter colors as our first shipment will be for spring and summer seasons.

Shoes were selected in white with colored stripes, except for Reebok, which comes in pastels and black. More shoes will be ordered in the midrange sizes. Our inventory with wholesale and retail prices is listed.

Financing

The four partners in Bodywear, Etc., will each invest $20,000, for a total investment of $80,000. This amount is more than adequate for business start-up, including inventory and a cash reserve equal to two months' expenses.

We have contacted the principal loan officer at American Bank where we will maintain our checking account and have established a $25,000 line of credit. The financial information of the corporation listed below is part of this document.

Summary and conclusion

The Bodywear, Etc., owners and directors carefully and thoroughly collected information on a variety of topics to aid in determining whether to start a business, what business to start, and where it should be located.

Organization, management structure, personnel

Our decision to form our business as a Subchapter S corporation will enable us to spread the profits and/or losses among the shareholders. This should prove beneficial to all shareholders.

Financing Requirements—Initial Startup Costs

1. Deposits
2. Organizational expenses
3. Promotional expenses
4. Building improvements
5. Fixed assets
6. Inventory

Monthly Budget (working capital)
Income statement

We chose a simple, straightforward organizational structure with minimum tiers and maximum span of control. The organization will require a minimum amount of time from each owner-director yet keep him or her involved in the operations of the business.

Market demographics and psychographics

Our investigation showed that the south Brevard area was by far the best area for the development of a new business.

Location

We decided to locate in a small mall in a growing area.

Building improvements

The initial layout and design of our store was based strictly on aesthetic considerations. Since the cost was greater than we had anticipated, we elected to change some of the materials and do some of the work ourselves. We intend to keep the cost around $12,000.

Environmental merchandising

The "look" of our store will be clean, modern, and appealing.

Advertising

We will heavily promote our grand opening with flyers and advertisements. We will keep our name before the public with a regular planned advertising campaign.

Inventory

Our inventory will be well balanced and appealing to a variety of customers.

Financing

The four partners are prepared to each invest $20,000 for a total investment of $80,000, more than adequate for business startup.

Conclusion

All of our research indicates that Bodywear, Etc., has a real chance of success. We feel we have put enough research and capital into the business to carry it through the rough startup stage and into a solid and profitable operation.

This appendix was prepared by the following students from Barry University: Vicky K. Lorick, Patricia A. Lowry, Tommie L. Scarbro, and James A. Whaley.

**bodywear,
etc.**

Section II (Continued)

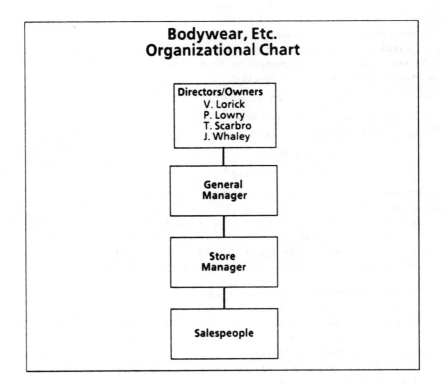

**Bodywear, Etc.
Organizational Chart**

Directors/Owners
V. Lorick
P. Lowry
T. Scarbro
J. Whaley

**General
Manager**

**Store
Manager**

Salespeople

Articles of Incorporation

BODYWEAR, ETC.

The undersigned subscribers to these articles of incorporation, each a natural person competent to contract, hereby associate themselves together to form a corporation under the laws of the State of Florida.

ARTICLE I

CORPORATE NAME

The name of this corporation is BODYWEAR, ETC.

ARTICLE II

NATURE OF BUSINESS

The general nature of the business to be transacted by this corporation is:

(a) To operate a retail outlet, or multiple outlets, for the display and sale of specialized exercise clothing and equipment. To evaluate health industry trends and determine advanced marketing techniques to advertise and promote new products.

(b) To manufacture, purchase or otherwise acquire, and to own, mortgage, pledge, sell, assign, transfer or otherwise dispose of, and to invest in, trade in, deal in and with goods, wares and merchandise, real and personal property, and services of every class, kind and description.

(c) To conduct business in and have one or more retail outlets in the State of Florida.

(d) To contract debts and borrow money, issue and sell or pledge bonds, debentures, notes and other evidences of indebtedness, and execute such mortgages, transfers of corporate property or other instruments to secure the payment of corporate indebtedness as required.

5

Section II (continued)

Articles of Incorporation
(continued)

(e)   To guarantee, endorse, purchase, hold, sell, transfer, mortgage or otherwise acquire or dispose of the assets of any corporation or the shares of the capital stock of, or any bonds, securities or other evidences of indebtedness created by any other corporation, and while the owner of such stock to exercise all the rights, powers, and privileges of ownership, including the right to vote such stock.

(f)   The foregoing clauses shall be construed both as objects and powers, the enumeration of which shall not be held to limit or restrict in any manner the powers or activities of this corporation which shall have the power to engage in any activity which may be necessary or profitable and generally shall have and enjoy all powers, privileges and immunities of businesses incorporated under the laws of the State of Florida.

ARTICLE III

CAPITAL STOCK

The maximum number of shares of stock that this corporation is authorized to have outstanding at any one time is one hundred (100) shares of common stock without nominal or par value. The consideration to be paid for each share shall be fixed by the Board of Directors.

ARTICLE IV

INITIAL CAPITAL

The amount of capital with which this corporation will begin business with is one (1) dollar.

TERM OF EXISTENCE

This corporation shall exist perpetually unless sooner dissolved according to law.

ARTICLE V

ADDRESS

The initial post office address of the principal office of this corporation in the State of Florida is:

6

Section II (continued)

Articles of Incorporation
(continued)

```
        Bodywear, Etc.
        Melbourne Square Promenade
        1900 Evans Road
        Melbourne, Florida 32935
```

The Board of Directors may from time to time move the principal office to any other address in Florida.

ARTICLE VI

DIRECTORS

This corporation shall have four directors, initially. The number of directors may be increased or diminished from time to time by By-Laws adopted by the stockholders, but shall never be less than four.

ARTICLE VII

INITIAL DIRECTORS

The names and post office addresses of the members of the first Board of Directors are:

VICKY K. LORICK   700 Friday Road #61   Cocoa, Florida 32926

PATRICIA A. LOWRY 1393 Pineapple Avenue   Melbourne, Florida 32935

TOMMIE L. SCARBRO 195 Treasure Street #104 Merritt Island, Fla. 32952

JAMES A. WHALEY   88 Fairglen Drive   Titusville, Florida 32796

ARTICLE VIII

SUBSCRIBERS

The names and post office addresses of the subscribers of these Articles of Incorporation are:

VICKY K. LORICK   700 Friday Road #61   Cocoa, Florida 32926

PATRICIA A. LOWRY 1393 Pineapple Avenue   Melbourne, Florida 32935

TOMMIE L. SCARBRO 195 Treasure Street #104 Merritt Island, Fla. 32952

JAMES A. WHALEY   88 Fairglen Drive   Titusville, Florida 32796

7

Section II (continued)

Articles of Incorporation
(continued)

ARTICLE IX

AMENDMENT

These Articles of Incorporation may be amended in the manner provided by law. Every amendment shall be approved by the Board of Directors, proposed by them to the stockholders, and approved at a stockholders' meeting by a majority of the stockholders entitled to vote thereon, unless all the directors and all the stockholders sign a written statement manifesting their intention that a certain amendment to these Articles of Incorporation be made.

VICKY K. LORICK

PATRICIA A. LOWRY

TOMMIE L. SCARBRO

JAMES A. WHALEY

**bodywear,
etc.**

Section V (continued)

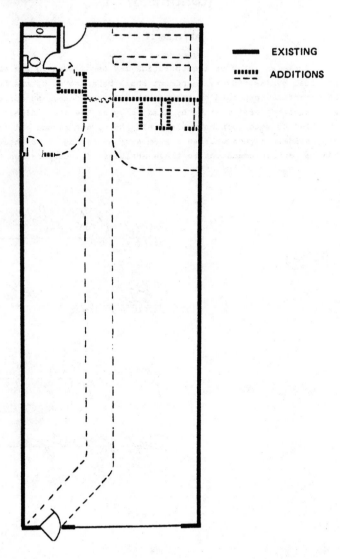

EXISTING

ADDITIONS

bodywear, etc.

Section VI (continued)

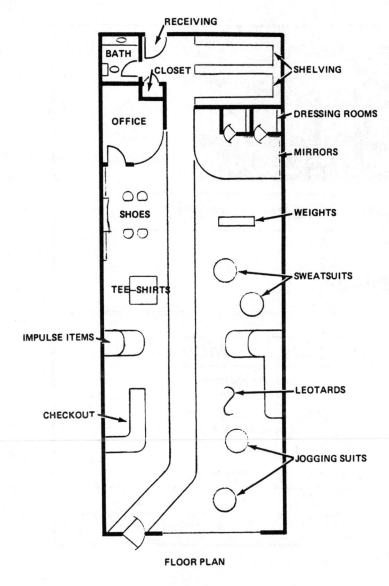

RECEIVING

BATH

CLOSET

SHELVING

DRESSING ROOMS

OFFICE

MIRRORS

SHOES

WEIGHTS

SWEATSUITS

TEE-SHIRTS

IMPULSE ITEMS

LEOTARDS

CHECKOUT

JOGGING SUITS

FLOOR PLAN

17

bodywear,
etc.

Section VII (continued)

JOIN THE CROWD! at the

Grand Opening

of

bodywear,
etc.

May 23 - May 26

Melbourne Mall Promenade
426-0000

One-stop shopping for all your
Exercise and Aerobics...

● Clothing ● Accessories ● Equipment

● Nike ● Adidas ● Reebok ● Danskin ● Unitard

WIN	**FREE**
1 Year Membership at Atlantic Nautilus	Tee-Shirt with Purchase of $25 . or more (first 100 people)

19

Section VII (continued)

**Vicky K Lorick
Owner/Director**

bodywear,
etc.

Melbourne Mall Promenade ● 426-0000

Sample Business Card

bodywear,
etc.

**One -Stop Shopping for all
your exercise and aerobics
● clothing ● accessories ● equipment**

Melbourne Mall Promenade   426-0000

Yellow Pages Advertisement

bodywear, etc.

Inventory - Jogging Suits (men)

Description	Quantity	Sizes	Colors	Wholesale Each	Retail Each	Wholesale Total	Retail Total
Adidas, nylon	22	S, M, L, XL	Gray/navy Gray/ burgundy	30.00	60.00	660.00	1320.00
Adidas, acrylic knit	22	S, M, L, XL	Navy/gray burgundy/ gray	37.00	74.00	808.00	1616.00
Nike, nylon	28	S, M, L, XL	gray/black gray/navy beige/ brown	32.00	64.00	896.00	1792.00

Inventory - Jogging Suits (women)

Description	Quantity	Sizes	Colors	Wholesale Each	Retail Each	Wholesale Total	Retail Total
Adidas, nylon	24	S, M, L	Pink/gray Lt. blue/gray	28.50	57.00	684.00	1368.00
Adidas, acrylic knit	18	S, M, L	Navy, gray, burgundy	35.00	70.00	630.00	1260.00
Nike, nylon	18	S, M, L	Lt. blue, pink, gray	30.00	60.00	540.00	1080.00

bodywear, etc.

Inventory - Shoes (men)

Description	Quantity	Sizes	Colors	Wholesale Each	Retail Each	Wholesale Total	Retail Total
Adidas, canvas	54	6-12	white	20.00	40.00	1080.00	2160.00
Adidas, nylon/suede	54	6-12	white	20.00	40.00	1080.00	2160.00
Nike, canvas	54	6-12	white gray black	22.50	45.00	1215.00	2430.00

Inventory - Shoes (women)

Description	Quantity	Sizes	Colors	Wholesale Each	Retail Each	Wholesale Total	Retail Total
Adidas, canvas	55	5-10	white	17.00	34.00	935.00	1870.00
Adidas, nylon/suede	55	5-10	white	19.50	39.00	1072.50	2145.00
Nike, canvas	55	5-10	white	22.50	34.00	1237.50	1870.00
Nike, nylon/suede	55	5-10	white	20.00	39.00	1100.00	2145.00
Reebok, leather	55	5-10	white, pink, black, gray, lt. blue	17.00	45.00	935.00	2475.00
Reebok, nylon/suede	55	5-10	same	19.50	40.00	1072.50	2200.00

bodywear, etc.

Inventory - Sweatsuits

Description	Quantity	Sizes	Colors	Wholesale Each	Retail Each	Wholesale Total	Retail Total
Fleecewear, long sleeve shirt	96	XS, S, M, L XL	White, pink, M. Blue, Orchid, Yellow, gray, red, navy, black	5.50	11.00	528.00	1056.00
Fleecewear, short sleeve shirt	96	same	same	4.50	9.00	432.00	864.00
Fleecewear, elastic waist pants	96	same	same	5.50	11.00	528.00	1056.00
Fleecewear, elastic waist shorts	96	same	same	4.50	9.00	432.00	864.00

Inventory - Leotards

bodywear, etc.

Description	Quantity	Sizes	Colors	Wholesale Each	Retail Each	Wholesale Total	Retail Total
Aerobic Wear, nylon-lycra, T-back	32	S, M, L	Pink, yellow, lilac, black	12.00	24.00	384.00	768.00
Danskin, nylon-lycra, sleeveless	45	S, M, L	gray, pink, orchid, white	9.00	18.00	405.00	810.00
Danskin, nylon-lycra, sleeveless	24	S, M, L	stripes (same)	11.00	22.00	264.00	528.00
Nautilus, poly/cotton, sleeveless	36	S, M, L	gray, white, yellow, black	12.00	24.00	432.00	864.00
Unitard, nylon/lycra	45	S, M, L	black, white, pink, yellow, gray	17.50	35.00	787.50	1575.00

bodywear, etc. =========================

Inventory - Tights

Description	Quantity	Sizes	Colors	Wholesale Each	Retail Each	Wholesale Total	Retail Total
Danskin, super sheen	90	S, M, L	yellow, pink, white, gray, orchid, navy, lt. blue, black	7.50	15.00	675.00	1350.00
Danskin, high gloss	90	S, M, L	yellow, pink, white, gray, orchid, navy, lt. blue, black, flesh	6.00	12.00	540.00	1080.00

bodywear, etc.

Inventory - Socks (men)

Description	Quantity	Sizes	Colors	Wholesale Each	Retail Each	Wholesale Total	Retail Total
Adidas, orlon/acrylic/nylon	48	9-11 10-13	white with navy, green, burgundy, yellow, all gray	2.25	4.50	108.00	216.00

Inventory - Socks (women)

Description	Quantity	Sizes	Colors	Wholesale Each	Retail Each	Wholesale Total	Retail Total
Electric Sox, sport	72	S, M, L	Yellow, white, orchid, pink, lt. blue	1.75	3.50	126.00	252.00
Electric sox, knee	72	S, M, L	same	1.88	3.75	135.36	270.70

30

Inventory - Weights

bodywear, etc.

Description	Quantity	Sizes	Colors	Wholesale Each	Retail Each	Wholesale Total	Retail Total
Biosoft - wrist	4	3lb	n/a	6.00	12.00	24.00	48.00
Biosoft - wrist	4	5lb	n/a	7.50	15.00	30.00	60.00
Biosoft - leg	4	3lb	n/a	6.00	12.00	24.00	48.00
Biosoft - leg	4	5lb	n/a	7.50	15.00	30.00	60.00
Excel - chrome-plated	4	set	n/a	24.50	49.00	98.00	196.00
Excel - chrome-plated, bells	4	3lb	n/a	7.50	15.00	30.00	60.00
Excel - chrome-plated, bells	4	5lb	n/a	10.00	20.00	40.00	80.00
Excel - chrome-plated, bells	4	10lb	n/a	12.50	25.00	50.00	100.00
Marcy - steel bar	8	set	n/a	50.00	100.00	400.00	800.00
Triangle - fiberglass	16	set	n/a	34.50	69.00	552.00	1104.00

bodywear, etc.

Inventory - Miscellaneous

Description	Quantity	Sizes	Colors	Wholesale Each	Retail Each	Wholesale Total	Retail Total
Bags, duffle, equipment, nylon	9	n/a	black, navy, gray	3.50	7.00	31.50	63.00
Bags, duffle, equipment, canvas	9	n/a	same	4.50	9.00	40.50	81.00
Belts, stretch, cinch, women	45	S, M, L	yellow, white, pink, gray, lt. blue	2.50	5.00	112.50	225.00
Gloves, Triangle, leather	24	n/a	gray, white	10.00	20.00	240.00	480.00
Jump rope, heavy rope, rubber	3	3 1/2 lbs	black	12.50	25.00	37.50	75.00
Jump rope, heavy rope, rubber	3	5lbs	black	15.00	30.00	45.00	90.00
Jump rope, aerobic	6	n/a	white	5.00	10.00	30.00	60.00
Legwarmers, Softouch	72	n/a	yellow, white, pink, orchid, gray, black, navy, lt. blue, off-white	7.00	14.00	504.00	1008.00

Inventory - Miscellaneous (continued)

bodywear, etc.

Description	Quantity	Sizes	Colors	Wholesale Each	Retail Each	Wholesale Total	Retail Total
Sweatbands, Biosoft, head	33	n/a	white, yellow, pink, lt. blue, orchid, fushia, lt. green, gray, red, navy, black	2.50	5.00	82.50	165.00
Sweatbands, Biosoft, wrist	48	n/a	same	1.50	3.00	72.00	144.00
Tee-shirts, unisex	192	XS, S, M, L, XL	white, yellow, pink, lt. blue, orchid, gray, fushia, red, navy, black, lt. green	4.50	9.00	864.00	1728.00
Total				705.88	1411.75	23,039.86	46,119.70

34

bodywear,
etc.

Section IX (Continued)

A. Financing Requirements - Initial Start-up Costs

1. <u>Deposits</u>

Telephone	$150.00	
Electric	300.00	
Lease Security	<u>1800.00</u>	
Total Deposits		$2250.00

2. <u>Organizational Expense</u>

Fee for incorporating	250.00	
Registration of Fictitious Name	10.00	
License Fees		
City of Melbourne	50.00	
Brevard County	15.00	
Application for Sales Tax Number	5.00	
Total Organizational Expense		330.00

3. <u>Promotional Expenses</u>

Advertising		
Sunday (1/4 page black, one time, Florida Today only)	894.30	
Daily (1 column inch black, six times, Florida Today, the Times and The Tribune)	160.20	
Printing and Distributing Flyers (1000)	146.85	
SPA Membership	150.00	
Tee Shirts (100)	447.00	
Miscellaneous	<u>300.00</u>	
Total		2098.35

**bodywear,
       etc.** ═══════════════════════════════

Section IX (Continued)

Initial Start-up Costs (Continued)

4.   <u>Building Improvements</u>   12,000.00

5.   <u>Fixed Assets</u>
     <u>Furniture</u>
     Chair, Desk   79.95
     Chairs, (4) arm, multi-purpose   400.00
     Chair, straight back, office   64.95
     Desk   300.00
     File Cabinet, 4 Drawer, Letter   <u>174.00</u>
          Sub-total   1018.90

     <u>Equipment</u>
     Calculator   59.95
     Cash Register   <u>400.00</u>
          Sub-Total   459.95

     <u>Fixtures</u>
     Sign   850.00
     Racks   544.50
     Hangers   <u>215.00</u>
          Sub-Total   1609.50

          Total Fixed Assets   13,088.35

6.   <u>Inventory (including freight)</u>   <u>23,039.86</u>

     Total Start-Up Costs   **$52,806.56**

bodywear,
etc. ===============================

Section IX (Continued)

B. Monthly Budget (Working Capital)

Rent	1877.00
Telephone	50.00
Utilities	150.00
Salaries	1807.67
Miscellaneous	300.00
Insurance	16.66
Advertising	222.06
Office/Store Supplies	50.00
TOTAL	**$4473.39**

bodywear, etc.

bodywear, etc.
Income Statement (Estimated)
for 9 months ended December 31, 19XX

Revenue:

Gross Sales			$150,000
Less: Sales Returns and Allowances			750
Less: Service Charges (VISA/MC)			113
Net Sales			149,137

Cost of Goods Sold:

Merchandise Inventory, April 1, 19XX		23,040	
Purchases	92,160		
Less: Purchases returns and allowances	205		
Net Cost of purchases		91,955	
Goods Available for sale		114,995	
Merchandise Inventory, December 31, 19XX		39,995	
Cost of Goods Sold			75,000
Gross Profit from Sales			$74,137

Operating Expenses:

Salaries and Payroll Expenses	16,269		
Rent Expense	16,893		
Advertising Expense	2094		
Office & Store Supplies	450		
Utilities	1800		
Insurance	1500		
Depreciation Expense	576		
Miscellaneous	2700		
Total Operating Expenses			42,282
Net Income			**$31,855**

APPENDIX C
What's Hot and What's Not

Recent surveys by *INC.* magazine give an indication of small business activity by place and classification.

One survey (March, 1990) ranked the cities by business activity using a combination of job growth statistics, business start-ups, and performance of high-growth companies. The top twenty cities were as follows:

1. Las Vegas, NV	11. Charlotte, NC
2. Washington, DC	12. Hickory, NC
3. Orlando, FL	13. Wilmington-Jacksonville, NC
4. Tallahassee, FL	14. Ventura, CA
5. San Jose, CA	15. Nashville, TN
6. Atlanta, GA	16. San Diego, CA
7. Charleston, SC	17. Chattanooga, TN
8. Lincoln, NE	18. Greenville-Spartanburg, SC
9. Raleigh-Durham, NC	19. Fort Myers, FL
10. Anaheim, CA	20. Sioux Falls, SD

The same survey showed the cities with the most business start-ups as:

1. Las Vegas, NV
2. Orlando, FL
3. Charleston, SC

The cities with the most fast-growth companies were:

1. Lincoln, NE
2. Washington, DC
3. Sioux Falls, SD, and Reading, PA

Small business growth and opportunity follow the economic trends of the country. Sunbelt areas continue to show positive growth while many industrial areas continue to show the effects of the recession.

Results of previous *INC.* surveys (January 1988) show the upsurge of service businesses in the small business sector. The most frequently started types of businesses were:

1. Miscellaneous business services
2. Eating and drinking places
3. Miscellaneous shopping goods
4. Automotive repair services
5. Residential construction
6. Machinery and equipment wholesalers
7. Real estate services
8. Miscellaneous retail stores
9. Furniture retailers
10. Computer and data processing services

Businesses directed toward saving others time are outperforming independent retail establishments who have been hit hard by the recession and the influx of mass merchandisers and discounters.

Franchises continue strong growth, particularly the fast-food operations: Little Caesar's Pizza, Subway Sandwiches, Hardee's, and Arby's lead the list. Of the less-expensive franchises showing growth are Mail Boxes Etc., Worldwide Refinishing Systems Inc., Coverall, Chem-Dry, and Jani-King.

Evidence of the growth of service industries is in their dominance of the 25 fastest-growing franchises (from *Entrepreneur* magazine, January 1991):

1. Subway Sandwiches (fast food)
2. Jani-King (commercial cleaning)
3. Coverall North America Inc. (commercial cleaning)

 4. Intelligent Electronics Inc. (computer-related products and services)
 5. Chem-Dry (carpet, upholstery, and drapery cleaning/dyeing)
 6. Little Caesar's Pizza (fast food)
 7. Mail Boxes Etc. USA (packing, mailing, and shipping services)
 8. Jazzercise Inc. (fitness centers)
 9. Choice Hotels & Motels Int'l. (hotels and motels)
10. Hardee's (fast foods)
11. Electronic Realty Associates (real estate services)
12. Heel/Sew Quick (shoe repair)
13. Sport It (sports equipment)
14. Nutri-System (diet and weight-control centers)
15. Worldwide Refinishing Systems Inc. (porcelain/marble restoration)
16. Arby's Inc. (fast foods)
17. Servicemaster (commercial cleaning)
18. Decorating Den (miscellaneous decorating products and services)
19. Days Inns of America Franchising Inc. (hotels and motels)
20. ABC Seamless Inc. (siding)
21. Help U-Sell Real Estate (real estate services)
22. Handle With Care Packaging Store (packing, mailing, and shipping services)
23. Jackson Hewitt Tax Service (income tax services)
24. I Can't Believe It's Yogurt (fast food)
25. Floor Coverings Int'l. (decorative products)

APPENDIX D

Small Business Development Centers

The following is a listing by state of central Small Business Development Center offices. Call or write these offices for the location of the center closest to you. There are over 600 SBDC offices nationally to assist you with no charge counseling services or low-cost seminar programs.

Alabama Small Business
  Development Center
University of Alabama at
  Birmingham
Medical Towers Building
1717 11th Avenue South,
  Suite 419
Birmingham, Alabama 35294
(205) 934-7260
FAX: (205) 934-7645

Alaska Small Business
  Development Center
University of Alaska Anchorage
430 West 7th Avenue, Suite 115
Anchorage, Alaska 99501
(907) 274-7232
FAX: (907) 274-9524

Arizona Small Business
  Development Center
108 North 40th Street, Suite 148
Phoenix, Arizona 85034
(602) 392-5224
FAX: (602) 392-5300

Arkansas Small Business
  Development Center
University of Arkansas at Little
  Rock
Little Rock Technology Center
  Building
100 South Main, Suite 401
Little Rock, Arkansas 72201
(501) 371-5381
FAX: (501) 375-8317

Colorado Small Business
  Development Center
1625 Broadway, Suite 1710
Denver, Colorado 80202
(303) 892-3840
FAX: (303) 892-3848

Connecticut Small Business
  Development Center
University of Connecticut
School of Business
  Administration
Box U-41, Room 422
368 Fairfield Road
Storrs, Connecticut 06268
(203) 486-4135
FAX: (203) 486-1576

Delaware Small Business
  Development Center
University of Delaware
Purnell Hall, Suite 005
Newark, Delaware 19716
(302) 451-2747
FAX: (302) 451-6750

District of Columbia Small
  Business Development Center
Howard University
6th and Fairmount Street, N.W.
Room 128
Washington, D.C. 20059
(202) 806-1550
FAX: (202) 797-6393

Florida Small Business
  Development Center
University of West Florida
Building 38, Room 107
Pensacola, Florida 32514
(904) 474-3016
FAX: (904) 474-2030

Georgia Small Business
  Development Center
University of Georgia
Chicopee Complex
1180 East Broad Street
Athens, Georgia 30602
(404) 542-5760
FAX: (404) 542-6776

Hawaii Small Business
  Development Center
University of Hawaii at Hilo
523 West Lanikaula Street
Hilo, Hawaii 96720-4091
(808) 933-3515
FAX: (808) 933-3683

Idaho Small Business
  Development Center
Boise State University
College of Business
1910 University Drive
Boise, Idaho 83725
(208) 385-1640
FAX: (208) 385-3877
1-800-225-3815

Illinois Small Business
  Development Center
Department of Commerce &
  Community Affairs
620 East Adams Street, 5th Floor
Springfield, Illinois 62701
(217) 524-5856
FAX: (217) 785-6328

Indiana Small Business
Development Center
Economic Development Council
One North Capitol, Suite 200
Indianapolis, Indiana 46204
(317) 634-1690
FAX: (317) 264-6855

Iowa Small Business
Development Center
Iowa State University
College of Business
Administration
Chamberlynn Building
137 Lynn Avenue
Ames, Iowa 50010
(515) 292-6351
FAX: (515) 292-0020

Kansas Small Business
Development Center
Wichita State University
Campus Box 148
Wichita, Kansas 67208
(316) 689-3193
FAX: (316) 689-3770

Kentucky Small Business
Development Center
University of Kentucky
20 Porter Building
Lexington, Kentucky 40506-0205
(606) 257-7668
FAX: (606) 257-8938

Louisiana Small Business
Development Center
Northeast Louisiana University
College of Business
Administration
Adm. 2-57
Monroe, Louisiana 71209
(318) 342-5506
FAX: (318) 342-5161

Maine Small Business
Development Center
University of Southern Maine
99 Falmouth Street
Portland, Maine 04103
(207) 780-4420
FAX: (207) 780-4810

Maryland Small Business
Development Center
Dept. of Economic and
Employment Development
217 East Redwood Street,
10th Floor
Baltimore, Maryland 21202
(301) 333-6996
FAX: (301) 333-6608

Massachusetts Small Business
Development Center
University of Massachusetts
205 School of Management
Amherst, Massachusetts 01003
(413) 545-6301, Ext. 303
FAX: (413) 545-1273

Michigan Small Business
Development Center
Wayne State University
2727 Second Avenue
Detroit, Michigan 48201
(313) 577-4848 or 4850
FAX: (313) 963-7606

Minnesota Small Business
Development Center
Department of Trade and
Economic Development
900 American Center Building
150 East Kellogg Boulevard
St. Paul, Minnesota 55101
(612) 297-5770
FAX: (612) 296-1290

Mississippi Small Business
Development Center
University of Mississippi
Suite 216
Old Chemistry Building
University, Mississippi 38677
(601) 232-5001 or 968-2794
FAX: (601) 232-5650

Missouri Small Business
Development Center
University of Missouri
Suite 300, University Place
Columbia, Missouri 65211
(314) 882-0344
FAX: (314) 884-4297

Montana Small Business
Development Center
Department of Commerce
1424 Ninth Avenue
Helena, Montana 59620
(406) 444-4780
FAX: (406) 444-2808

Nebraska Small Business
Development Center
University of Nebraska at Omaha
60th & Dodge Street
CBA, Room 407
Omaha, Nebraska 68182
(402) 554-2521
FAX: (402) 554-3363

Nevada Small Business
Development Center
University of Nevada Reno
College of Business
Administration
Room 411
Reno, Nevada 89557-0100
(702) 784-1717
FAX: (702) 784-4305

New Hampshire Small Business
Development Center
University of New Hampshire
University Center
400 Commercial Street,
Room 311
Manchester, New Hampshire
03101
(603) 625-4522
FAX: (603) 624-6658

New Jersey Small Business
Development Center
Rutgers University
Graduate School of Management
Ackerson Hall, 3rd Floor
180 University Avenue
Newark, New Jersey 07102
(201) 648-5950
FAX: (201) 648-1110

New Mexico Small Business
Development Center
Santa Fe Community College
P.O. Box 4187
Santa Fe, New Mexico
87502-4187
(505) 438-1362
FAX: (505) 438-1237

Upstate New York Small
Business Development Center
State University of New York
(SUNY)
SUNY Plaza, S-523
Albany, New York 12246
(518) 443-5398
FAX: (518) 465-4992

Downstate New York Small
Business Development Center
State University of New York
(SUNY)
SUNY Plaza, S-523
Albany, New York 12246
(518) 443-5398

North Carolina Small Business
Development Center
University of North Carolina
4509 Creedmoor Road, Suite 201
Raleigh, North Carolina 27612
(919) 733-4643
FAX: (919) 787-9284

North Dakota Small Business
Development Center
University of North Dakota
Gamble Hall, University Station
Grand Forks, North Dakota
58202-7308
(701) 777-3700
FAX: (701) 223-3081

Ohio Small Business
Development Center
Department of Development
30 East Broad Street
23rd Floor
P.O. Box 1001
Columbus, Ohio 43226
(614) 466-2711
FAX: (614) 466-0829

Oklahoma Small Business
Development Center
Southeastern Oklahoma State
University
P.O. Box 4229, Station A
Durant, Oklahoma 74701
(405) 924-0277 or
(800) 522-6154
FAX: (405) 924-8531

Oregon Small Business
Development Center
Lane Community College
99 West 10th, Suite 216
Eugene, Oregon 97401
(503) 726-2250
FAX: (503) 345-6006

Pennsylvania Small Business
Development Center
University of Pennsylvania
The Wharton School
444 Vance Hall
Philadelphia, Pennsylvania 19104
(215) 898-1219
FAX: (215) 898-1299

Puerto Rico Small Business
Development Center
University of Puerto Rico
Mayaguez Campus
P.O. Box 5253, College Station
Building B
Mayaguez, Puerto Rico 00709
(809) 834-3590
FAX: (809) 834-3790

Rhode Island Small Business
Development Center
Bryant College
1150 Douglas Pike
Smithfield, Rhode Island
02917-1284
(401) 232-6111
FAX: (401) 232-6319

South Carolina Small Business
Development Center
University of South Carolina
College of Business
Administration
1710 College Street
Columbia, South Carolina 29208
(803) 777-4907
FAX: (803) 777-4403

South Dakota Small Business
Development Center
University of South Dakota
School of Business
414 East Clark
Vermillion, South Dakota 57069
(605) 677-5272 or 5279
FAX: (605) 677-5427

Tennessee Small Business
  Development Center
Memphis State University
330 Fogelman Executive Center
Memphis, Tennessee 38152
(901) 678-2500
FAX: (901) 678-2983

University of Houston
Small Business Development
  Center
601 Jefferson, Suite 2330
Houston, Texas 77002
(713) 752-8444
FAX: (713) 752-8484

Utah Small Business
  Development Center
University of Utah
102 West 500 South, Suite 315
Salt Lake City, Utah 84101
(801) 581-7905
FAX: (801) 581-7814

Vermont Small Business
  Development Center
University of Vermont
Extension Service
Morrill Hall
Burlington, Vermont 05405
(802) 656-4479
FAX: (802) 656-8642

Virgin Islands Small Business
  Development Center
University of the Virgin Islands
Grand Hotel Building, Annex B
P.O. Box 1087
St. Thomas, U.S. Virgin Islands
  00804
(809) 776-3206
FAX: (809) 775-3756

Virginia Small Business
  Development Center
Commonwealth of Virginia
Department of Economic
  Development
P.O. Box 798
1021 East Cary Street, 11th Floor
Richmond, Virginia 23219
(804) 371-8258
FAX: (804) 371-8137

Washington Small Business
  Development Center
Washington State University
441 Todd Hall
Pullman, Washington 99164-4740
(509) 335-1576
FAX: (509) 335-0949

West Virginia Small Business
  Development Center
Governor's Office of Community
  and Industrial Development
1115 Virginia Street, East
Capitol Complex
Charleston, West Virginia 25310
(304) 348-2960
FAX: (304) 348-0127

Wisconsin Small Business
  Development Center
University of Wisconsin
432 North Lake Street,
  Room 423
Madison, Wisconsin 53706
(608) 263-7794
FAX: (608) 262-3878

Wyoming Small Business
  Development Center
111 West 2nd Street
Suite 416
Casper, Wyoming 82601
(307) 235-4825
FAX: (307) 473-7243

Index

About the Author

James W. Halloran is director of the Small Business Development Center, Clayton State College, Atlanta, Georgia. A small business and marketing consultant since 1980, Mr. Halloran is himself a successful entrepreneur and retailer whose first-hand knowledge and experience make him a true expert in starting a successful business. He is the author of *The Right Fit: The Entrepreneur's Guide to Finding the Perfect Business* and *Why Entrepreneurs Fail: Avoid the 20 Fatal Pitfalls of Running Your Business*.